The Art of Jewish Living

SHABBAT

2nd Edition

The Family Guide to Preparing for and Celebrating the Sabbath

Ron Wolfson

A project of
the Federation of Jewish Men's Clubs
and the University of Judaism

JEWISH LIGHTS Publishing
Woodstock, Vermont

My son, preserve the commandments of your father;
Do not forsake the teachings of your mother;
Bind them continually on your heart....
(Proverbs 6:20–21)

To
Bernice and Alan Wolfson
my beloved parents
for giving me the gift of Shabbat

Shabbat, 2nd Edition:
The Family Guide to Preparing for and Celebrating the Sabbath

2003 Second Edition, Second Printing
2002 Second Edition, First Printing
© 2002 by the Federation of Jewish Men's Clubs

1996 First Edition, First Jewish Lights Publishing Printing

Library of Congress Cataloging-in-Publication Data
Wolfson, Ron.
[Seder lel Shabat]
Shabbat : the family guide to preparing for and celebrating the Sabbath / Ron Wolfson. — 2nd ed.
      p. cm. — (The art of Jewish living series)
Includes bibliographical references.
ISBN 1-58023-164-0
1. Sabbath. 2. Judaism—Customs and practices. I. Title. II. Series.
BM685 .W584 2001
296.4'1—dc21

                                                  2001006806

10 9 8 7 6 5 4 3 2

Manufactured in Canada
Hebrew text used with permission of Davka Corporation.

Published by Jewish Lights Publishing
A Division of LongHill Partners, Inc.
Sunset Farm Offices, Route 4, P.O. Box 237
Woodstock, VT 05091
Tel: (802) 457-4000   Fax: (802) 457-4004
www.jewishlights.com

CONTENTS

FOREWORD

Omaha, Nebraska, is where I learned to "make *Shabbes.*"

Today, when I tell people of my origins in Omaha, I usually get stares of disbelief or some sort of deprecating comment like "There are Jews in Omaha?" Few know that one of the finest small Jewish communities in the country thrives there.

My bubbie and zadie, Ida and Louis Paperny, *zikhronam livrakhah* (*z"l*—may they rest in peace), were among the first Jews in Omaha. They came from White Russia in the earliest years of the twentieth century, as family lore has it, with nothing more than the clothes on their backs and a few coins in their pockets. But far more important than material goods, they brought with them a deep commitment to Jewish values and traditions. They sought to transplant their rituals into this new soil and raise a family in a Jewish home on the plains of the Midwest.

It wasn't easy. With the pressures of making a living in a retail business, the time available for Jewish pursuits was limited. Certainly, the major Jewish holidays were observed and a kosher kitchen maintained. But the day-to-day rituals fell by the wayside. Except one.

The Friday night table ritual was the one weekly Jewish time my grandparents insisted on retaining in their family. My mother, Bernice, as one of four daughters, recalls this time with great fondness. Although her father was busy building a fruit stand into a grocery store, keeping hours unfit for normal living, she looked forward to Friday night with great anticipation, knowing that he would be with the family, no matter what.

When she married and established her own home, this commitment to a Friday night Shabbat dinner continued. Although her husband, Alan, had rebelled against the rigid Orthodox environment he had endured as a child, she convinced my father to go along with the Shabbat dinner ritual once I arrived on the scene. So, for as long as I can remember, Friday night has meant candles, Kiddush, *hallah,* special dinners, and, perhaps most important, the family together.

Even though my mother "made Shabbes" in our home, ironically it was my father who taught me the importance of this time for our family. It happened when I was a junior high school student, a fourteen-year-old. Like most of the kids, I was eager to be seen with the "in" crowd. One Friday afternoon, I joined the group hanging out at the local shopping mall. Somehow the time got away, and I came home several hours late. My parents were livid. When told that I had missed Shabbat dinner, I dismissed my tardiness as only an adolescent could: "What's the difference? Dad doesn't believe in this stuff anyway." During the subsequent conversation with my father, I learned that while he had his doubts about Jewish theology, he had acquired a tremendous regard for the power of Jewish ritual in his family. Like his father-in-law before him, he worked long, crazy hours in the grocery business. Friday night was the busiest time of the week for him. Yet, in order to maintain our family Shabbat dinner, he arranged to work Saturday nights every week, giving up numerous social opportunities. As a young teenager just beginning the process of dating, I was profoundly impressed by this revelation. Yet, I had to ask him the obvious question: "But why is Shabbat dinner so important to you?"

I cannot recall the exact comments he made then, but the importance and meaning of his words have stayed with me since. He talked at length about his own experiences with Shabbat in a home ruled by the strict hand of Orthodoxy. For him as a child, Shabbat was a series of "no's." "No, you can't go to the movies." "No, you can't listen to the radio." The Shabbat table image he most vividly remembered was of his father, sitting alone, deeply immersed in his private world of prayer. Shabbat was something to be suffered through until the liberation of Saturday night.

He admitted to me that it took a lot of persuasion from my mother to start a Friday night ritual in his own home "for the sake of the children." But, now, three boys and fourteen years later, he confessed that despite the sacrifice of social evenings and the pressures of the business, Friday night had become the single most important moment of his week. For it was then, surrounded by the aura of Jewish ritual, that his family was together. After a long week of pickup meals and brief encounters with his children, the Shabbat dinner had become his family time. A time to catch up with his children and their exploits, to interact with his wife, and to enjoy a relaxing, festive meal. A time for laughter and fun. A time to be a human being.

His words drilled through me, and suddenly I realized what was at stake for him. I understood his anger and disappointment at my casual dismissal of the importance of being home for this time. Did it matter that he still stumbled through the Kiddush? Did it matter that he probably never understood the meanings of the ritual actions he made? Not at all! For him and for my mother, the Shabbat Seder had a deeper—I dare say more profound—meaning. By welcoming the Shabbat on a weekly basis, they sought to ensure quality time in their family and to transmit part of the Jewish heritage to their children.

This understanding of the value of Shabbat has now been shared in our family through four generations. As Susie and I established our own home, we too began the process of establishing this time as our weekly Jewish family time. When our children, Havi and Michael, came on the scene, the lessons I learned about Shabbat from my parents and grandparents gained even more profound importance.

So it should be understandable that when my work as a professor of Jewish education took me into the field of family and adult education, one of my first subjects was teaching people about Shabbat—its meanings, its practices, and its importance to family life. My first attempt was to compile a Shabbat Seder booklet for use at numerous scholar-in-residence weekends I staffed as part of an outreach program for the University of Judaism. The response to the material in the booklet was encouraging. When I was asked to teach a course on Shabbat at my congregation, Valley Beth Shalom in Encino, California, I rushed to the task. During my work with numerous individuals and couples, the outline for the book you now hold in your hands slowly took shape.

Then one day I received a call from my colleague Dr. David Gordis, then vice president of the University of Judaism. He told me of a conversation he had just had with a man named Jules Porter, a well-known leader in the Los Angeles Jewish community. Jules was in line to become the president of the Federation of Jewish Men's Clubs, an important group of congregational men's organizations that support the work of the Conservative Movement. Jules had told David of the successful Hebrew Literacy

Campaign sponsored by the Men's Clubs, which had taught more than 50,000 people how to read the Hebrew of the Friday night worship service. It was time to take the next step, and he was looking for ideas.

David Gordis spoke to him about the need to reach out to the congregational membership with programs that teach both the meaning of Jewish observance and the practice. Jules suggested that a likely target was the home celebration of Jewish holidays. David knew of my work in this area and suggested that the three of us get together. Out of that meeting came *The Art of Jewish Living* project.

The Federation of Jewish Men's Clubs has been an outstanding sponsor of this program. First and foremost, I must thank Jules Porter, international president of the Federation of Jewish Men's Clubs, who has seen a dream come true. He has been the spiritual godfather of this project. He has been fund-raiser, consultant, photographer, designer, and chief cheerleader. My only hope is that the response to his dream will be commensurate with the unceasing effort he has contributed to ensure its success.

The leaders of the FJMC also deserve a note of thanks. While he was president of the Federation of Jewish Men's Clubs, Mr. Joseph Gurmankin was instrumental in the early stages of the project. Rabbi Joel S. Geffen *(z"l)*, spiritual advisor to the FJMC, offered encouragement along the way, and Rabbi Charles Simon, executive director, has been an efficient and supportive colleague. Without the initial grant from the Century Club of the Federation, the project would not have proceeded.

On behalf of the FJMC, we gratefully acknowledge the many individuals who have contributed financially to *The Art of Jewish Living* project. Special recognition is due Mr. Arnold C. Greenberg of West Hartford, Connecticut, for his generous support.

The Art of Jewish Living series enjoys the endorsement of every arm of the Conservative Movement. We wish to thank the late Chancellor Gerson Cohen *(z"l)* of the Jewish Theological Seminary of America; Mr. Marshall Wolke, president of the United Synagogue of America; Mrs. Selina Weintraub, president of the Women's League for Conservative Judaism; and Rabbi Alexander Shapiro, president of the Rabbinical Assembly of America, for their support.

A project of this magnitude cannot see the light of day without the help and guidance of numerous colleagues and friends. To Dr. David Gordis, my sincerest gratitude for initially suggesting me for the project. The manuscript of the Teacher's Guide was carefully reviewed by Rabbi Abraham Eckstein, whose comments were both timely and thoughtful. Other colleagues I wish to thank for their assistance with the manuscripts are Rabbi Alan Silverstein of the Rabbinical Assembly; Rabbis Elliot Dorff, Joel Rembaum, and Bob Wexler; Dr. Eliezer Slomovic of the University of Judaism; and, most especially, Dr. David Lieber, president emeritus of the University of Judaism, for his advice and encouragement. My staff at the Clejan Educational Resources Center of the UJ, Judy Bin-Nun, Sharene Johnson, Rick Burke, and Toby Camarov, were extremely helpful. A special thanks to Jan and Alan Shulman *(z"l)* for their help with the initial conceptualization of the course and to Sally Weber and JoAnne Leinow, program directors of Adat Ari El and Sinai Temple in Los Angeles, respectively, who led me to the people whose comments grace these pages.

I want to especially thank the families who allowed us into their homes to ask about their Shabbat experiences: Sally and Bob Shafton, Sandy and Bill Goodglick, Suzan and Irwin Weingarten, Karen Vinocor, Wendy and Asher Kelman, Elaine and Carl Albert, Judi Strauss, Wilma Brooks, Debra and Larry Neinstein, Janice and Ben Reznik, Bonnie and Ira Goodberg, Bev and Steve Weise, and, of course, all their children. I hope that the honesty and sincerity of their stories will be excellent models for those readers beginning their own Shabbat experiences.

The development team on this project has been outstanding. The staff of Jules Porter Photographers, particularly Lewis Gottesman, has been professional and timely in providing the majority of the photography in the book. *The Art of Jewish Living*'s original design firm, Torah Aura Productions, is quickly becoming the leading innovator of exceptionally creative curricular materials for Jewish education. My sincerest thanks to Jane Golub and Alan Rowe for all their efforts.

Joel Grishaver, the creative genius behind Torah Aura, is another story. Working under impossible deadlines, with his unmatched design, editing, and writing skills, Joel has had an incalculable impact on the content, focus, and shape of this work. I am deeply indebted to him for being a great editor and a good friend.

Finally, I want to thank my partners in "making Shabbes": my wonderful wife, Susie, and our two fabulous children, Havi Michele and Michael Louis. They are a continual source of inspiration and joy to me—as a professional, as a husband, and as a father. May we enjoy many, many *Shabbatot* together!

Ron Wolfson
Los Angeles, California

An artist cannot be continually wielding his brush. He must stop at times in his painting to freshen his vision of the object, the meaning of which he wishes to express on his canvas.

Living is also an art. We dare not become absorbed in its technical processes and lose our consciousness of its general plan....

The Shabbat represents those moments when we pause in our brushwork to renew our vision of this object. Having done so, we take ourselves to our painting with clarified vision and renewed energy. This applies to the individual and to the community alike.

MORDECAI M. KAPLAN

USING THIS TEXT

This text consists of multiple layers of information about the Shabbat Seder—the Friday night home table service. Each layer offers a new perspective or set of skills for the learner.

Chapter 1, The Art of Shabbat, is an introduction to the process of making Shabbat. It also introduces the people who share their Shabbat experiences throughout the book.

The complete text of the Shabbat Seder is presented in chapter 2. This rendition is designed to be a convenient resource for use during the Shabbat table ceremony itself. The detailed explanations of each of the ten steps of the Shabbat Seder are the focus of the next ten chapters of the text.

Each of these chapters follows a consistent outline. To begin with, we hear from the people we interviewed for this project as they talk about the various steps of the Shabbat Seder, how they practice the ritual, and what it means to them. It is important to note that they are all laypeople, not "professional" Jews. We hope their struggles and triumphs with making Shabbat resonate with those who are just learning to do so.

Then, each chapter offers an introductory essay about the particular step of the Shabbat experience under discussion. This sets the tone for the detailed information to come.

The chapter is then divided into three sections: Concepts, Objects and Practice. The Concepts section offers the reader an explanation of the major themes of each step of the Shabbat Seder. In the Objects section, we discuss the various items necessary for the Shabbat Seder celebration and their requirements. The Practice section gives explicit directions for the actual performance of the rituals.

Next, the texts of the blessings are presented in a rather unique format. First, the texts have been divided into small word phrases and numbered in a linear fashion. Second, there are three columns of texts. From right to left, they are (1) the English transliteration of the text, (2) the English translation of the text, and (3) the Hebrew text. This format allows those who are able to read Hebrew to work with the Hebrew and English translation columns, while those who cannot read Hebrew can work with the English transliteration and translation columns. Since one of our goals is for the reader to learn and use the Hebrew texts of the Shabbat Seder, this linear presentation should assist the learner in deciphering the meanings of the Hebrew words.

The Hebrew transliteration scheme we use in the texts generally follows that used by the Rabbinical Assembly of America in its new prayerbooks. Here is a key to pronouncing these transliterations:

ai = as in "i"—*Adonai* = ah-doe-nigh

ei = as in "hay"—*Eloheinu* = eh-low-hay-new

i = as in "see"—*lehadlik* = leh-hahd-leek

o = as in "low"—*shalom* = shah-lowm

e = as in "red"—*Elohim* = eh-low-heem

a = as in "Mama"—*bara* = bah-rah

u = as in "blue"—*vanu* = vah-nu

kh = as in the sound you make when trying to dislodge a fishbone from the roof of your mouth

h̲ = as kh above

A word about translations. Many of the Hebrew blessings of the Shabbat Seder refer to God using the masculine gender. For example, the word *bemitzvotav* literally translated means "through His commandments"; the *av* ending indicates third person masculine singular. In our attempt to present as literal a translation as possible in the teaching texts, we have retained the masculine gender in the translations that refer to God. However, in the Shabbat Seder presentation in chapter 2, which is designed for use at the table, we have used an egalitarian translation of the blessings. We have substituted the masculine terms with nonsexist terminology or with a repetition of the Divine Name. Thus, *bemitzvotav* becomes "through the commandments." While this results in two different translations of the same blessings, we feel strongly that the learner should understand both how the Hebrew language works in the original and how new translations that are sensitive to the spiritual feelings of all Jews can be used.

After the blessing texts, a section entitled Practical Questions and Answers poses and answers common questions about the steps in the Shabbat Seder.

Each chapter concludes with Some Interesting Sources, usually texts from rabbinic literature, that we hope will stimulate further discussion and study about the Shabbat Seder experience.

Added to this new edition is a chapter featuring the home celebration of the Shabbat day, including a section on *Havdalah,* the ceremony separating the Sabbath from the rest of the week.

The chapter "The Shabbat Gallery" offers the reader a wide variety of Shabbat enrichment activities. Craft projects and recipes for making before Shabbat, games and discussion ideas for the Shabbat table, and several creative suggestions for Shabbat celebration are presented.

We have followed these chapters with an Afterword, the complete version of the *Birkat Hamazon,* and a Selected Bibliography of Shabbat resources for future reading.

Behatzlahah! We wish you "good success" in learning the art of Jewish living!

The Art of Shabbat

For people who have never been exposed to this before, it's very hard for someone to whom this is very common and ordinary to understand how really foreign this was. You know it's yours, but it's like the Zulus would come in and say: "Now you have to do this tribal rite." You know you're really a Zulu and this is what you have to do to become a Zulu and you'd say: "Well, I know, I guess I'm a Zulu but I don't know—this has no meaning to me and I have no connection to this whatsoever."

ELAINE ALBERT

On Making Shabbes

In Jewish English, the common phrase is "make Shabbes." It seems logical enough: one person asks another, "Who's making Shabbes this week: you or your in-laws?" Immediately it conjures up images of cooking, cleaning, shopping, and organizing. A whole progression of labor is involved in the creation of the day of rest. The idea of making Shabbes is a practical concept. It reflects a pragmatic social reality: in order to celebrate a day of rest, someone has to do a lot of work.

The idea of making Shabbes is really biblical. The Torah commands the Jewish people to "Guard Shabbat—making Shabbat throughout their generations" (Exodus 31:17). From the beginning, a Jewish vision of rest had little to do with a recreational use of leisure time. Starting with the beginning of the Torah, rest was defined as a process of RE-CREATION. God spent six days creating. Then the Torah says, שָׁבַת וַיִּנָּפַשׁ.... "God made Shabbat and God rested." The word for rest here is וַיִּנָּפַשׁ, *vayinafash*. It is a form of the word *nefesh*, which means "soul." When God rests, the world has soul. When we are commanded to imitate God (living up to the image in which we were created), the expectation is that our rest, too, will be soulful. Creating that kind of rest is something at which we must work.

Scientists define work as something that burns calories. Their view is rational: labor is anything that uses energy. Something at rest uses no energy. When the Rabbis of the Talmud looked for a definition of work, they viewed it differently. They connected work to creation. Work was changing the natural (created) world. Rest was leaving that world unchanged—allowing it to change us. Mordecai Kaplan explained it this way: "An artist cannot be continually wielding his brush. He must stop at times in his painting to freshen his vision of the object, the meaning of which he wishes to express on his canvas.... The Shabbat represents those moments when we pause in our brushwork to renew our vision of this object. Having done so, we take ourselves to our painting with clarified vision and renewed energy." Expanding on the same theme, Abraham Joshua Heschel said: "Six days a week we wrestle with the world, wringing profit from the earth; on the Sabbath we especially care for the seed of eternity planted in our soul.

Six days a week we seek to dominate the world; on the seventh day we try to dominate the self."

Shabbat is something we make. _Ḥallot_ are bought. Meals are prepared. Tables are set. Children are herded to the table. We stand. We sit. Prayers are said. Rituals are performed. The execution of a Shabbat is the coordination of a myriad of small details and the application of a series of diverse skills. Yet, the physical making of Shabbes is only the foundation on which we create Shabbat. The connection between a white tablecloth, the moisture collecting on the outside of a silver Kiddush cup filled with cold wine, the buildup of wax drippings on the candlesticks—and the "seed of eternity"—is at once both profoundly tangible and wonderfully mythic. The real world of Shabbat is made up of tablecloths stained with repeated use, family jokes that are so well known that just a look triggers a laugh, hugs, and the feel and taste of warm _ḥallah_. It is this real-world Shabbat that bonds couples closer together, that creates significant family moments, that roots Jewish identity. These are the payoffs, the rewards of devoting a day to "dominate the self."

The Talmudic rabbis had a very simple principle: if you really want to know how something is to be practiced, go and look at what Jews really do. In crafting a book on how to "make Shabbes," we decided to do just that. We went to several Jewish homes and asked people about their Shabbat experiences. We learned many things, and all of them have helped to shape this work:

> • _Shabbat is an art form._ Every family creates its own Shabbat. While candles, Kiddush, and _ḥallah_ were part of every Shabbat celebration (along with lots of other common elements), every family we visited had a very different Shabbat experience. The art of making Shabbat means finding your own way of using the traditional tools and practices to compose your own "picture" of the Shabbat ritual.
> • _Shabbat is an evolving creation._ Families change the way they celebrate Shabbat. New practices are often discovered and integrated. Eventually, children grow into and out of stages and needs, and families evolve through changing rhythms of expression. Also, there seems to be a spontaneous and subtle process of constant change that simply marks growth.

• *You can start a Shabbat experience by doing just one or two things.* Surprisingly, most of the families we interviewed did not come from strong experiences of Shabbat. Most had to develop their own sense of Shabbat and establish their own mode of practice. Usually they began by adopting just one or two practices as their weekly ritual. Slowly, these families learned about and considered other options, evolving their own particular Shabbat practice.

• *The modern American experience has added to Shabbat.* Wonderful new practices have been created because of our lifestyles. Consider the practices of phoning a child at college every Friday afternoon to give him the traditional parental blessing, or baking three months' worth of *hallah* and filling the extra freezer.

• *Shabbat is a long-term investment.* Not every single Shabbat is a great experience. Some weeks, celebrating Shabbat is a strain. Sometimes the experiences are less than ideal. Yet, wherever we found Shabbat taken seriously, it had a profound effect. Every family we visited told us stories of individually difficult Shabbatot, and all talked of the significant impact of the Shabbat experience on their home. Nevertheless, celebrating Shabbat seems to add up. This was an ongoing message. It is the sum total of Shabbatot that makes an impact.

Sally and Robert Shafton

When you spend Shabbat with the Shaftons, you know that you are going to spend some time studying Torah. Their friend Sandy Goodglick warned us, "They sometimes even give you homework—something you have to study before you come." When dinner is over and the food has been cleared away from Bob and Sally's Shabbat table, the Hertz Humashim and other Torah commentaries are taken out, and a serious discussion of the weekly Torah portion begins. This happens every Shabbat—even when the children aren't visiting, even when there is no company, even when it is just the two of them.

Sally and Bob are a couple whose children have grown up and left home. Today they are active members of the Jewish community, heavily involved in both the life of their synagogue and several Jewish organizations.

But theirs is a story of transformation and evolution. Shabbat was something they discovered when their children were young—and it has remained an important element in their lives.

BOB: The word which comes to both of our minds when we think of Shabbat is "yawn." Not because it is boring, but because the real sense of rest comes to me every time we say the blessing over the wine. We get to about "*attah*" and I yawn. It used to be something I was embarrassed about, but now I know it's true. That it is really greeting the Sabbath Queen. I mean—she's beautiful, and I yawn.

SALLY: When the kids were too young to do much else except the blessings, we wrote a little original family song, which was sung to the tune of "Old McDonald": "Shabbes candles we love you (E-I-E-I-O)."

BOB: And we would go around and tickle the kids and tackle the kids and end up rolling on the ground....

SALLY: It was just a physical kind of happiness, and the littlest one would always end up on the bottom of the heap, screaming her head off. It got pretty raucous—dancing around the Shabbat lights. That and the *bera-khot* was the extent of our Shabbat.

SALLY: I started looking at the *parashah* [weekly Torah portion] on Tuesday or Wednesday, not understanding a thing that I was reading, because it was new to me. I would try to find one simple concept that I thought would appeal to the family, and then I would take one child in my room and the other two were closed out. That way we created a mystique because the other two couldn't wait for their turn. They would come in with me and we would read part of the Torah portion, and I would lead them to that one concept that I thought would appeal. That child became responsible to come to the Shabbat table and "lead" the Shabbat discussion.

BOB: It wasn't always idyllic. At various stages, the kids were not always anxious to participate. We didn't make it "you must be there," "you must prepare," but we let them know we were going to be there and that those who wanted to participate were most welcome. The other problem we had was that our extended family did not always want to participate, and that was a disappointment.

SALLY: One of the joys was that I saved the things that the children wrote about the *parashah*, and when a kid would be preparing for Shabbat, she would always ask to look at what the other had written last year about that *parashah*. I would show them and they would come to the table and say, "She was all wrong last year. That is not what it says."

SALLY: Now it is wonderful. Bob has a very busy schedule—we both have a very busy schedule—and during the week, we are lucky if there is one night at home. Friday night is always at home, no matter what, for the two of us. Although many of our family complain that the kids are gone—it's just the two of us and we're all alone—honestly, it's pretty nice. We look forward to that quiet Friday night together. Just the two of us. We still look at the *parashah*, and the two of us will often discuss it together.

BOB: Friday night is a nice quiet time. I was kidding about the yawning. It is a time that should be of peace, and calmness, and some introspection—some community, obviously, but also some introspection. We usually each have an individual prayer that we say aloud for the family, wherever they may be. No matter who's around this table, they're all a part of what went into this.

Suzan, Dinah, Tovah, Mindle, and Irwin Weingarten

The Weingarten family is a series of wonderful combinations. Suzan and her now nine-year-old daughter Dinah converted to Judaism. Since her marriage to Irwin, two other children have been born: Mindle, age fourteen months, and Tovah, who is eight weeks old. This is a truly "blended" family. As a convert, Suzan approaches Jewish practice with a sense of discovery and wonder at these elements added to her life. She has gained a profound understanding of Jewish ritual, achieved through careful and consistent study. As a new family they find that Shabbat provides a medium for experimentation and exploration. It is a weekly time block that seems full of opportunities to further develop their sense of family. The juggling of two infants adds even more flavor to this celebration. While their practice is underscored by real commitment, there is a playful joy in the way that Suzan, Dinah, Tovah, Mindle, and Irwin create Shabbat.

SUZAN: It is a really nice moment when you yell, "Turn the TV off. It's candlelighting time!" It's a real nice feeling because it gets quiet. I don't know what it will be like in the next few years, but it's really a nice time, and I look forward to the quiet of the evening.

IRWIN: What's really nice, I think, is that it is the culmination of our week. Physically, it is really different. I walk into the house, the table is set beautifully, and Dinah is usually dressed in a nice dress. Sometimes Dinah and I walk to shul. It gives us a chance to unwind and to talk. We come back, and it's just a completely different feeling in this household than on any other night. You know that there are not going to be any phone calls coming in about business. It's time to get shut off. So it's a pretty nice feeling when you walk in the house.

SUZAN: After lighting the candles, we sit down and wait fifteen minutes for Irwin to find the page in the *siddur* (prayerbook).

DINAH: He never looks it up in advance.

SUZAN: He knows it by heart, but he always has to find the page. He always gets the book, and he never remembers the page. He'll flip pages, and we watch and get kind of impatient, saying, "Come on. You gotta remember the page."

DINAH: He usually says the first part, and then I say the *berakhah* over the wine.

IRWIN: Right! We're slowly weaning myself off the Kiddush. I think in another half year or so, Dinah will be able to say the whole thing. She knows a little bit of the beginning and all of it after that.

DINAH: Because we do it at school [a Jewish day school].

IRWIN: So maybe my responsibilities will come to just a directorship soon. And it will be passed down.

SUZAN: Dinah and I converted about three years before Irwin and I got married. The first year, I had never been invited to a Friday night. I didn't know what they were. After I converted, I think I had dinner with Irwin's family one night, and so I got to see what it was about. Then I ended up getting a job at a Jewish institution. That's where my training really began. The place actually locked up in the afternoon, or a good two or three hours before Shabbes was going to start. I used to go for my boss, or my boss would go for me, and get the *ḥallah* in the morning. I always knew when it was time to go home and prepare a meal, and that was when I started to realize that you had to plan things ahead of time. When I got into making cholent,* I knew I had to start making it at 6:30 in the morning before I left for work. I had to have it all ready and started and the meal planned—even if it was just for Dinah and me. And that was one of my favorite things: making cholent.

DINAH: I don't like cholent.

SUZAN: I used to make it all the time because I thought it was so neat to make something the day before so you didn't have to do anything the next day. I enjoyed that.

SUZAN: When I had Mindle, I had everything packed in my suitcase, and I went into labor or whatever and was in the hospital for Shabbes. We had portable candlesticks and the candles.

IRWIN: In Glendale Adventist Hospital we did a little Kiddush, Suzan and I, with Mindle, because it was Friday night.

---

*Cholent is a traditional Jewish dish made of beef, potatoes, and vegetables that is allowed to slow-cook on the stove from Friday until Saturday lunch. This way, a hot meal can be served without work being done.

Ariel, Emil, Jeremiah, Wendy, and Asher Kelman

We classified the Kelman family as our "traditional" family—traditional in the sense that the father is still the spokesperson for the family and "directs" the family ritual, and traditional in the sense that the Kelman Shabbat experience is an expression of family continuity and not something that was adopted or significantly redefined by this generation. Yet, we were uncomfortable labeling the Kelman family as a traditional family (even though they would clearly identify with that image). While the elements of their Shabbat Seder are traditional, and while the role definition is also traditional, there is an element of insight, flexibility, and questioning that impressed us. Our final thought was that the Kelman family is indeed a traditional family, but our preconception of "traditional" was far too narrow.

The other overriding element in their Shabbat is the energy that comes from three boys: Ariel (eleven), Jeremiah (nine), and Emil (seven).

EMIL: I like doing the blessing over the bread. I try to say it with my dad.

ARIEL: My mother always makes special food. Chicken, sometimes soup, usually rice, and sometimes we even have artichokes, which I like. After that we usually have a special dessert. We also have bread, which is ḥallah.

JEREMIAH: My father always tells my brothers to bring the *kipah*s and then tells us to settle down.

ASHER: When I was young, of course, there were fewer things to do. We didn't have computers. I don't think that when we grew up we had television for most of the time. Many, many less distractions. I think that to have Shabbat today, one needs to have a real discipline, a commitment. One of my views of Shabbat is that this is a time in which I have made a commitment together with Wendy that we are going to spend valuable, rich time with our children. We know that if we don't do this, the children will miss out on one of the richest parts of Judaism.

WENDY: I like following all the traditions that have been followed for many years, and feeling that our family is keeping these traditions, and that my husband and I have taught our children how to follow these traditions and to keep our religion and those traditions alive.

EMIL: I always have homework, and I am afraid that I won't get it done because I have Shabbat.

ARIEL: While we're eating, my Dad talks about things. Sometimes he tells us about a lot of Jewish questions, like about Pharaoh and stuff. In the middle we enjoy our food. I like the food that my Mom makes. I especially like cow tongue.

EMIL: I love Shabbat. It's fun. Sometimes I get afraid that I'll do everything wrong when I am doing the blessings, the prayers, I mean....

JEREMIAH: My favorite thing, I like food. That's the best part. It's better than listening to all these prayers that you don't understand.

ASHER: My favorite thing is just sitting down and, when Wendy is not realizing it, just lowering my head and seeing the candles next to her, and that, to me, is having my family around me. It is very warm, and I feel that this family is playing a role, a private, magical role, being in a chain and keeping the tradition going.

Wilma Brooks and Judi Stauss

Wilma and Judi are single Jewish women. Both of them are involved in their synagogue and in a singles ḥavurah. While they each grew up in homes that embodied a measure of Jewish observance, Wilma and Judi became seriously involved with Jewish life as young adults. Although each approaches Shabbat observance from a different angle, they have faced the challenge of making Shabbes as a single person with unusual honesty and sensitivity.

WILMA: I begin to think about Shabbat on Thursday. That's when my cleaning help comes. She always comes on Thursday, because I am afraid if she doesn't show up on Friday, I'm dead.

JUDI: I was raised in a semitraditional home. We were not Friday night shul-goers; we had Shabbes dinner at home. Right now, I find it extremely difficult to make Shabbat dinner by myself, and therefore I don't. I go to *ḥavurah* dinners, and I love doing Shabbat dinners for other people. It's always been a special time, never a big date night. But I can't do it by myself. It's rare that I light candles for myself. When I do, of course, I follow with Kiddush. I did this week because I was giving the commentary on Saturday morning.

WILMA: The first time I made my own Shabbat, the first time I lit candles, I felt as if I was in somebody else's body. It was something I wanted to do, but I was very uptight about it. It took me a long time; it was months before I would light candles in front of anybody. I don't have a problem making Friday night dinner by myself. Sometimes I just get tired of inviting people. I set the table. I light Shabbes candles. It's a Shabbes table whether it's just me or other people are there.

I also have my dogs. I mean, "Shabbat Shalom" to Mish and Fluff is a must.

JUDI: The biggest problem is finding a Shabbes community. I have people out here who are very close, and they are my adopted family. I'll share Shabbat with them quite often. Or, I'll have dinner at home and then go to the synagogue. I feel that's my community, too.

Wilma Brooks

WILMA: The first time I made Shabbat dinner was for the singles *havurah* at Adat Ari El. When I got involved with the *havurah*, I was looking to have some kind of Shabbes in my life, but I never thought it would be what it became. I just thought, once in a while, I'll have Friday night—never on a weekly basis. At that first *havurah* Shabbat, we did Drexler's (a kosher catering service). With Drexler's, you can have a whole Shabbes meal and not lift a finger!

JUDI: I love to go to Shabbat dinner at homes with children. I love children, and it is very joyous for me to have Shabbat with kids—to see them do the blessings, take part in the discussions, and that sort of thing. It would be a big mistake to limit my Shabbes experiences to just singles.

Judi Strauss

WILMA: Absolutely. The mix of singles and couples in my Shabbat network is very important. The first time I led *bensching* (the blessing after food) was at Jerry and Sally Weber's. When I first heard it, it seemed so long that I wondered how anyone could know it all. I mean, I never thought I would ever lead bensching. But one Shabbes, Jerry turned to me and said, "Your turn." And once I did it, I got real comfortable with it.

JUDI: To me, the most meaningful part of Shabbat is candles. After I say the blessing in both Hebrew and English, then I have my private little chat with God. I also like the *hallah*-pull. We say the blessing, and then everybody grabs a part of the *hallah*.

13

Elisa, Matthew, David, Elaine, and Carl Albert

We called the Alberts our "together" family. At their Shabbat Seder, every-one does everything together. But this sense of togetherness goes deeper—it has to do with the way this family thinks and talks. When we went back to our tapes to edit this transcript, it was really impossible to isolate mono-logues or statements. What we had recorded was conversation, a process whereby the family had told us its story by intertwining the perspectives of each member.

Like many of the families we visited, the Alberts have created their own sense of Shabbat out of traditional elements. This creation was something the family could document, because the changes were recent. Theirs is an "institutional" success story, in that programs designed "to influence Jew-ish identification and behavior" (specifically the Brandeis-Bardin Institute and the Holiday Workshop Series) had motivated their involvement in Jew-ish practice. Yet, more than that, it is the story of how a family learned from outside influences and then collectively used these insights to compose its own Shabbat experience.

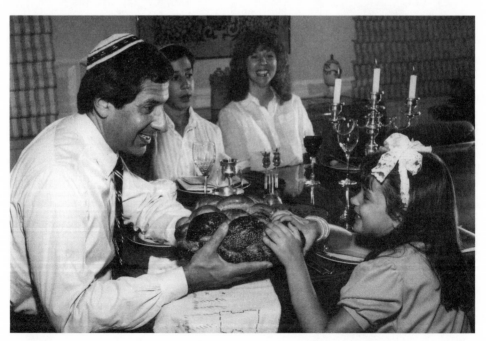

The Albert family is Elisa (seven), Matthew (thirteen), David (sixteen), Elaine, and Carl.

ELAINE: Neither Carl nor I grew up with this in our home. Originally I guess the spark of it came from a question that was posed to us by an introductory weekend at Brandeis (the Brandeis-Bardin Institute) by Dennis Prager: "Do you want your grandchildren to be Jewish?" We had two small boys at the time, and we said to each other that day that we wanted our children to be Jewish, and we didn't even know why! That question really haunted us.

CARL: Even more basic, I think we asked ourselves, "What does it mean to be Jewish?" And I couldn't answer that. I don't think either of us could.

MATTHEW: I remember when Mom came home and said we're having Shabbat. I didn't know what it was. I said: "Fine."

ELAINE: The reaction when we started to do this was that we had two very giggly children.

CARL: Me, too. I was giggly, too. I was uncomfortable with this.

ELAINE: I guess we all were. Neither of us had ever really seen it or done it, and what we ended up doing was saying, "What do we do? Where do we go?" Someone directed me to Patti Golden and her Holiday Workshop Series, and I took it that fall. It gave us something—it gave us tools.

For people who have never been exposed to this before, it's very hard for someone to whom this is very common and ordinary to understand how really foreign this was. You know it's yours, but it's like the Zulus would come in and say, "Now you have to do this tribal rite." You know you're really a Zulu and this is what you have to do to become a Zulu, and you'd say, "Well, I know, I guess I'm a Zulu, but I don't know—this has no meaning to me and I have no connection to this whatsoever."

CARL: That's exactly what we felt at the time.

ELAINE: In the beginning we just did the four things that Patti recommended: candles, Kiddush, *ḥallah*, and a very short *Birkat Hamazon*.

CARL: We read it off the paper in front of us.

MATTHEW: Until the brains took over...

ELAINE: Until, just like Matthew said, until the brains take over and you do a little more reading and...

MATTHEW: I was talking about me and David.

ELAINE: It took a long time.

CARL: For me, Shabbat is a very different night. It separates the week. It's the night to say the week is over, and it's a night that we're home together as a family. And that we know exactly what we're doing, and that is that. There is no rushing around. There are no appointments, and nobody is running away to other people's homes, the movies, etc. It's just a quiet night, and we know what it is going to be.

DAVID: It's relaxing. Nobody jumps up during dinner to answer the phone.

ELISA: Except me.

ELAINE: The telephone is still not quite a resolved problem.

DAVID: It's just a relaxing end of the week. No more school; it's just really quiet. Well, it's a family thing. It's not women do candles—men do wine. It's like a family kind of thing. Everybody has to be there to make it special.

ELAINE: The payoff, I hope, is that we will have three Jewish children who will create Jewish families for themselves. That really would be the payoff. But that is really yet to be seen. That's ultimately, but there is also a more immediate payoff. I hope that this makes us a closer family. I hope that this communicates certain values that both Carl and I want to communicate to our children, and Shabbat seems like an effective way of communicating these values.

Erin, Ari, and Karen Vinocor

The latest research says that fewer than half of the children born today will grow up in a household that has not been altered by divorce. We knew that to be honest about the making of Shabbat, we needed to look at how a single-parent family makes Shabbat. Shabbat is a time that resonates with the theme of family, when traditional roles are waiting to be fulfilled, and when the changes in a family's lifestyle seem to stand out. Likewise, Shabbat is also a healing force, a time of harmony and peace. Erin (seven), Ari (ten and a half), and Karen welcomed us into their home and frankly discussed their Shabbat Seder. Their Shabbat (held every other week when Karen has custody of the children) is an affirmation of their Jewish commitments, a celebration of the warmth and closeness of their relationship; yet, it contains frank acknowledgments of the divorce and its impact. As they repeatedly stressed to us, their Shabbat practice is an honest expression of who they are. It contains candles, Kiddush, a baseball cap, hugs, blessings, Birkat Hamazon, and a sense of renewed continuity.

KAREN: Shabbat usually begins the Sunday before Shabbat when I go shopping and have to buy the food for the week. I have to know exactly what I want. Shabbat is second nature for me. I've been doing it since before I remember what I was doing, because I was brought up in a very, very religious home. Shabbat is no big deal to me. I don't have to put in extra energy for it, because it's part of the routine.

I observe Shabbat every other week when I have my children. When my children are with their father, I do not observe Shabbat. It doesn't have that family feeling any more, so I don't observe it. I might light candles. I might make Kiddush.... I vowed that that would never happen to me, but it did.

We've been transforming how the Kiddush goes. Number one, the Kiddush for us does not begin at the blessing *Barukh attah Adoshem...borei peri hagafen*. That's a half-Kiddush. We start from *Vayehi erev vayehi voker*.

ARI: No, we start at *Yom hashishi*.

KAREN: And the children do not know that from school. That is something that they've learned from home.

ARI: No, from the book.

KAREN: Well from the siddur. We follow it in the siddur. And then we, Ari and I usually, sing it together. I told Ari that he has to start singing with me because I want him to feel comfortable doing it before his Bar Mitzvah.

ARI: And I get to drink more.

KAREN: That's right. You say more, you drink more.

ERIN: What about me?

KAREN: Your time will come. It's at the point now where Erin is learning how to read Hebrew, so now she follows the siddur. Ari doesn't need the siddur any more. It's a bit of a transformation. I used to say the whole thing by myself.

ARI: Now I say the whole thing by myself.

YOUR AUTHOR: Tell us about your Kiddush cup.

ARI: We don't have one. We use glasses.

KAREN: And why do we use glasses?

ERIN: So me and Ari can have the exact same shape. But instead of putting wine in, most of the time we put in grape juice, because me and my brother don't like wine. He doesn't like it, but I a little bit like it.

KAREN: So as an incentive to say Kiddush, we put in something they like to drink—grape juice. I never got another Kiddush cup after my divorce. That went in the divorce. It went out the door, and I never got another one.

ARI: That's fine by me. It's the same no matter what kind of glass you use twice a month.

KAREN: It's the feeling that goes along with it, not necessarily the object.

KAREN: I do Jewish things all day long. When I say "good night" to my kids every day, it's with the *Sh'ma*. That's a Jewish thing. When I wake up my children in the morning, I say "*Modeh Ani.*" That is Jewish. That's consistent. I don't do extra Jewish things on Shabbat. When we go outside and we see a rainbow, we quickly run inside to get a siddur so we can say the correct *berakhah* to say over seeing a rainbow. That's Jewish. It's not all Shahbat. It's Jewishness all the time.

The best part of Shabbat for me is when I bless my children. I get to hug them and kiss them, and they have to stand there and take it whether they like it or not. Shabbat is the end of the week. It's just a special feeling—a unique feeling that I made it through the week and this is my reward. And it's nice. We don't have fights at this meal. It's never been said that you don't get to fight on Shabbat—we just don't. It's the one meal where we sing. It's pleasant—there's a whole pleasantness about it.

Sandy and Bill Goodglick

North American Jews have a mythic belief that one performs Jewish rituals for the children because it is good for the children. The Goodglick family is one whose style of Jewish life was changed by their children. It started when their son Todd (now a doctor) was twelve years old and demanded a more intensive Jewish education. In order to keep up with their children (Todd, Tracey, and Lee), Sandy and Bill began to study as well. Their present Shabbat experience evolved through both study and involvement in the community.

Perhaps the nicest part of our interview with the Goodglicks was a hands-on sense of tradition. There is a principle in the Talmud: a person who repeats something in the name of the person who originally said it brings the redemption (Talmud Ta'anit 15a). In our talk with Sandy and Bill, they made it clear that this is an ongoing practice. In our discussion of their Shabbat Seder, we heard of friends and children who had introduced them to specific practices, camps, and synagogues where they had learned particular melodies, and teachers and rabbis who had helped them understand a particular concept or custom. The Goodglicks' Shabbat Seder has been assembled and arranged like a very special collection of precious objects.

SANDY: Friday is always a hectic day. I think any Jewish housewife will tell you that. First you have to look good. Then you have to have the house look good, and have the table look good, and have the food look good. On Friday I have the first morning appointment at the hairdresser.

BILL: Sandy said something important. She has her hair done on Friday. There was a time in our vivid memory when she used to go on Saturday.

SANDY: Shabbes really starts for me now at 2:45, when I place a call to Providence, Rhode Island, where our youngest son is studying, and he and I have a nice little pre-Shabbes chat, and then the mood takes over for me. I begin to relax and wait for Bill to come home. We always have Mom Goodglick with us on Shabbes, and varying numbers of kids, depending on what's up for them. And we try to have guests—sometimes the kids' age group, sometimes our age group, sometimes a mix, and sometimes there are just the three of us—Bill, Mom, and myself.

SANDY: Then the responsibility for Shabbat shifts to Bill. We sit down, he'll pour the wine, put out the prayerbooks, and then it's his show.

BILL: Sandy says it becomes "my show." It becomes a bit of a show, but someone has to take charge at that point. It has to be a structured kind of affair. If you notice this book, it has fifteen paper clips and bits of paper so I know where I'm going in the book, but no one else does. I do try to vary the readings.

SANDY: If Tracey is here, we sing the blessing. If Tracey is not here, I say the blessing in Hebrew. If we have people who aren't familiar with Shabbat, I'll translate. Sometimes Bill's mom will light the candles. Sometimes we have Tracey light…. When we first lit the candles, Tracey was just a baby, and I didn't even know why we lit them. I just did the transliteration out of the book and didn't really know what I was saying. When we finally got into it, Tracey had learned the blessing to music and she has a nice voice, so when she's here it's natural to sing, and when she's not I just kind of go back to my old ways.

BILL: Our background is not one of deep religious schooling, so this is all learned over the years by observation. For instance, I learned about saying *Eishet Hayil* ("A Woman of Valor") from Phil and Sonia Silverman. They had a profound effect on us, which they know. Sonia is gone now, but Phil used to stand behind Sonia, and they would hold hands. I sit at one end of the table and Sandy sits at the other. It sounds formal, but it isn't. I feel it is important to sing *Eishet Hayil* and to sing it in the presence of all who are there. I think she enjoys it and gets a kick out of it. And usually the meal improves. It works! What can I say?

Practical Questions and Answers

How do I start to "make Shabbat"?

For many, the first motivation to start some sort of Shabbat observance comes from children. The kids come home from nursery or Hebrew school, excited by the "pretend" Shabbat they experience on Friday morning, asking for some sort of Shabbat celebration in the home. "Daddy, can you say Kiddush? Mommy, can we light candles?" Suddenly, we parents who earlier counted on the school to provide these experiences for the child come to understand that some sort of effort is required. Feeling ourselves unskilled at Jewish practice, though open to learning, we seek help to create a Shabbat ritual in the family.

This type of beginning is less than auspicious, particularly since most of us are highly educated professionals who suddenly find ourselves in a situation requiring specific skills and behaviors that are totally foreign and lacking. If we have seen any modeling of the Shabbat ritual, it has probably been by the skilled teacher or professional at a religious school function—not exactly the best role models for those of us who are just starting. It is so easy to be embarrassed for lacking skills that we have no reason to know. Yet, in the face of this impending embarrassment, it is very difficult to ask for help. One begins to "make Shabbes" by deciding that it is important to struggle through this embarrassment and begin.

I can't teach my child Judaism. Isn't it enough that I send my child to religious school?

Not at all. One must not fall into the trap of thinking that only professionals can teach our children religious values and behaviors. It is a truth that parents are successful teachers of many subjects—health, behavior, budgeting, driving a car—although they are not doctors, psychologists, accountants, or mechanics. Yet we are afraid to teach our children Judaism.

We are afraid that we don't know enough, that we won't have the right answers, that we will be embarrassed in front of our children—who may, in fact, know more than we do. To combat this psychological block, we parents must make a conscious decision to become Jewish teachers. This should be a matter of choice, arrived at after careful thought and deliberation. Ideally, both parents will agree on what steps to take in establishing this Jewish time in the family. Clearly, the choice must be made, affirmed, and acted upon rather than left to happenstance.

The second step must involve learning about Shabbat *for oneself*. The more we know about Shabbat, the more comfortable we will be with it in our homes. The more comfortable we are with the blessings and behaviors, the more capable we become as teachers of our own family. Moreover, we need to be personally committed to the observance for effective learning to take place. "This Shabbat Seder is important to me—it is not simply a show for my children."

None of this comes without effort. *The Art of Jewish Living* series has been designed to give adults the environment, the materials, and the guidance to learn the whys and hows of Jewish observance in the home. This is where the process of starting Shabbat truly begins—with a commitment to learn for oneself.

Do we have to do it all from the beginning?

Absolutely not. If Jewish observance is something new, we should not let the seeming enormity of it overwhelm the initial effort. It is not only possible but advisable to begin to assume Jewish ritual life one step at a time. When the famous Jewish philosopher and teacher Franz Rosenzweig was once asked whether he observed certain Jewish rituals, he replied, "Not yet."

Shabbat: Preparing for and Celebrating the Sabbath presents a great deal of material, encompassing the entirety of the traditional Shabbat eve home observance and Shabbat day. Although you will learn about all the steps in the Shabbat Seder, if you are just starting a Shabbat observance, you will be well advised to begin with a few of the basic rituals—for example, candlelighting, blessing of children, Kiddush, *Hamotzi*, and a short version of the *Birkat Hamazon*. Once you become comfortable with the first steps, the other parts of the Seder will fall into place. Remember, every family we interviewed indicated that the evolution of the Shabbat Seder is a fact of Jewish life in the home.

Doesn't the full Shabbat Seder take a long time to do?

We asked the families we visited to estimate how much time it takes them from candlelighting to the *Hamotzi*, just before serving the meal. The average was fifteen to twenty minutes. Depending on which parts of the Shabbat Seder you include in your own composition of the ritual, it might take more time or it might take less.

You should be able to conduct a nearly complete Shabbat Seder, including the meal, *Zemirot*, and *Birkat Hamazon*, within one hour. One hour a week: a worthy investment in your Jewish family.

What if I can't have a Shabbat Seder every week?
Try to put your learning about and celebration of Shabbat in the larger perspective of your life commitments. No one is asking you to make a commitment to observe Shabbat in a certain way the rest of your life. Consider this period of learning one of experimentation, of trying on the various ritual behaviors. Some may fit quite nicely right away; others will feel too tight. Things will likely loosen up down the road. Or you may try to alter the traditional ritual to something that fits you and your family better. This learning, experimenting, and trying-on process can last a lifetime; if it does, it will be a healthy sign of religious maturity and growth.

What if my spouse doesn't go along with this?
A reluctant spouse can be a major obstacle for anyone wishing to begin a Shabbat observance in the home. It is important for you to discuss with your spouse the reasons for this effort and your feelings about needing support. You will also need to listen carefully to your spouse's negative feelings and perhaps try to identify the source of the negativism. Many people who grew up in an oppressive religious environment have a great deal of anger to work out before they can approach Jewish observance with a fresh outlook. It is also embarrassing and at times intimidating for those who lack the skills to make Shabbat to begin. Some spouses will go along passively; others may get enthusiastic as time goes on. Try to encourage him or her to learn with you. If you have serious problems with this, seek the advice of friends, or consult with a rabbi.

What should I do when my children are teenagers and have Friday night social opportunities?
We asked this question of our interviewees as well. They seemed to reflect a consensus that attendance at the family Friday night dinner was not optional. There was an expectation that everyone would be home for this time. One family told us that their teenagers were required to be at home Friday night, but they were always welcome to invite friends to be a part of the evening at home. Another set of parents told us that this expec-

tation was stated, but the teenagers had the right not to attend. However, *their* Shabbat celebration would continue regardless. Although the parents told us they would be disappointed if the child chose not to be there, they felt strongly that their teenagers had to have this freedom of choice. A third family told us that attendance at dinner was required; what the teenager did afterwards was up to him or her. This is not an easy issue for a family with teenagers. Yet, those families who seemed to be successful in establishing a Shabbat dinner ritual full of participation, meaning, good food, and fun had little trouble in keeping this their "sacred" family time of the week.

What if my close relatives don't appreciate our Shabbat celebration?
This can be a frustrating and disappointing problem. One family told us that after many attempts at involving their brother's family in their Shabbat ritual, they simply gave up. The relatives would be invited to Shabbat dinner and would make fun of the sincere effort being made. Finally the family decided that it would be best to be with these relatives on American holidays such as Thanksgiving or the Fourth of July.

I am a single person. How can I make Shabbat?
While it is true that parts of the Shabbat Seder revolve around children, this should not discourage the single person from celebrating Shabbat. As you consider what elements of the Shabbat Seder to include in your own composition of the ceremony, you may want to discard steps such as *Birkhot Hamishpaḥah* (family blessings), which may not be relevant to your situation. The important thing to remember is that it is difficult for anyone to make Shabbat alone. So, find some family or friends to help you establish this time in your life. Some singles we spoke to make Shabbat in their own homes, often inviting guests. Some prefer to celebrate Shabbat at the homes of family members. An increasingly encouraging phenomenon is the development of singles *ḥavurot* that make Shabbat evenings a part of their programming.

I am a "Jew by Choice," recently converted to Judaism. I learned about Shabbat in the conversion class, but I have had little real experience with it. I am nervous about beginning. What should I do?
First of all, *mazal tov* on becoming a member of the Jewish people! Like any Jew just beginning to adopt Shabbat as a regular part of his or her reli-

gious life, you should take it slowly but consistently. While learning the material in the text, try to visit the homes of people who observe the Shabbat ritual. Look for opportunities to participate in a Shabbat dinner celebration in a synagogue, *havurah*, or special support groups for Jews by Choice. You may want to seek the advice of other converts who have had more experience in establishing the Shabbat home ritual in their families. If you are married, try to secure the cooperation of your spouse. It will take some time, but consistent practice will go a long way in helping you to make Shabbat an important part of your new Jewish lifestyle.

In our family, my spouse is not Jewish and has not converted. Should I recite all the blessings myself?
Decisions about religious celebration in an interfaith family are indeed difficult to reach. In one family we met, the father is not Jewish, so the mother conducts the Shabbat ritual. She not only lights candles, she blesses the children and recites Kiddush as well. Her children are beginning to learn some of the easier parts of the ceremony and help her with *Hamotzi*. The father in this family does not actively participate in the Shabbat Seder, although he is present at the table.

If your situation is one in which both Jewish and non-Jewish holidays are celebrated, it may be even more important to include a regular Shabbat Seder in your family's religious observance schedule.

The challenges facing these families are considerable. However, many Jewish institutions now have people, programs, and counseling available to Jews by Choice and interfaith couples looking to establish a meaningful, tension-free religious environment in their homes. If need be, don't hesitate to seek them out.

How do I create my own Shabbat Seder?
Begin by learning the basic steps of the Shabbat table ritual, their meaning, and their practice. It is very difficult to become an "artist" without first knowing the basic strokes and the theory of composition. Once you have learned these ten steps, you will be able to judge for yourself which of them is most important to you. Building on the fundamental steps of candlelighting, blessing the children, Kiddush, *Hamotzi*, and *Birkat Hamazon*, you should be able to compose a Shabbat table celebration that is comfortable and meaningful to you.

Do I have to recite all of the prayers in Hebrew?

The Hebrew language is known as *leshon hakodesh*—"the holy tongue." For generations, the Hebrew words of these prayers tied the Jews of the world to their heritage and their community. Clearly, Jews in every land during the Diaspora experience have translated these blessings into the local language. And yet, something does seem to get lost in the translation. If you cannot read Hebrew, try to say the blessings using the English transliterations. This will feel stilted at first, but with practice you should become more comfortable with the words. If that doesn't work, then by all means use the English translations of the blessings. An easy-to-use booklet of the Shabbat Seder blessings is available from Jewish Lights Publishing: (800) 962-4544.

I don't have a very good voice. Do I have to chant the blessings?

As we will learn later, singing is a very important part of a successful Shabbat Seder. The chanting of the blessings adds greatly to the beauty and the aura of the ritual. Certainly, it is acceptable to recite rather than sing these prayers. However, do try to learn the tunes; the investment of effort will pay tremendous dividends. An audiotape cassette of the chanted blessings is available from Jewish Lights Publishing: (800) 962-4544. And don't worry about your voice. It's very nice!

I love the Shabbat home service, but sometimes my kids complain on Friday night that they have already "celebrated" Shabbat in school during the day. What do I do?

If your children attend a Jewish nursery or day school, the chances are very good that they will experience some sort of "Shabbat" observance in school on Friday. Even though most Jewish educators carefully explain that this is a "pretend" Shabbat or practice for the home ceremony, some children will feel that they have already "had Shabbat" in school.

There are two problems here. One is that young children can mistakenly think that Shabbat begins on Friday morning. It should be made clear to them that Shabbat actually begins just before sundown on Friday night and ends just after sundown on Saturday night. The practice session in school can be very helpful for children to learn the ritual, but it is no substitute for the Shabbat Seder at home. The second problem is that parents could have reluctant participants at the table on Friday night. Tell your children that Shabbat really begins on Friday night and that having the family participate in this ceremony together is very important. Beyond this, try to make your Shabbat Seder something to look forward to each week. Favorite foods, meaningful rituals, and some of the activities suggested in "The Shabbat Gallery" chapter can go a long way to making your home Shabbat celebration an eagerly awaited experience for the kids, even if they did practice the Shabbat rituals at school.

I want my children to learn the Shabbat blessings at home so they will be ready for their Bar and Bat Mitzvah celebrations. Is there anything wrong with letting them do the rituals?

Clearly, most families we spoke to embodied this notion in their Shabbat celebrations. On the other hand, some pointed out that the children never "take over" the entire celebration. One parent told us straight out that Shabbat was for the adults as much as it was for the children. In this family the kids take the lead in certain blessings, or sing along with others, but they never take on total responsibility for the entire service. There is an important point here. The best models children can have for learning to conduct the Shahbat Seder are their parents. Moreover, kids quickly learn that the Shabbat Seder will take place because the parents want to celebrate it *for themselves* as much as "for the sake of the children." Encourage the kids to learn by joining you, and they will learn much more than just the blessings and behaviors.

Starting Shabbat in my family is not going to be easy. How else might I help along the process?

One of the best things to do is enlist others to support your efforts. Invite sympathetic guests, friends who are also learning, and family members who will admire and appreciate your efforts to your home for Shabbat eve. It is extremely important to invite these supportive friends and family at first. A basic principle is in operation here: Jews need other Jews to be Jewish. Surround yourselves with support.

2

סֵדֶר לֵיל שַׁבָּת

Seder Leil Shabbat
The Shabbat Seder

It gives us a chance to unwind and to talk. We come back, and it's just a completely different feeling in this household than on any other night. You know that there are not going to be any phone calls coming in about business. It's time to get shut off. So it's a pretty nice feeling when you walk in the house.

IRWIN WEINGARTEN

Seder is a word most of us recognize. We automatically think of a Passover Seder. It is one of the outstanding moments of the Jewish year. In the Jewish tradition, there is also a weekly Seder that takes place at the Shabbat dinner table. Although not formally a Seder like the Passover Seder, for reference purposes we will call this Friday night celebration the Shabbat Seder.

Seder means "order." At the Passover Seder, the order of the service and meal is organized and guided by the Haggadah, the prayerbook used for that celebration. On Friday night, the Shabbat celebration follows a "Seder" as well: a *Seder Leil Shabbat,* a Seder for Shabbat eve, an ordered set of rituals and blessings that welcome the Shabbat in the home.

This Shabbat Seder is made up of ten steps, which we will explain in detail shortly. First, let us describe them briefly:

1. הֲכָנָה לְשַׁבָּת *Hakhanah leShabbat:* **Preparing for Shabbat**
   Shabbat doesn't just happen. While the Shabbat begins at a fixed time every Friday, for a Jew to participate and fully experience it there needs to be preparation. The house, the table, and the individual are all prepared. With these physical preparations comes a psychological readiness, because Shabbat is also a state of mind. Among the important steps in this Shabbat preparation is the giving of *tzedakah* (alms).

2. הַדְלָקַת נֵרוֹת *Hadlakat Nerot:* **Candlelighting**
   The act of kindling the Shabbat candles actually begins the Shabbat. Lighting candles is a physical act, yet with the recitation of the *berakhah* (blessing), time is symbolically transformed. Weekday time enters a new state of being—Shabbat.

3. שָׁלוֹם עֲלֵיכֶם *Shalom Aleikhem:* **"Peace Be to You"**
   There is a Jewish legend that two angels visit every Jewish home at the beginning of each Shabbat. The traditional song *Shalom Aleikhem* greets these "ministering angels" and is a second echo of the beginning of Shabbat.

4. בִּרְכוֹת הַמִּשְׁפָּחָה *Birkhot Hamishpahah:* **Family Blessings**
   Shabbat is Jewish family time par excellence. This is emphasized by a series of blessings of daughters, sons, and spouses. Traditionally this included the recitation of *Eishet Hayil,* "A Woman of Valor" (Proverbs 31:10–31).

5. קִדּוּשׁ *Kiddush:* **Sanctification of the Day**

Through the recitation of a *berakhah* over a full cup of wine, the Shabbat day is sanctified. In a three-part prayer, we recall the creation of Shabbat, bless the fruit of the vine, and echo the reasons why we remember and observe the Shabbat day.

6. נְטִילַת יָדַיִם *Netilat Yadayim:* **Washing the Hands**

The Rabbis of the Talmud compared the Shabbat table to the Altar in the Temple. It was a holy place. To emphasize this, many of the activities surrounding the meal are designed to remind us of the practices in the ancient Temple in Jerusalem. We wash hands as a symbolic act of purification before breaking bread.

7. הַמּוֹצִיא *Hamotzi:* **Blessing over Bread**

Bread is the staff of life. In the Jewish tradition, the *Hamotzi,* the *berakhah* over bread, marks the beginning of the meal. On Shabbat, this *berakhah* is said over a special bread, *ḥallah.*

8. סְעוּדַת שַׁבָּת *Se'udat Shabbat:* **The Shabbat Meal**

The *Se'udat Shabbat,* the Shabbat meal, involves special food, special songs, and a special tone that make it unlike any other meal of the week.

9. זְמִירוֹת *Zemirot:* **Shabbat Songs**

The *Se'udat Shabbat* is a relaxed, unhurried dinner. The singing of *Zemirot,* special Shabbat songs, is often part of the meal, bringing an extra sense of *Oneg Shabbat* (Shabbat joy). Sometimes, Torah study is also added to the meal.

10. בִּרְכַּת הַמָּזוֹן *Birkat Hamazon:* **Blessing after Food**

The meal is concluded with a series of *berakhot* thanking God for the food that has been eaten. Additionally, some of these blessings praise God for the goodness shown to us in other ways, including the gift of Shabbat.

The Shabbat Seder

סֵדֶר לֵיל שַׁבָּת

The following is a complete text for the *Seder Leil Shabbat* (the Friday Night Table Service). It can be used weekly in your home as a resource for creating your own Shabbat. In the subsequent chapters, we will systematically focus on each step in this Seder, making each act clear and accessible.

1

HAKHANAH LESHABBAT   **PREPARATION FOR SHABBAT**   הֲכָנָה לְשַׁבָּת

A festive Shabbat celebration requires preparation: preparing the home, preparing the meal, preparing the self. In honor of Shabbat, we contribute *tzedakah* for the support of the Jewish community.

2

At least two candles are lit, the eyes are covered, and the blessing is recited. Upon completing the blessing, look at the lights and wish each other "Shabbat Shalom."

HADLAKAT NEROT

Barukh attah Adonai

Eloheinu melekh ha'olam

asher kidshanu bemitzvotav

vetzivanu lehadlik ner

shel Shabbat.

הַדְלָקַת נֵרוֹת

בָּרוּךְ אַתָּה יְיָ,

אֱלֹהֵינוּ מֶלֶךְ הָעוֹלָם,

אֲשֶׁר קִדְּשָׁנוּ בְּמִצְוֹתָיו,

וְצִוָּנוּ לְהַדְלִיק נֵר

שֶׁל שַׁבָּת.

CANDLELIGHTING

Praised are You, Adonai,

our God, Ruler of the universe,

who made us holy through the commandments

and commanded us to kindle

the Shabbat lights.

3

As we gather at the table we join in singing this traditional hymn welcoming the Shabbat:

SHALOM ALEIKHEM

Shalom aleikhem

malakhei hasharet

malakhei Elyon

mimelekh malkhei hamelakhim

Hakadosh barukh hu.

Bo'akhem leshalom

malakhei hashalom

malakhei Elyon

mimelekh malkhei hamelakhim

Hakadosh barukh hu.

Barkhuni leshalom

malakhei hashalom

malakhei Elyon

mimelekh malkhei hamelakhim

Hakadosh barukh hu.

Tzeitkhem leshalom

malakhei hashalom

malakhei Elyon

mimelekh malkhei hamelakhim

Hakadosh barukh hu.

PEACE BE TO YOU

Peace be to you,

ministering angels,

angels of the Most High

from the Ruler, the Ruler of Rulers,

The Holy One, the One to be praised.

Come in peace,

angels of peace,

angels of the Most High

from the Ruler, the Ruler of Rulers,

The Holy One, the One to be praised.

Bless me with peace,

angels of peace,

angels of the Most High

from the Ruler, the Ruler of Rulers,

The Holy One, the One to be praised.

Go in peace,

angels of peace,

angels of the Most High,

from the Ruler, the Ruler of Rulers,

The Holy One, the One to be praised.

שָׁלוֹם עֲלֵיכֶם

שָׁלוֹם עֲלֵיכֶם,
מַלְאֲכֵי הַשָּׁרֵת,
מַלְאֲכֵי עֶלְיוֹן,
מִמֶּלֶךְ מַלְכֵי הַמְּלָכִים,
הַקָּדוֹשׁ בָּרוּךְ הוּא:

בּוֹאֲכֶם לְשָׁלוֹם,
מַלְאֲכֵי הַשָּׁלוֹם,
מַלְאֲכֵי עֶלְיוֹן,
מִמֶּלֶךְ מַלְכֵי הַמְּלָכִים,
הַקָּדוֹשׁ בָּרוּךְ הוּא:

בָּרְכוּנִי לְשָׁלוֹם,
מַלְאֲכֵי הַשָּׁלוֹם,
מַלְאֲכֵי עֶלְיוֹן,
מִמֶּלֶךְ מַלְכֵי הַמְּלָכִים,
הַקָּדוֹשׁ בָּרוּךְ הוּא:

צֵאתְכֶם לְשָׁלוֹם,
מַלְאֲכֵי הַשָּׁלוֹם,
מַלְאֲכֵי עֶלְיוֹן,
מִמֶּלֶךְ מַלְכֵי הַמְּלָכִים,
הַקָּדוֹשׁ בָּרוּךְ הוּא:

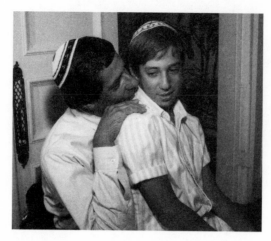

4

In the spirit of *shalom bayit*—"peace in the home"—we offer blessings for our children.

BIRKHOT HAMISHPAHAH

FAMILY BLESSINGS

For the Sons

Y'simkha Elohim
k'Efrayim vekhiMenashe.

(May) God make you
like Ephraim and Menasseh.

For the Daughters

Yesimekh Elohim
keSarah Rivka Rahel veLeah.

(May) God make you
like Sarah, Rebecca, Rachel, and Leah.

For All Children

Yevarekhekha Adonai
veyishmerekha.

(May) God bless you
and watch over you.

Ya'er Adonai panav
elekha vihuneka.

(May) God cause the Divine face to shine
upon you and be gracious to you.

Yisa Adonai panav elekha
veyasem lekha shalom.

(May) God lift up the Divine face toward you
and give you peace.

בִּרְכוֹת הַמִּשְׁפָּחָה

יְשִׂימְךָ אֱלֹהִים
כְּאֶפְרַיִם וְכִמְנַשֶּׁה.

יְשִׂימֵךְ אֱלֹהִים
כְּשָׂרָה רִבְקָה רָחֵל וְלֵאָה.

יְבָרֶכְךָ יְיָ
וְיִשְׁמְרֶךָ.
יָאֵר יְיָ פָּנָיו
אֵלֶיךָ וִיחֻנֶּךָּ.
יִשָּׂא יְיָ פָּנָיו אֵלֶיךָ
וְיָשֵׂם לְךָ שָׁלוֹם.

Turning to the parents, we offer words of praise.

EISHET HAYIL	A WOMAN OF VALOR (PROVERBS 31:10–31)
Eishet hayil mi yimtza	A good wife, who can find?
verahok mipeninim mikhrah.	She is more precious than corals.
Batah ba lev ba'lah	The heart of her husband trusts in her,
veshalal lo yehsar.	And he has no lack of gain.
Gemalat'hu tov velo ra	She does him good and not harm
kol yemei hayeha.	All the days of her life.
Darsha tzemer ufishtim	She seeks out wool and flax
vata'as beheifetz kapeha.	And works it up as her hands will.
Hayta ka'oniyot soher	She is like the ships of the merchant;
mimerhak tavi lahmah.	From afar she brings her food.
Vatakom be'od lailah	She arises while it is yet night,
vatiten teref leveita	And gives food to her household,
vehok lena'aroteha.	And a portion to her maidens.
Zamema sadeh vatikaheihu	She examines a field and buys it;
mipri khapeha nat'ah karem.	With the fruit of her hands she plants a vineyard.
Hagrah ve'oz motneha	She girds herself with strength,
vate'ametz zero'oteha.	And braces her arms for work.
Ta'amah ki tov sahrah	She perceives that her profit is good;
lo yikhbeh valailah nerah.	Her lamp does not go out at night.
Yadeha shilhah vakishor	She lays her hands on the distaff;
vekhapeha tamkhu falekh.	Her palms grasp the spindle.
Kapah parsah le'ani	She opens her hand to the poor,
veyadeha shilhah la'evyon.	And extends her hands to the needy.
Lo tira leveita mishaleg	She does not fear snow for her household,
ki khol beitah lavush shanim.	For all her household are clad in warm garments.

אֵשֶׁת חַיִל

אֵשֶׁת חַיִל מִי יִמְצָא
וְרָחֹק מִפְּנִינִים מִכְרָהּ:
בָּטַח בָּהּ לֵב בַּעְלָהּ
וְשָׁלָל לֹא יֶחְסָר:
גְּמָלַתְהוּ טוֹב וְלֹא־רָע
כֹּל יְמֵי חַיֶּיהָ:
דָּרְשָׁה צֶמֶר וּפִשְׁתִּים
וַתַּעַשׂ בְּחֵפֶץ כַּפֶּיהָ:
הָיְתָה כָּאֳנִיּוֹת סוֹחֵר
מִמֶּרְחָק תָּבִיא לַחְמָהּ:
וַתָּקָם בְּעוֹד לַיְלָה
וַתִּתֵּן טֶרֶף לְבֵיתָהּ
וְחֹק לְנַעֲרֹתֶיהָ:
זָמְמָה שָׂדֶה וַתִּקָּחֵהוּ
מִפְּרִי כַפֶּיהָ נָטְעָה כָּרֶם:
חָגְרָה בְעוֹז מָתְנֶיהָ
וַתְּאַמֵּץ זְרוֹעֹתֶיהָ:
טָעֲמָה כִּי־טוֹב סַחְרָהּ
לֹא־יִכְבֶּה בַלַּיְלָה נֵרָהּ:
יָדֶיהָ שִׁלְּחָה בַכִּישׁוֹר
וְכַפֶּיהָ תָּמְכוּ פָלֶךְ:
כַּפָּהּ פָּרְשָׂה לֶעָנִי
וְיָדֶיהָ שִׁלְּחָה לָאֶבְיוֹן:
לֹא־תִירָא לְבֵיתָהּ מִשָּׁלֶג
כִּי כָל־בֵּיתָהּ לָבֻשׁ שָׁנִים:

Marvadim astah lah	Coverlets she makes for herself;
shesh ve'argaman levushah.	Her clothing is fine linen and purple.
Noda bashe'arim ba'lah	Her husband is distinguished in the council
beshivto im ziknei aretz.	When he sits among the elders of the land.
Sadin astah vatimkor	She makes linen cloth and sells it;
vahagor natnah lakena'ani.	She delivers belts to the merchant.
Oz vehadar levushah	Strength and honor are her garb;
vatishak leyom aharon.	She smiles confidently at the future.
Piha pathah vehokhmah	She opens her mouth with wisdom,
vetorat hesed al leshonah.	And the teaching of kindness is on her tongue.
Tzofiya halikhot beitah	She looks well to the ways of her household;
velehem atzlut lo tokhel.	She eats not the bread of idleness.
Kamu vaneha vayashruha	Her children rise up and call her blessed,
ba'lah vayehalelah.	And her husband praises her:
Rabot banot asu hayil	"Many daughters have done excellently,
ve'at alit al kulanah.	But you excel them all."
Sheker hahen vehevel hayofi	Grace is deceptive and beauty is passing;
isha yirat Adonai hi tit'halal.	A woman revering Adonai, she shall be praised.
Tenu la mipri yadeha	Give her of the fruit of her hands,
viyhaleluha vashe'arim ma'aseha.	And let her own works praise her in the gates.

מַרְבַדִּים עָשְׂתָה־לָּהּ
שֵׁשׁ וְאַרְגָּמָן לְבוּשָׁהּ:
נוֹדָע בַּשְּׁעָרִים בַּעְלָהּ
בְּשִׁבְתּוֹ עִם־זִקְנֵי־אָרֶץ:
סָדִין עָשְׂתָה וַתִּמְכֹּר
וַחֲגוֹר נָתְנָה לַכְּנַעֲנִי:
עוֹז־וְהָדָר לְבוּשָׁהּ
וַתִּשְׂחַק לְיוֹם אַחֲרוֹן:
פִּיהָ פָּתְחָה בְחָכְמָה
וְתוֹרַת־חֶסֶד עַל־לְשׁוֹנָהּ:
צוֹפִיָּה הֲלִיכוֹת בֵּיתָהּ
וְלֶחֶם עַצְלוּת לֹא תֹאכֵל:
קָמוּ בָנֶיהָ וַיְאַשְּׁרוּהָ
בַּעְלָהּ וַיְהַלְלָהּ:
רַבּוֹת בָּנוֹת עָשׂוּ חָיִל
וְאַתְּ עָלִית עַל־כֻּלָּנָה:
שֶׁקֶר הַחֵן וְהֶבֶל הַיֹּפִי
אִשָּׁה יִרְאַת־יְיָ הִיא תִתְהַלָּל:
תְּנוּ־לָהּ מִפְּרִי יָדֶיהָ
וִיהַלְלוּהָ בַשְּׁעָרִים מַעֲשֶׂיהָ:

ASHREI ISH

Haleluyah.

Ashrei ish yarei et Adonai

bemitzvotav ḥafetz me'od.

Gibor ba'aretz yihyeh zar'o

dor yesharim yevorakh.

Hon va'osher beveito

vetzidkato omedet la'ad.

Zaraḥ baḥoshekh or laysharim

Ḥanun veraḥum vetzadik....

Mishmu'ah ra'ah lo yira

Nakhon libo batu'aḥ bAdonai.

Samukh libo lo yira....

Pizar natan la'evyonim

tzidkato omedet la'ad.

Karno tarum bekhavod....

HAPPY IS THE MAN (PSALM 112)

Halleluya!

Happy is the man who reveres Adonai,

Who greatly delights in God's commandments.

His descendants will be honored in the land;

The generation of the upright will be praised.

His household prospers,

And his righteousness endures forever.

Light dawns in the darkness for the upright;

For the one who is gracious, compassionate and just...

He is not afraid of evil tidings;

His mind is firm, trusting in Adonai.

His heart is steady, he will not be afraid....

He has given to the poor.

His righteousness endures forever;

His life is exalted in honor....

אַשְׁרֵי־אִישׁ

הַלְלוּיָהּ
אַשְׁרֵי־אִישׁ יָרֵא אֶת־יְיָ
בְּמִצְוֹתָיו חָפֵץ מְאֹד:
גִּבּוֹר בָּאָרֶץ יִהְיֶה זַרְעוֹ
דּוֹר יְשָׁרִים יְבֹרָךְ:
הוֹן־וָעֹשֶׁר בְּבֵיתוֹ
וְצִדְקָתוֹ עֹמֶדֶת לָעַד:
זָרַח בַּחֹשֶׁךְ אוֹר לַיְשָׁרִים
חַנּוּן וְרַחוּם וְצַדִּיק:
מִשְּׁמוּעָה רָעָה לֹא יִירָא
נָכוֹן לִבּוֹ בָּטֻחַ בַּיְיָ:
סָמוּךְ לִבּוֹ לֹא יִירָא
פִּזַּר נָתַן לָאֶבְיוֹנִים
צִדְקָתוֹ עֹמֶדֶת לָעַד
קַרְנוֹ תָּרוּם בְּכָבוֹד:

45

BIRKAT HAMISHPAHAH

Harahaman

hu yevarekh

otanu kulanu yahad

bevirkat shalom.

FAMILY BLESSING

May the Merciful One

bless

all of us together

with the blessing of peace.

בִּרְכוֹת הַמִּשְׁפָּחָה

הָרַחֲמָן

הוּא יְבָרֵךְ

אוֹתָנוּ כֻּלָּנוּ יַחַד

בְּבִרְכַּת שָׁלוֹם.

5

By reciting the Kiddush, we acknowledge the sanctity of Shabbat through blessing a cup of wine. The cup is lifted, and we say:

KIDDUSH

SANCTIFICATION OF THE DAY

VAYKHULU

Vayehi erev vayehi voker:	And there was evening and there was morning:
yom hashishi.	the sixth day.
Vaykhulu hashamayim	And the heavens were completed
Veha'aretz vekhol tzeva'am.	and the earth and all its components (were completed).
Vayekhal Elohim	And God completed
bayom hashvi'i	on the seventh day
melakhto asher asa;	the work which God had been doing;
Vayishbot bayom hashvi'i	and rested on the seventh day
mikol melakhto asher asa.	from all the work which had been done.
Vayevarekh Elohim	And God blessed
et yom hashvi'i	the seventh day
vayekadesh oto	and sanctified it,
ki vo shavat	because on it, God rested
mikol melakhto	from all the work
asher bara Elohim la'asot.	which God had created through doing.

BOREI PERI HAGAFEN

Barukh attah Adonai	Praised are You, Adonai,
Eloheinu melekh ha'olam	our God, Ruler of the universe,
borei peri hagafen.	Creator of the fruit of the vine.

קִדּוּשׁ

וַיְהִי־עֶרֶב וַיְהִי־בֹקֶר
יוֹם הַשִּׁשִּׁי.
וַיְכֻלּוּ הַשָּׁמַיִם
וְהָאָרֶץ וְכָל־צְבָאָם.
וַיְכַל אֱלֹהִים
בַּיּוֹם הַשְּׁבִיעִי
מְלַאכְתּוֹ אֲשֶׁר עָשָׂה
וַיִּשְׁבֹּת בַּיּוֹם הַשְּׁבִיעִי
מִכָּל־מְלַאכְתּוֹ אֲשֶׁר עָשָׂה.
וַיְבָרֶךְ אֱלֹהִים
אֶת־יוֹם הַשְּׁבִיעִי
וַיְקַדֵּשׁ אֹתוֹ
כִּי בוֹ שָׁבַת
מִכָּל־מְלַאכְתּוֹ
אֲשֶׁר־בָּרָא אֱלֹהִים לַעֲשׂוֹת.

בָּרוּךְ אַתָּה יְיָ
אֱלֹהֵינוּ מֶלֶךְ הָעוֹלָם
בּוֹרֵא פְּרִי הַגָּפֶן.

MEKADESH HASHABBAT

Barukh attah Adonai	Praised are You, Adonai,
Eloheinu melekh ha'olam	our God, Ruler of the universe,
asher kidshanu bemitzvotav	who made us holy through the commandments
veratza vanu.	and who is pleased with us.
VeShabbat kodsho	And the holy Shabbat,
b'ahava uvratzon	with love and satisfaction,
hinhilanu—	God gave us as an inheritance—
zikaron lema'asei vereishit.	a remembrance of the work of Creation.
Ki hu yom tehilah	For it was first among
lemikra'ei kodesh—	the sacred days of assembly—
zeikher litziyat Mitzrayim.	a remembrance of the Exodus from Egypt.
Ki vanu vaharta	For You have chosen us
ve'otanu kidashta	and You have sanctified us
mikol ha'amim;	from (among) all the peoples;
veShabbat kodshekha	and Your holy Shabbat
be'ahava uvratzon	with love and satisfaction.
hinhaltanu.	You gave us as an inheritance.
Barukh attah Adonai	Praised are You, Adonai,
Mekadesh Hashabbat.	Sanctifier of the Shabbat.

בָּרוּךְ אַתָּה יְיָ

אֱלֹהֵינוּ מֶלֶךְ הָעוֹלָם

אֲשֶׁר קִדְּשָׁנוּ בְּמִצְוֹתָיו

וְרָצָה בָנוּ

וְשַׁבַּת קָדְשׁוֹ

בְּאַהֲבָה וּבְרָצוֹן

הִנְחִילָנוּ

זִכָּרוֹן לְמַעֲשֵׂה בְרֵאשִׁית

כִּי הוּא יוֹם תְּחִלָּה

לְמִקְרָאֵי קֹדֶשׁ

זֵכֶר לִיצִיאַת מִצְרָיִם

כִּי בָנוּ בָחַרְתָּ

וְאוֹתָנוּ קִדַּשְׁתָּ

מִכָּל הָעַמִּים

וְשַׁבַּת קָדְשְׁךָ

בְּאַהֲבָה וּבְרָצוֹן

הִנְחַלְתָּנוּ.

בָּרוּךְ אַתָּה יְיָ

מְקַדֵּשׁ הַשַּׁבָּת.

6

As the Rabbis did in the days of the Temple, we ritually cleanse our hands in order to sanctify the act of eating. We cover our hands with water and recite:

NETILAT YADAYIM

Barukh attah Adonai

Eloheinu melekh ha'olam

asher kidshanu bemitzvotav

vetzivanu

al netilat yadayim.

נְטִילַת יָדָיִם

בָּרוּךְ אַתָּה יְיָ

אֱלֹהֵינוּ מֶלֶךְ הָעוֹלָם

אֲשֶׁר קִדְּשָׁנוּ בְּמִצְוֹתָיו

וְצִוָּנוּ

עַל נְטִילַת יָדָיִם.

WASHING THE HANDS

Praised are You, Adonai,

our God, Ruler of the universe,

who has made us holy through the commandments

and commanded us

concerning the washing of hands.

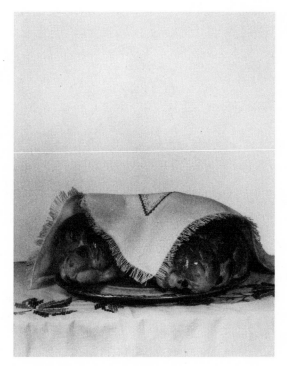

7

The two special Shabbat loaves, _Hallot_, are uncovered, and we say:

HAMOTZI	הַמּוֹצִיא
Barukh attah Adonai	בָּרוּךְ אַתָּה יְיָ,
Eloheinu melekh ha'olam	אֱלֹהֵינוּ מֶלֶךְ הָעוֹלָם
hamotzi lehem min ha'aretz.	הַמּוֹצִיא לֶחֶם מִן הָאָרֶץ.

BLESSING OVER BREAD

Praised are You, Adonai,

our God, Ruler of the universe,

who brings forth bread from the earth.

8

SE'UDAT SHABBAT   THE SHABBAT MEAL   סְעוּדַת שַׁבָּת

9

ZEMIROT	SHABBAT SONGS	זְמִירוֹת

During our festive meal, let us share in song:

SHABBAT SHALOM

Bim bam, bim bim bim bam,
Bim bim bim bim bim bam.
Shabbat shalom,
Shabbat shalom,
Shabbat, Shabbat, Shabbat,
Shabbat shalom.

בִּים בָּם
בִּים בָּם
שַׁבָּת שָׁלוֹם
שַׁבָּת שָׁלוֹם.

LEKHA DODI

Lekha dodi likrat kallah	Come, my friend, to greet the Bride.
Penei Shabbat nekablah.	Let's encounter the presence of Shabbat.
Shamor vezakhor bedibur ehad.	"Observe" and "Remember" in one word.
Hishmi'anu El hamyuhad.	The One God who caused us to hear.
Adonai ehad ushmo ehad.	Adonai is One and the Divine Name is One.
Leshem ultiferet velit'hilah.	To the Divine Name is the glory and the fame.
(Lekha dodi…)	
Likrat Shabbat lekhu venelkhah!	To greet the Shabbat, let us go!
Ki hi mekor haberakhah,	Because it is the source of blessing,
Meirosh mikedem nesukhah,	Conceived before life on earth began,
Sof ma'aseh bemahshavah	Last in God's work, first in God's thought.
tehilah. (Lekha dodi…)	
Hit'oreri hit'oreri,	Arise, arise, for your light has risen,
Ki va orekh kumi ori.	For the dawn has broken, the light has come.
Uri uri shir daberi;	Awake, awake, and joyously sing;
Kevod Adonai alayikh niglah.	The honor of Adonai is upon you and revealed.
(Lekha dodi…)	
Yamin usmol tifrotzi;	From the right to the left, you will prosper;
Ve'et Adonai ta'aritzi.	And you will always revere Adonai.
Al yad ish ben Partzi,	Through the person descended from Peretz (King David),
Venismeha venagilah.	We will rejoice and exult.
(Lekha dodi…)	
Bo'i veshalom ateret ba'lah,	Come in peace, crown of her husband,
Gam besimhah uvtzoholah.	Come in happiness and with good cheer.
Tokh emunei am segulah,	Amidst the faithful of the treasured people,
Bo'i khallah; bo'i khallah!	Come, Bride; Come, Bride!
(Lekha dodi…)	

לְכָה דוֹדִי לִקְרַאת כַּלָּה
פְּנֵי שַׁבָּת נְקַבְּלָה:

שָׁמוֹר וְזָכוֹר בְּדִבּוּר אֶחָד
הִשְׁמִיעָנוּ אֵל הַמְיֻחָד
יְיָ אֶחָד וּשְׁמוֹ אֶחָד
לְשֵׁם וּלְתִפְאֶרֶת וְלִתְהִלָּה:

לִקְרַאת שַׁבָּת לְכוּ וְנֵלְכָה
כִּי הִיא מְקוֹר הַבְּרָכָה
מֵרֹאשׁ מִקֶּדֶם נְסוּכָה
סוֹף מַעֲשֶׂה בְּמַחֲשָׁבָה
תְּחִלָּה:
הִתְעוֹרְרִי הִתְעוֹרְרִי
כִּי בָא אוֹרֵךְ קוּמִי אוֹרִי
עוּרִי עוּרִי שִׁיר דַּבֵּרִי
כְּבוֹד יְיָ עָלַיִךְ נִגְלָה:

יָמִין וּשְׂמֹאל תִּפְרוֹצִי
וְאֶת־יְיָ תַּעֲרִיצִי
עַל יַד אִישׁ בֶּן פַּרְצִי
וְנִשְׂמְחָה וְנָגִילָה:

בּוֹאִי בְשָׁלוֹם עֲטֶרֶת בַּעְלָהּ
גַּם בְּשִׂמְחָה וּבְצָהֳלָה
תּוֹךְ אֱמוּנֵי עַם סְגֻלָּה
בּוֹאִי כַלָּה, בּוֹאִי כַלָּה:

YISMEHU VEMALAKHUTEKHA

Yismehu vemalakhutekha	Rejoice in Your reign.
Shomrei, shomrei, shomrei Shabbat,	Observe the Shabbat.
vekorei oneg Shabbat.	Call the Shabbat a delight.

EILEH HAMDAH LIBI

Eileh hamda libi	Be merciful, my beloved, and pray,
Husa na ve'al na tit'alem.	do not hide from us.

TZUR MISHELO

Tzur mishelo akhalnu	Our Rock, from whose goodness we have eaten,
Barkhu emunai	Let us praise our God, my faithful ones.
Sava'nu vehotarnu	We have satisfied ourselves and we have left over (food)
Kidvar Adonai.	According to the word of Adonai.

Hazan et olamo	You feed the world,
Ro'einu avinu	Our Shepherd, Our Parent.
Akhalnu et lahmo	We eat of God's bread,
Veyeino shatinu.	Of Your wine we drink.
Al ken nodeh lishmo	For this, we give thanks to God
Unehalelo befinu.	And praise God with our mouths.
Amarnu ve'aninu;	We say and we answer:
Ein kadosh kAdonai.	None is as holy as Adonai.
(Tzur mishelo…)	
Beshir vekol todah	With song and a voice of thanks,
Nevarekh leloheinu.	We praise our God,
Al eretz hemdah	For the spacious land,
Shehinhil la'avoteinu.	Which is the inheritance of our ancestors.
Mazon vetzeidah	Food and sustenance
Hisbi'a lenafsheinu.	is rich reward to our souls.
Hasdo gavar aleinu	God's gracious love determines all,
Ve'emet Adonai. (Tzur mishelo…)	And the truth of Adonai.

יִשְׂמְחוּ בְמַלְכוּתְךָ
שׁוֹמְרֵי שַׁבָּת
וְקוֹרְאֵי עֹנֶג שַׁבָּת.

אֵלֶּה חָמְדָה לִבִּי
חוּסָה נָא וְאַל נָא תִּתְעַלֵּם.

צוּר מִשֶּׁלּוֹ אָכַלְנוּ
בָּרְכוּ אֱמוּנַי
שָׂבַעְנוּ וְהוֹתַרְנוּ
כִּדְבַר יְיָ.

הַזָּן אֶת־עוֹלָמוֹ
רוֹעֵנוּ אָבִינוּ
אָכַלְנוּ אֶת־לַחְמוֹ
וְיֵינוֹ שָׁתִינוּ
עַל כֵּן נוֹדֶה לִשְׁמוֹ
וּנְהַלְלוֹ בְּפִינוּ
אָמַרְנוּ וְעָנִינוּ
אֵין קָדוֹשׁ כַּיְיָ.

בְּשִׁיר וְקוֹל תּוֹדָה
נְבָרֵךְ לֵאלֹהֵינוּ
עַל אֶרֶץ חֶמְדָּה טוֹבָה
שֶׁהִנְחִיל לַאֲבוֹתֵינוּ
מָזוֹן וְצֵידָה
הִשְׂבִּיעַ לְנַפְשֵׁנוּ
חַסְדּוֹ גָּבַר עָלֵינוּ
וֶאֱמֶת יְיָ.

HINEI MAH TOV

Hinei mah tov umah na'im
shevet aḥim gam yaḥad.

הִנֵּה מַה־טּוֹב וּמַה־נָּעִים
שֶׁבֶת אַחִים גַּם־יָחַד.

Behold, how good and pleasant it is
For brethren to dwell together in unity.

DAVID MELEKH YISRA'EL

David, Melekh Yisra'el,
Ḥai, ḥai, vekayam!

דָּוִד מֶלֶךְ יִשְׂרָאֵל
חַי וְקַיָּם.

David, King of Israel,
lives forever!

LO YISA GOY

Lo yisa goy el goy ḥerev,
Lo yilmedu od milḥamah.

לֹא־יִשָּׂא גוֹי אֶל־גּוֹי חֶרֶב
לֹא־יִלְמְדוּ עוֹד מִלְחָמָה:

Nation shall not lift up sword against nation,
Neither shall they learn war any more.

10

BIRKAT HAMAZON   **BLESSING AFTER FOOD**   בִּרְכַּת הַמָּזוֹן

To complete our Shabbat Seder, we praise God for providing us good food, our families and friends, and the Shabbat itself:

SHIR HAMA'ALOT

Shir Hama'alot:	A song of ascents:
Beshuv Adonai	When Adonai restores
et shivat Tzion	the fortunes of Zion,
hayinu keholmim.	we will be as in a dream.
Az yimalei sehok pinu	Then our mouths will be filled with laughter
ulshoneinu rina.	and our tongues (filled with) songs of joy.
Az yomru vagoyim:	Then they will say among the nations:
"Higdil Adonai la'asot	"Adonai did great things
im eileh."	for them."
Higdil Adonai la'asot imanu;	Adonai will do great things for us;
hayinu semeihim.	we will be happy.
Shuva Adonai et sheviteinu	God will restore our fortune
ka'afikim baNegev.	like streams in the Negev.
Hazor'im bedim'a	Those who sow in tears,
berina yiktzoru;	with songs they shall reap;
Halokh yeleikh uvakho	One who walks along and weeps,
nosei meshekh hazara—	carrying a sack of seeds—
bo yavo verina,	that one will come back with song,
nosei alumotav.	carrying sheaves.

שִׁיר הַמַּעֲלוֹת
בְּשׁוּב יְיָ
אֶת־שִׁיבַת צִיּוֹן
הָיִינוּ כְּחֹלְמִים:
אָז יִמָּלֵא שְׂחוֹק פִּינוּ
וּלְשׁוֹנֵנוּ רִנָּה
אָז יֹאמְרוּ בַגּוֹיִם
הִגְדִּיל יְיָ לַעֲשׂוֹת
עִם־אֵלֶּה:
הִגְדִּיל יְיָ לַעֲשׂוֹת עִמָּנוּ
הָיִינוּ שְׂמֵחִים:
שׁוּבָה יְיָ אֶת־שְׁבִיתֵנוּ
כַּאֲפִיקִים בַּנֶּגֶב:
הַזֹּרְעִים בְּדִמְעָה
בְּרִנָּה יִקְצֹרוּ:
הָלוֹךְ יֵלֵךְ וּבָכֹה
נֹשֵׂא מֶשֶׁךְ־הַזָּרַע
בֹּא־יָבוֹא בְרִנָּה
נֹשֵׂא אֲלֻמֹּתָיו:

ZIMMUN

The *Zimmun* is recited responsively when three or more adults are present. The word *Eloheinu* is added to the *Zimmun* if ten or more adults are present.

Leader:

Haverai nevarekh.　　　　　　　My friends, let us praise.

Everyone:

Yehi shem Adonai mevorakh　　　May Adonai's name be praised

meiattah ve'ad olam.　　　　　　from now and until forever.

Leader:

Yehi shem Adonai mevorakh　　　May Adonai's name be praised

meiattah ve'ad olam.　　　　　　from now and until forever.

Birshut haverai,　　　　　　　　With the consent of my friends,

nevarekh (Eloheinu)　　　　　　let us praise (our God) the One

she'akhalnu mishelo.　　　　　　whose food we have eaten.

Everyone:

Barukh (Eloheinu)　　　　　　　Praised is (our God) the One

she'akhalnu mishelo　　　　　　whose (food) we have eaten,

uvtuvo hayinu.　　　　　　　　and by whose goodness we live.

Leader:

Barukh (Eloheinu)　　　　　　　Praised is (our God) the One whose

she'akhalnu mishelo　　　　　　(food) we have eaten,

uvtuvo hayinu.　　　　　　　　and by whose goodness we live.

Everyone:

Barukh hu uvarukh shemo.　　　Praised be God and praised be God's name.

חֲבֵרַי נְבָרֵךְ:

יְהִי שֵׁם יְיָ מְבֹרָךְ
מֵעַתָּה וְעַד עוֹלָם:

יְהִי שֵׁם יְיָ מְבֹרָךְ
מֵעַתָּה וְעַד עוֹלָם:
בִּרְשׁוּת חֲבֵרַי
נְבָרֵךְ (אֱלֹהֵינוּ)
שֶׁאָכַלְנוּ מִשֶּׁלּוֹ.

בָּרוּךְ (אֱלֹהֵינוּ)
שֶׁאָכַלְנוּ מִשֶּׁלּוֹ
וּבְטוּבוֹ חָיִינוּ.

בָּרוּךְ (אֱלֹהֵינוּ)
שֶׁאָכַלְנוּ מִשֶּׁלּוֹ
וּבְטוּבוֹ חָיִינוּ.

בָּרוּךְ הוּא וּבָרוּךְ שְׁמוֹ:

HAZAN ET HAKOL

Barukh attah Adonai	Praised are You, Adonai,
Eloheinu melekh ha'olam	Our God, Ruler of the universe,
hazan et ha'olam	who feeds the world,
kulo betuvo	all of it with goodness,
behen behesed uvrahamim.	with graciousness, with love, and with compassion.
Hu notein lehem lekhol basar	God provides food to every creature
ki le'olam hasdo.	because divine love (endures) forever.
Uvtuvo hagadol	And through it, God's great goodness
tamid lo hasar lanu	has never failed us,
ve'al yehsar lanu mazon	and food will not fail us
le'olam va'ed	ever,
ba'avur shemo hagadol.	for the sake of God's great name.
Ki hu El zan umfarnes lakol	Because God who feeds and provides for all,
umeitiv lakol	and does good for all,
umeikhin mazon	and prepares food
lekhol beriyotav asher bara.	for all creatures that God created.
Barukh attah Adonai	Praised are You, Adonai,
Hazan et hakol.	the Provider of food for all.

בָּרוּךְ אַתָּה יְיָ
אֱלֹהֵינוּ מֶלֶךְ הָעוֹלָם
הַזָּן אֶת־הָעוֹלָם
כֻּלּוֹ בְּטוּבוֹ
בְּחֵן בְּחֶסֶד וּבְרַחֲמִים.
הוּא נוֹתֵן לֶחֶם לְכָל־בָּשָׂר
כִּי לְעוֹלָם חַסְדּוֹ
וּבְטוּבוֹ הַגָּדוֹל
תָּמִיד לֹא חָסַר לָנוּ
וְאַל יֶחְסַר לָנוּ מָזוֹן
לְעוֹלָם וָעֶד
בַּעֲבוּר שְׁמוֹ הַגָּדוֹל
כִּי הוּא אֵל זָן וּמְפַרְנֵס לַכֹּל
וּמֵטִיב לַכֹּל
וּמֵכִין מָזוֹן
לְכָל־בְּרִיּוֹתָיו אֲשֶׁר בָּרָא:
בָּרוּךְ אַתָּה יְיָ
הַזָּן אֶת הַכֹּל:

AL HA'ARETZ VE'AL HAMAZON

Nodeh lekha, Adonai, Eloheinu,	We thank You Adonai, Our God,
al shehinhalta la'avoteinu:	for Your inheritance to our ancestors:
eretz hemda, tovah, urhavah,	a land—desirable, good, and spacious,
berit veTorah, hayim umazon.	the covenant and the Torah, life and food.
Yitbarakh shimkha	May Your name be praised
befi khol hai	by the mouth of every living thing,
tamid le'olam va'ed.	always and forever.
Kakatuv:	As it is written:
"ve'akhalta vesavata	"and (when) you have eaten, and are satisfied,
uverakhta et Adonai Elohekha	you shall praise Adonai, Your God,
al ha'aretz hatovah	for the good land
asher natan lakh."	which God gave to you."
Barukh attah Adonai	Praised are You, Adonai,
al ha'aretz ve'al hamazon.	for the land and for the sustenance.

BIRKAT YERUSHALAYIM

Uvnei Yerushalayim	Rebuild Jerusalem,
ir hakodesh	the Holy City,
bimheirah veyameinu.	soon, and in our days.
Barukh attah, Adonai,	Praised are You, Adonai,
boneih verahamav Yerushalayim,	who with compassion rebuilds Jerusalem,
Amen.	Amen.

נוֹדֶה לְּךָ יְיָ אֱלֹהֵינוּ
עַל שֶׁהִנְחַלְתָּ לַאֲבוֹתֵינוּ
אֶרֶץ חֶמְדָּה טוֹבָה וּרְחָבָה
בְּרִית וְתוֹרָה, חַיִּים וּמָזוֹן.
יִתְבָּרַךְ שִׁמְךָ
בְּפִי כָל-חַי
תָּמִיד לְעוֹלָם וָעֶד.
כַּכָּתוּב,
וְאָכַלְתָּ וְשָׂבָעְתָּ
וּבֵרַכְתָּ אֶת יְיָ אֱלֹהֶיךָ
עַל הָאָרֶץ הַטֹּבָה
אֲשֶׁר נָתַן לָךְ.
בָּרוּךְ אַתָּה יְיָ
עַל הָאָרֶץ וְעַל הַמָּזוֹן:

וּבְנֵה יְרוּשָׁלַיִם
עִיר הַקֹּדֶשׁ
בִּמְהֵרָה בְיָמֵינוּ.
בָּרוּךְ אַתָּה יְיָ
בּוֹנֵה בְרַחֲמָיו יְרוּשָׁלָיִם.
אָמֵן:

69

BIRKAT HATOVAH

Barukh attah Adonai	Praised are You, Adonai,
Eloheinu melekh ha'olam	Our God, Ruler of the universe,
hamelekh hatov	the Ruler who is good
vehametiv lakol.	and does good for all.
Hu heitiv hu meitiv	God has been good, God is good,
hu yeitiv lanu.	God will be good to us.
Hu gemalanu	God bestowed upon us,
hu gomleinu	God bestows upon us,
hu yigmleinu la'ad	God will bestow upon us forever,
hen vahesed verahamim	grace, kindness, and compassion,
vizakeinu limot hamashiah.	and gain for us the days of the Messiah.

HARAHAMAN

Harahaman hu yanhileinu	(May) the Merciful One give us as an inheritance
yom shekulo Shabbat	a day that is completely Shabbat,
umenuha lehayei ha'olamim.	and rest in life everlasting in the world to come.

OSEH SHALOM

Venisa verakhah	Then shall we receive blessing
mei'et Adonai	from Adonai
utzedakah	and justice
mElohei yish'einu.	from the God of our deliverance.
Venimtza hein	And may we find favor
veseikhel tov	and good understanding
be'einei Elohim ve'adam.	in the eyes of God and people.
Oseh shalom	The One who makes peace in the
bimromav	heavens,
hu ya'aseh shalom aleinu	(May) God make peace for us
ve'al kol Yisra'el ve'imru, Amen.	and for all Israel, and let us say, Amen.

בָּרוּךְ אַתָּה יְיָ
אֱלֹהֵינוּ מֶלֶךְ הָעוֹלָם,
הַמֶּלֶךְ הַטּוֹב
וְהַמֵּטִיב לַכֹּל
הוּא הֵטִיב, הוּא מֵטִיב
הוּא יֵיטִיב לָנוּ
הוּא גְמָלָנוּ
הוּא גוֹמְלֵנוּ
הוּא יִגְמְלֵנוּ לָעַד
חֵן וָחֶסֶד וְרַחֲמִים
וִיזַכֵּנוּ לִימוֹת הַמָּשִׁיחַ.

הָרַחֲמָן הוּא יַנְחִילֵנוּ
יוֹם שֶׁכֻּלּוֹ שַׁבָּת
וּמְנוּחָה לְחַיֵּי הָעוֹלָמִים.

וְנִשָּׂא בְרָכָה
מֵאֵת יְיָ
וּצְדָקָה מֵאֱלֹהֵי יִשְׁעֵנוּ
וְנִמְצָא חֵן
וְשֵׂכֶל טוֹב
בְּעֵינֵי אֱלֹהִים וְאָדָם:

עֹשֶׂה שָׁלוֹם בִּמְרוֹמָיו
הוּא יַעֲשֶׂה שָׁלוֹם
עָלֵינוּ וְעַל כָּל יִשְׂרָאֵל
וְאִמְרוּ אָמֵן:

3

הֲכָנָה לְשַׁבָּת

Hakhanah leShabbat
Preparing for Shabbat

I start to think about Shabbat when I get hassled at work. The earlier I get hassled at work, the sooner I start thinking about it. I think this week, I was thinking about it on Monday. I couldn't wait until Friday night.

LARRY NEINSTEIN

From a Ḥavurah Meeting

YOUR AUTHOR: When is the first time in the week that you think about Friday night?

LARRY NEINSTEIN: I start to think about Shabbat when I get hassled at work. The earlier I get hassled at work, the sooner I start thinking about it. I think this week, I was thinking about it on Monday. I couldn't wait until Friday night.

DEBRA NEINSTEIN: As the homemaker for a family unit, I think about it in the middle of the week when I want to do the shopping and start asking the children which kugel they would like and how they would like their chicken. I think also about it when they ask, "Hey, Mom, will you bake *ḥallah* Friday?" and I say, "No." I had this habit for about a month that I was going to make *ḥallah* every Friday, which is really, really wonderful and they enjoyed it, but I haven't done it in a long time. They liked to help make it.

BEN REZNIK: Now we celebrate Shabbat more at home because we have the kids. But before, when we used to go to my parents or Janice's parents, we probably thought about it three weeks in advance in order to decide whose house we would go to.

JANICE REZNIK: It depends on whether we're having company.

LARRY NEINSTEIN: I think what's made me think about Shabbat sooner than I used to is the fact that we started keeping more of a Shabbat. When we weren't having a Shabbat, and weren't having a Friday night and I wasn't staying home and we were driving on Saturday, I didn't think about it—it was no big deal. But after we started not driving on Saturday, and there was a whole block of time, twenty-four hours or more, that we were just going to be together doing things, I was looking forward to it more, so I started thinking about it sooner.

According to one tradition, the leading Rabbis during Talmudic times would help in the preparation of Shabbat. The Talmud (*Shabbat* 119a) tells that one Rabbi would prepare the greens, another would gather wood, a third would make the fire, and another would prepare the house for the guest—the Shabbat. That Rabbi would bring out the Shabbat dishes and utensils and put away the weekday utensils. When asked why he was doing this work, the Rabbi would answer: "Were my guest one of the great sages of our age, I would personally prepare the reception. With Shabbat as my guest, I do the same." The Talmud teaches that everyone should feel honored to be able to share in the work of preparing for Shabbat.

Real Jewish tradition taught that both men and women actively prepared for the celebration of Shabbat. It was a special honor. De facto "tradition" has allowed Shabbat preparation to fall to the women. It was our hope that we would find a renewed sense of egalitarian responsibilities in the preparation for Shabbat among the families we interviewed. While our limited sample did reflect a tendency towards egalitarian table rituals, in this arena they voiced a "great appreciation" of the women who took responsibility for preparing Shabbat.

CARL ALBERT: All the preparation is done by the "queen" of the house.

ELAINE ALBERT: I get help from someone setting the table.

ASHER KELMAN: The big burden of making Shabbat is on Wendy. Not only is the house spanking clean, the kids prepared (having put on better clothing), the tablecloth is white and everything is in order. The silver is polished and the _hallah_ is warm.... I don't think the man makes Shabbat.

BILL GOODGLICK: Shabbat begins with Sandy. She sets the mood. That is traditional.

SANDY GOODGLICK: Friday is always a hectic day. I think any Jewish housewife will tell you that. First you have to look good, then you have to have the house look good, and have the table look good, and have the food look good.

BOB SHAFTON: Sometimes we ask ourselves what would Shabbat be like in Israel, and I try to bring flowers home. However, it doesn't start at 2:00 in the afternoon. I really admire people who are able to break out early in the afternoon, earlier than normal, and come home and relax and take a nap like they do in Jerusalem.

SALLY SHAFTON: Friday mornings when I come down, the first thing I do, even before I have a cup of coffee, is take out the Shabbat candles. Don't ask me why. I get the Shabbat candles out; Bob's *kipah* goes on his chair. The rest of the stuff comes out later, but the candles stay out all day. The candlesticks we use are really wonderful. There are three sets of them, all given to us by the kids. The Kiddush cups have all been brought back from Israel. The *hallah* covers—each one represents a different trip. They have great meaning every time they're pulled out, and wonderful memories are associated with all of them.

The traditional final act of Shabbat preparation was the giving of *tzedakah*. Here is the Albert family's description of their adaptation of that practice.

ELISA ALBERT: We give *tzedakah* before candlelighting.

MATTHEW ALBERT: We take the change out of our pockets, or we bring it down to the table before. We have a little *tzedakah* box, and we put our money in it.

YOUR AUTHOR: Is it your money that you put in, or do you ask Mom and Dad?

MATTHEW ALBERT: If we forget, we ask.

ELISA ALBERT: I've got to ask Mommy because Mommy says it's not appropriate to put pennies in—and that's all I've got.

YOUR AUTHOR: What do you do with the *tzedakah*?

CARL ALBERT: That's a good question—we talk about it sometimes.

ELISA ALBERT: We just put money in, and then my Mom has to give it all to whatever and then send it.

DAVID ALBERT: Elisa came home with this *tzedakah* box that the school sent for Ethiopian Jews. We started filling that one up—and we filled it up with other ones we had around the house, and sent it to school with Elisa.

Concepts

Preparation

Shabbat is often portrayed as a "bride" or a "queen," a most special guest who visits our home weekly. In order to properly receive this special guest, and to ensure that we are organized for the celebration to come, the celebration of Shabbat must begin with preparation. In fact, preparation for Shabbat is in and of itself a mitzvah—a commandment. These are physical acts: cleaning, laying out ritual objects, setting the table, changing clothes, etc. But this is also a psychological and spiritual process: a way of preparing our own transition from the tensions and obligations of the workday week to the rest and peace of Shabbat. For some, Shabbat preparation also includes a spiritual dimension, with time set aside for reading, studying, or just reflecting.

Work and Rest

In the Torah, the mitzvah to observe Shabbat stipulates one basic principle: refrain from work *(melakhah)*. "Six days you shall labor and do all your work, but the seventh day is a Shabbat of the Lord your God. You shall not do any work—you, your son or daughter, your male or female slave, or your cattle, or the stranger who is within your settlement" (Exodus 20:9–10).

This biblical commandment makes it clear that the prohibition of work applies not only to an individual but to his or her family, helpers, guests, and even beasts of burden. The Torah creates the Shabbat experience for the entire household. Later, we will see that this intent expands to giving nature itself a day free from the interference of humanity.

While the Torah forbids "work," it gives us no definition of *melakhah*—the kind of work that is prohibited. While certainly there are some obvious indications of what the term meant to the biblical mind, it took the Talmudic Rabbis and later codifiers of Jewish law to define the actions that are specifically *melakhah* and therefore prohibited on Shabbat. Rabbinic law defined thirty-nine categories of *melakhah*. These were isolated by analyzing the jobs needed to build the Tabernacle, the portable sanctuary used in the wilderness, which are also called *melakhah* in the Torah. If the work of building the Tabernacle was forbidden on Shabbat, then certainly any similar work for less than that holy purpose would be restricted on the day of rest.

In the *Mishnah*, a list of thirty-nine *melakhot* (categories) of labor can be found. The Talmud makes it clear that these thirty-nine types of work— sewing, hammering, tearing, etc.—are just to serve as general categories under which specific acts could be evaluated. In looking at this list, Erich Fromm, a modern thinker, pointed out that what is really forbidden is any act that changes the physical world. When we rest on Shabbat, we stop manipulating nature; we stop building and moving and changing the physical. That makes Shabbat a time to focus on the eternal, on that which cannot be changed through human action.

Much of the job of preparing the home for Shabbat is done so that we do not have to "work" during the holiday. For example, since both lighting a fire and cooking are *melakhot* (forbidden categories of labor), all cooked food is prepared before Shabbat begins.

Embellishing a Commandment

Jews value the mitzvot, the commandments God taught them through the Torah. *Hiddur mitzvah* is an expression of this regard. It is a Jewish practice to embellish a mitzvah and to make it as beautiful and pleasant as possible. Shabbat is no exception. White tablecloths, fresh flowers, fine china, and nice clothes all contribute to a feeling of specialness at the beginning of the holiday. Many families have ritual objects that have been specially collected or that come with a unique family history, and their use enhances the observance of Shabbat. The holiday meal (be it traditional foods or special treats), eating in the dining room, and other acts can all be expressions of *hiddur mitzvah*.

Tzedakah

Tzedakah, the obligation to share one's resources to help others in need, is a Jewish passion. Jews have ingeniously woven the giving of *tzedakah* into the celebration of every holiday and every *simḥa* (joyous event). In the case of Shabbat, wherein the handling of money is prohibited, it became a practice to make the giving of *tzedakah* the culmination of preparation for the holiday. It is a common practice to drop a few coins in a *tzedakah* box just before lighting the candles. This can be done with the ubiquitous Jewish National Fund "blue box," an object d'art crafted especially for this purpose; a canister your children made at religious school; or even an old jar. In some families it has become a practice to include a discussion of how these *tzedakah* funds should be used.

Objects

The preparation for Shabbat and the enhancement of the Shabbat home and table is an area wide open for creativity. Homemade *ḥallah* covers and tablecloths, candlesticks that have been in the family for four generations, a Kiddush cup purchased at a special moment, a cutting board for the *ḥallah* made in a junior high school shop class—all enhance the Shabbat experience in their own way. We have been in homes where the Kiddush cups, candlesticks, and other ritual objects are of museum quality and were carefully collected over years of searching. We have been in other homes where the table objects reflected each family member's trip to Israel. Other families have told us of the *simḥa* for which each piece was purchased.

Here is a basic checklist of the objects you will want to have ready. In subsequent chapters, we will describe the requirements for each in detail.

1. *Tzedakah* box
2. Candlesticks
3. Candles
4. Matches
5. Kiddush cup(s)
6. Wine
7. *Ḥallah* bread (two unsliced loaves) and salt
8. *Ḥallah* plate, cover, and knife
9. *Kipot* (head coverings)
10. Shabbat Seder booklets

For *hiddur mitzvah*, the enhancement of Shabbat, consider the following:

1. White tablecloth
2. Special china, silver, and crystal
3. Fresh flowers
4. Traditional and/or favorite holiday foods
5. Nice clothes

Practice

We have seen that the preparation for Shabbat serves two purposes even though it is not part of the formal table ritual. First, in order to observe Shabbat within the framework of Jewish law, the home must be organized to eliminate the need for "work" during Shabbat. This includes the completion of all shopping (so that money need not be spent), the preparation of hot food (so that actual cooking won't take place during the holiday), etc. Second, there is a psychological benefit to preparation: helping people to enter into the Shabbat spirit.

Our experience in looking at Shabbat in the homes we visited tells us (with some admitted guilt from both partners) that women still bear the greater burden of Shabbat preparation. We've also learned that in those families where everyone has a role, Shabbat preparation seems to have a greater impact. Those husbands who fly through the front door just as Shabbat is beginning have a much harder time making the transition than those who have managed to help prepare at least the final details. Likewise, those children who have regular roles in preparing for Shabbat seem to value the Shabbat experience more intensely than those for whom this is just another thing parents have done for them. Therefore, we recommend that the responsibilities for preparing for Shabbat be shared as widely as possible.

Practical Questions and Answers

Why do we contribute *tzedakah* money before lighting candles?

Once the candles have been lit, Shabbat has begun. Since the use of money (including the giving of *tzedakah*) is considered a violation of the Shabbat, it must be done before candlelighting. In Eastern Europe, it was often a custom for children to go through their parents' pockets just before Shabbat and remove any coins that might have been accidentally (or intentionally) forgotten. Any money found would be added to the *tzedakah* box. Moreover, as we celebrate this joyous day with our family we are reminded of those in need.

Who should put money in the box?

Everyone, if possible. Children can be encouraged to save allowance money for their contributions. Even if parents give coins to the children to contribute, we recommend that the adults also put money in the box to model the appropriate behavior.

Do we say a *berakhah* when contributing *tzedakah*?

There is no blessing for this act, but you might want to discuss the meaning of giving *tzedakah* or share feelings about doing so.

What shall we do with the box once it is full?

Opening a *tzedakah* box and counting the money collected is lots of fun and a good family activity. If you have a full Jewish National Fund box, or one belonging to another specific institution, set an appointment for your family to take the box to the local office or representative for counting. If you have collected money in a homemade box, discuss with your family which *tzedakah* cause(s) you would like to support. Of course, do this activity before or after Shabbat.

Where should we keep the *tzedakah* box?

Since the box contains money, do not leave the box on the Shabbat table after passing it around.

Why is white the traditional color for Shabbat tablecloths, candles, ḥallah covers, and clothes?

One account of this tradition of wearing and using white objects came from the Kabbalists of Safed (Tzfat) in Israel, Jewish mystics who considered white a symbol of purity and joy. If you have ever been to a Jewish summer camp or visited in Israel on Shabbat when nearly everyone wears white, you know how truly impressive this practice can be—even in your own home.

Some Interesting Sources

The Torah draws a comparison between God's creation of the world and Israel's building the Tabernacle, their portable sanctuary in the wilderness. Just as God rested from the process of creation, Israel was commanded to rest from its creation of the Tabernacle.

When the Rabbis of the Talmud searched for a definition of work, to know what acts must be prohibited on Shabbat, they thought of the building of the Tabernacle. They listed the thirty-nine kinds of work used in building their sanctuary as a reference to the kinds of work that were to be forbidden on Shabbat:

1. Ploughing
2. Sowing
3. Reaping
4. Binding sheaves
5. Threshing
6. Winnowing
7. Selecting
8. Sifting
9. Grinding
10. Kneading
11. Baking
12. Shearing sheep
13. Bleaching
14. Combining raw materials
15. Dyeing
16. Spinning
17. Weaving
18. Making two loops
19. Weaving two threads
20. Separating into threads
21. Tying a knot
22. Untying a knot
23. Sewing
24. Tearing
25. Trapping
26. Slaughtering
27. Skinning
28. Tanning
29. Scraping pelts
30. Marking out
31. Cutting to shape
32. Writing
33. Erasing
34. Building
35. Demolishing
36. Kindling a fire
37. Extinguishing a fire
38. Finishing a product with a final hammer blow
39. Carrying from the private to the public domain (or vice versa).

Erich Fromm explained that the Jewish view of work is "any interference by people, be it constructive or destructive, with the physical world. Rest is a state of peace between people and nature." How do these thirty-nine categories of labor conform to his definition?

One of the purposes of Shabbat preparation is to prevent the need for any labor on Shabbat. Things are prepared so that work need not be done. What kind of preparation could enhance your rest experience on Shabbat?

Here is one other aspect to "prohibitions" of Shabbat.

> The mitzvah of Shabbat, like, all other mitzvot, must be set aside if human life is in danger. If a person is dangerously ill, whatever treatment a skilled local physician considers necessary may be done for him or her on Shabbat. If it is not clear whether the Shabbat needs to be violated (for instance if one physician says that it is necessary and another says that it is not), the Shabbat should be violated, just to prevent any possibility of danger to a human life. This overrides the Shabbat.
> Maimonides, *Mishneh Torah*, The Laws of Shabbat, 1:1

The other major purpose of Shabbat preparation is to enhance or honor the Shabbat. Preparation allows us to honor the Shabbat and welcome it as a guest into our homes. In this text, Maimonides speaks of Shabbat preparation.

2. What is meant by "honor"? This is what is meant by the Rabbis when they taught: It is a mitzvah (obligation) to wash one's face, hands, and feet with hot water on Friday to honor the Shabbat. One should wrap oneself in a fringed garment and sit with honor waiting to receive the Shabbat, just as if one were going to meet a king. The sages of old used to gather their students on Friday, dress in their best clothes, and say: "Come let us go out and meet Shabbat, the King."

3. Honoring the Shabbat means wearing clean clothes, so as to not wear the same clothes on both weekdays and Shabbat. If one does not own a change of clothes, one should let down his/her

cloak, so that it does not look the same as it does on weekdays. Ezra the Scribe fixed the rule that in honor of Shabbat, people should wash their clothes on Thursdays.

5. One should set his or her table properly on Friday night, even if he or she feels no need for more than a little food…. One should also prepare one's room in honor of Shabbat. Before sundown one should have a lamp lit, a table laid, and the bed properly prepared. These are all part of honoring the Shabbat.

6. Even if one is a person of very high rank and does not usually get involved in the marketing or other household chores, one should perform one of these tasks by himself or herself in preparation of Shabbat, for this is a personal way of honoring it. There were among the Rabbis of old, those who split firewood for cooking, others cooked or salted meat, fixed wicks, lit lamps, went to market to buy food or drink for the Shabbat. While none of these Rabbis usually did these tasks on a weekday, this made it more of an act of special preparation.

Maimonides, *Mishneh Torah*, The Laws of Shabbat, 1:30

How can these rabbinic images of Shabbat preparation be brought into your home? In what other ways can your preparation serve to honor Shabbat?

4

הַדְלָקַת נֵרוֹת

Hadlakat Nerot
Candlelighting

What I love is when the kids have gone to sleep and the house is dark and the candles are still burning on the table.

DEBRA NEINSTEIN

After the kids are in bed and the house is dark and the table is cleared and there is only a half inch of the candles left, the glow is so beautiful.

BONNIE GOODBERG

Lights. Flames seem to evoke a sense of wonder. That is part of what makes candlelight special. The Rabbis associated Shabbat candles with the light of Torah; they connected Shabbat candlelighting to a verse in Proverbs (6:23): "The mitzvot are a candle, the Torah is light." Our own experience shows the continuity of this wonder—perhaps enhanced by the uniqueness of candles in a world lit by electricity. One of our vivid recollections is of our daughter Havi at one year of age. One weekday night we went to a local pizza restaurant. It was intentionally dark, and on the tables were patio candles. Havi reacted immediately. She began to circle her hands, in imitation of her mother's weekly ritual, and bless this candle. At a *havurah* meeting filled with parents of young children, we learned that Havi's perception was not unique. We were told stories of children whose natural reaction to birthday candles was the *berakhah lehadlik ner* and of a three-year-old who regularly stops at the dining room table, picks up a candlestick left there, and sings *Bim Bam* to it. The Rabbis of the Talmud looked into a candle and saw a Jewish experience: the light of Torah. It seems that today children who are raised with the weekly lighting of candles find an equally Jewish experience in the mystery of a candle flame.

It was usual, a generation or two ago, for the lighting of candles to be a woman's private moment. Often, while the men were off at synagogue welcoming the Shabbat through a worship service, women had a private spiritual moment at home. It was a time for personal prayers and meditations; it was an extemporaneous expression.

BEN REZNIK: Friday night was always good for a real good cry from my mother, because there was never *bensching* (blessing) candles without tears coming down her eyes. Every Friday night we would stand around and watch her bless the candles and cry. And she still does it to this day—anybody she saw during the week who was less fortunate then we, she put in her prayers. She sobbed over the candles for all the relatives that she lost, for her mother and her brother who died. And she cried for happiness, too. Ever since we had the children, she does a prayer for them. She looks at them and starts to cry. There's always a sigh of relief when she takes off the veil and says "Shabbat Shalom."

Today, a North American sense of family has brought the candlelighting ceremony to the table. Whether performed by a single family member or collectively, it has been transformed into a public act. With it come new opportunities and a new sense of bonding. In his book *The Mask Jews Wear* Eugene Borowitz points out that the "good Shabbes kiss" that follows the end of the rabbinic benediction at public worship services is a unique creation of the North American Jewish community. It became a possibility when husband and wife began to sit together during services. In the same way, the incorporation of candlelight as part of a table service brings about a new set of experiences.

SUZAN WEINGARTEN: We take a match, and we cover our heads. Dinah and I have a special head covering that we both use. We light the candles, and we bring in the light. It's twirling your hands around and bringing the light toward you and covering our eyes. I have tried to figure out exactly what it does, and I think it moves the air around so that when you uncover your eyes, none of the candles are out. The air moves and keeps the fire going. We cover our eyes and say the blessing more like a whisper. Then we all kiss. We try to all kiss lips at the same time.

ELISA ALBERT: I have a special candle. My Mom gives me a match, and I light it. And there are three other big candles that my Mom lights.

CARL ALBERT: Six, if we have company.

ELAINE ALBERT: We have my mother's candlesticks. There are two candlesticks with three in each one. I know that sometimes it is a custom to light one candle for each member of the family. We've worked it out that we have two plus three children is five, plus one for Elijah. That's how we account for the six, although then Elisa has a special little one.

ELISA ALBERT: Yeah, my brother gave me the candle holder for my birthday.

ELAINE ALBERT: Matthew just got an exceptional gift in honor of his Bar Mitzvah. It's a set of oil lamps for Shabbat lights.

YOUR AUTHOR: It sounds like Matthew is going to start to light candles.

MATTHEW ALBERT: I do, anyways.

ELAINE ALBERT: We have all these candles to light, so whoever would like to light is welcome. Then we all sing the blessing.

Sometimes there are one or more of my family that I go into Shabbat not having the best relationship with. Sometimes I think I can't bear it.... I'm not going to be able to make it through Shabbat dinner tonight. I don't know how I'm going to do it. But somehow or another, after I light the candles, something magical happens or something special happens and I find that I can. It's a way to exorcise any demons that have been plaguing us.

Participation in candlelighting seems to be a wonderfully joyful act. We've seen some creative personal celebrations, like the Shaftons' early practice of singing "Shabbes candles we love you (E-I-E-I-O)." But as we listened carefully to our interviews, we learned that there is also a wonderful impact in *watching* the candles.

SANDY GOODGLICK: On different Shabbatot I have different thoughts. Most days I think that we were blessed to have all our parents around the table: all four. In the last seven years, we have lost three, so we feel that very keenly. And I think when we started making Shabbes and my parents were here from Seattle, we knew we were lucky. You know that it may not always be so, although you can't envision it. But I think that is what Shabbes reminds you of: that life is short, and it's a very special time, and you have to relish it. Sometimes I just enjoy looking at everyone around the table, with kind of unfocused eyes. Sometimes I just think of what has got to come out of the oven.

Bill sits across the table from me. I see him through the candles, which I think is magnificent. And I can see his emotion just drilling through those flames. Of all the impressions of Friday night, I think that is the one that lasts until Wednesday.

ASHER KELMAN: When we sit down Friday night, the candles are in the middle of the table, and I sometimes move my head down and I can see a candle on either side of my wife's face. It's symbolic, somehow, of millions of Jewish wives that have made the Shabbat. My favorite thing is just sitting down and, when Wendy is not realizing it, just lowering my head and seeing the candles next to her. That to me is having my family around me. It is very warm, and I feel that this family is playing a role, a private magical role: being in a chain, keeping the tradition going.

SUZAN WEINGARTEN: Before we were married, but after I converted, we used to go to Irwin's parents'. I remember it came time to light candles, and his mother would go in another room and light candles. She would go in there alone. Nobody else would go. It was like, "What is she doing in there?" I knew about candlelighting, but it was like, "Why does she do it all by herself?" I thought that was very interesting. I didn't understand it. I didn't ask, but it was an exciting feeling, like being let into the club.

IRWIN WEINGARTEN: You mean the tribe.

Concepts

The Symbol of Light

The lighting of candles is a major Jewish ritual act. We light candles on the festival of Ḥanukkah, on the anniversary of the death of a family member (the *Yahrzeit* candle), and to begin major Jewish holidays. We even keep a light—the *ner tamid*—eternally burning in the synagogue.

The lighting of candles is a symbolic act. Kindling is an act of exploration; it involves illuminating the dark or the unknown. Without light, there is no opportunity for study, for knowledge, or for joy. Light also symbolizes the creation. God's first creative act was the creation of light. Shabbat is a celebration of creation, and the lighting of candles conjures up the first act of creation. Just as God began creation by saying, "Let there be light," we begin our Shabbat celebration by lighting and blessing the Shabbat lights.

Candlelighting also had a practical implication. Light was needed for the evening celebration. Since no fire can be kindled after Shabbat begins, it was very important in the days before electricity to light candles that would burn during the evening.

Objects

Candlesticks

Although Jewish law requires only the kindling of one Shabbat light (candle), it is traditional to use at least two candlesticks and to light at least two candles.

In the Torah, the Ten Commandments are presented twice: first in the book of Exodus and then in the book of Deuteronomy. While the two sets of commandments are functionally identical, the only major difference falls in the fourth commandment: that for Shabbat. In Exodus (20:8) the commandment reads, "*Remember* (Zakhor) *the Shabbat day to keep it holy,*" and the commandment is justified by the statement "*for in six days Adonai made heaven and earth... and He rested on the seventh day."* In Deuteronomy (5:12) the fourth commandment is stated as *"Observe (Shamor) the Shabbat day to keep it holy,"* and it is explained, *"remember that you were a slave in the land of Egypt, and Adonai your God freed you from there...."* Tradition connects the two candlesticks to the two forms of the Shabbat commandment: "Remember" and "Observe." The two *ḥallah* breads also evoke this twofold command. These two themes of "creation" and "exodus" form the core of the Shabbat Kiddush. Even the first verse of the Shabbat hymn *Lekha Dodi* begins: "'Observe' and 'Remember' in one breath..."

There are no physical requirements for the candlesticks themselves, although generally families have acquired silver or brass ones. Many candlesticks are quite elaborate in design, while others are very simple. Some are short; some are tall. Some families light more than two candles, in many cases using one for each member of the family.

Many families use candlesticks that are family heirlooms. If you are purchasing candlesticks for the first time—or, for that matter, any of the other Shabbat ritual items—try to acquire the most beautiful objects you can afford. Or, you might want to use candlesticks you or your children have made. The point is not the expense, but the beauty and meaningfulness of the ritual objects.

Candles

The mitzvah to kindle the Shabbat light was originally directed toward oil lamps. The *Mishnah* goes into great detail about the right kind of wicks to be used in the lamp. Today, the mitzvah is commonly performed with candles. Although there are special Shabbat candles, just about any kind of candle can be used. White candles are traditional. The candles simply need to last long enough to burn throughout the meal. Either white utility candles or white tapers are commonly used. Birthday candles or Ḥanukkah candles will not burn long enough, which disqualifies them for use as Shabbat candles.

Practice

The procedure for lighting the Shabbat candles is as follows:

1. Place the candlesticks wherever you wish. The candles should not be moved after they are lit until Shabbat is over, so choose your place carefully. Most families place the candles directly on the Shabbat dinner table or nearby.

2. Put the candles into the candlesticks. If you have difficulty making them stay put, burn the bottom of the candle to allow some hot wax to drip into the receptacles. This should help the candles stick in the holders.

3. It is common practice to cover the head before lighting candles.

4. Strike a match and light the candles. Make sure that all the candles are well lit before you recite the blessing. This may take some time, especially if children are involved. You may need to strike several matches to get all the candles lit. That's fine, as long as all lighting is done before the blessing is recited. Do *not* use one candle to light another as in the candlelighting for Ḥanukkah!

5. Circle the flames with your hands once or three times, beginning with your hands parallel to your body and reaching out over the candles in a circular motion back toward your body. When the circling is completed, place your hands over your eyes or in front of the candles to block your view of them.

6. Recite or chant the blessing for the candles.

7. Do not say "Amen" at the end of the blessing. Although many people are used to saying "Amen" at the conclusion of a blessing, technically it is unnecessary. The word "Amen" literally means "so be it," a formal acknowledgment that one agrees with what has just been said. This was done for those who were unfamiliar with the prayers, and it served to include them in the process of praying. If, however, you are reciting a particular blessing, it is superfluous to say "Amen" to your own prayer.

8. Spend a few seconds in private prayer with your eyes covered.

9. Uncover your eyes, look at the flames in order to complete the act that the blessing you just recited specified, and wish everyone "Shabbat Shalom" with appropriate kisses, hugs, and handshakes.

Practical Questions and Answers

Why does the Shabbat day begin on Friday night?

The Jewish calendar is based in part on a lunar system, so the Jewish day begins at dusk, when the moon can first be seen. The first chapter of Genesis makes this clear. At the end of the first day of creation, that day is reviewed with these words: *Vayehi erev, vayehi voker—yom ehad*—"And there was evening, and there was morning—one day" (Genesis 1:5). Always remember: a Jewish day begins the night before.

When are the candles lit?

According to Jewish law, candles are to be lit no later than eighteen minutes before sundown.

How can I find the exact candlelighting time?

Most Jewish calendars include candlelighting times for your city. On some calendars, the time is listed next to the symbol of two candlesticks in the date box. Other calendars have charts listing the candlelighting times week by week.

What if I don't have a Jewish calendar?

Candlelighting time can be determined by anyone with a local newspaper. Simply find the Friday weather page, which lists the times for sunrise and sunset. Candlelighting will be eighteen minutes before the listed sunset time. For example, if the newspaper lists sunset at 6:18 P.M., candlelighting will be no later than 6:00 P.M.

Why are there different candlelighting times in different cities?

Sunset comes at different times, depending on the geographic location of a particular place in relation to the solar cycle. Note also that while some calendars adjust for Daylight Savings Time, others list only Standard Time. In the latter case, one hour must be added to the listed time when Daylight Savings Time is in effect.

When does Shabbat end?

Shabbat is, of course, celebrated for a full day. It does not end with the completion of the Friday night Shabbat Seder. Shabbat officially concludes with the *Havdalah* ("separation") ceremony, which literally separates Shabbat time from the rest of the week. It is recited when three stars are visible in the Saturday evening sky, or at least forty-two minutes after the sunset time listed for that day. For more information on the rituals of the Shabbat day, see page 213.

Who should light the Shabbat candles?

While it may come as a surprise to many, both men and women are equally obligated to light Shabbat candles. According to the *Shulḥan Arukh* (The Code of Jewish Law):

> Men and women are both obligated to have a candle lit in their homes on Shabbat.
>
> *Oraḥ Ḥayim* 263:2

The reason women traditionally lit the Shabbat candles is found in the very next line of the Code:

> Women are more obligated in this mitzvah then are men, because they are usually at home and they deal with the household needs.

The *Shulḥan Arukh* was written more than four hundred years ago, when this explanation reflected a sociological reality. In those days, women were at home preparing the Shabbat dinner while men were at synagogue welcoming the Shabbat through an early evening service. Today, however, with many women pursuing careers outside the home, and with household responsibilities being shared, the emphasis given by the *Shulḥan Arukh* may no longer apply. Also, it is important to note that the setting for candlelight-

HADLAKAT NEROT	CANDLELIGHTING
1. *Barukh attah Adonai*	Praised are You, Adonai,
2. *Eloheinu melekh ha'olam*	our God, Ruler of the universe,
3. *asher kidshanu bemitzvotav*	who made us holy through God's commandments
4. *vetzivanu lehadlik*	and commanded us to kindle
5. *ner shel Shabbat.*	the Shabbat lights.

ing has changed. Once, women tended to light candles alone in the corner of a room. It was a kind of private spiritual moment. Today, candlelighting tends to be a public ritual, often taking place at the dinner table or nearby.

While every family will make its own determination concerning the roles different members will occupy, it is clear that according to Jewish law, if the woman of the house is not at home in time to light Shabbat candles, the man of the house is obligated to do so. This suggests that any (or all) family member(s) may kindle the Shabbat lights and recite the *berakhah*.

We also know that in many families, one adult lights the candles and the entire family joins in chanting or reciting the *berakhah*.

Must I cover my head during candlelighting?
Covering the head is a sign of reverence for God above. Men are expected to wear head coverings called *kipot* (yarmulkes) during the entire Shabbat Seder. Women traditionally covered their heads with a lace cloth or scarf (known as a *tikhel* in Yiddish) while lighting the candles, just as they would wear a similar head covering in the synagogue. While this practice has fallen out of use among many women, others retain it as a sign of respect. In fact, some women are now adopting the *kipah* as part of their religious wardrobe.

Why are the eyes covered and the hands waved during candlelighting?
The eyes are covered while reciting the blessing to block the view of the candles. Normally, in Jewish ritual practice an act is done immediately after a specific blessing is said. For example, we will recite the Kiddush and immediately drink the wine; we will recite the *Hamotzi* and immediately eat the *ḥallah* bread. With candles it must be different because of the prohibition of lighting fire

1. בָּרוּךְ אַתָּה יְיָ,
2. אֱלֹהֵינוּ מֶלֶךְ הָעוֹלָם,
3. אֲשֶׁר קִדְּשָׁנוּ בְּמִצְוֹתָיו,
4. וְצִוָּנוּ לְהַדְלִיק
5. נֵר שֶׁל שַׁבָּת.

on Shabbat. Since the blessing itself officially ushers in the Shabbat, we cannot light the fire after the blessing is said. Therefore, the Rabbis came up with a kind of legal fiction. We light the candles first so the fire is prepared for the Shabbat. Then we block the candles from our sight while we recite the blessing. During this moment, it is as if the candles had not been lit. When the blessing is completed, we uncover our eyes—and behold, the candles are lit.

To enhance this action, it became traditional to wave the hands in a circular pattern over the candles just before reciting the blessing. Various reasons are given for this. Some say it is to bring the warmth of the flames into the aura of the person reciting the blessing. Others say it is to ensure that the flames are well lit, avoiding the possibility of the candles extinguishing themselves before the flame has caught the wick. Others point to the inherent mystical sensation of the act. Whatever the reasons, it became traditional to circle the flames—some say once, others say three times—just before blocking the view of the candles.

There are three ways to block the view of the candles while reciting the blessing:

1. Place your hands over your eyes with palms toward you.
2. Place your hands over your eyes with palms away from you toward the flames.
3. Place your hands with palms toward the flames directly in front of the candles, blocking them from view.

Everyone seems to have a favorite position. Those who cover the eyes seem to feel the privacy of the moment more. Those whose hands are close to the candles feel the warmth on the palms. Rest assured that little children will peek through their fingers at whatever is going on.

What happens if not everyone can get home in time for candlelighting?
With busy schedules and work obligations, some families find it difficult to gather together at the official candlelighting time. This is especially true during the winter months, when candlelighting can be as early as 4:00 P.M.

Jewish law insists that candles not be kindled after the beginning of Shabbat. To do so is to overtly violate the Shabbat by "kindling," which is one of the forbidden categories of labor.

While we know that it takes advance planning and careful adjustment of work and school schedules, it is important to respect this requirement of Jewish law. In case the entire family cannot gather for candlelighting, one of these options can be considered:

1. One adult lights the candles at the official time and recites the blessing. When the family gathers together at the table, the Shabbat Seder begins with *Shalom Aleikhem*.
2. Do not light candles that week, and begin the Shabbat Seder with *Shalom Aleikhem*.

Are there other rules about candlelighting?

Once lit, the candles should not be moved. The reason is that the candlesticks are considered an instrument of work and are not to be touched lest one be tempted to use or adjust them during the Shabbat. Therefore, choose a place for them carefully. Unless you will not completely clear the table during the length of Shabbat, do not place them on the table itself. Put them nearby the table on a buffet server, on a separate table just for candles, or in the kitchen.

Candles are never blown out; to do so would be an act of labor (by rabbinic definition). Allow the candles to burn down. A tray underneath the candlesticks will help catch wax drippings. Special wax catchers that are put into the bottom of candlesticks can also be used. Before lighting the wicks and saying the blessing, it is permissible to heat the bottoms of the candles to help them stick in the candlesticks. A tip on cleaning candlesticks: soak them in hot water to loosen the wax drippings, and you won't need to dig out the hardened wax.

If a wick burns out after a blessing has been said, do not relight it.

Use new candles each week. They should be completely new with fresh wicks. Buy candles in bulk cartons to make sure a supply is always on hand.

What happens if we leave home before the candles burn out?

This is a serious question. More than one home has been severely damaged by fire from falling candles. Plan ahead. It is perfectly legal to cut the candles down to a length that will enable the flames to last through dinner, but not late into the night. The standard utility candles for Shabbat seem to last approximately three to four hours. By cutting the candles in half before lighting them, you can reduce the burn time proportionately. If you must leave the burning candles unattended, place them in a safe area before lighting, e.g., on the kitchen tile or in the sink. Put aluminum foil in a tray under the candlesticks. Be certain that if the candles should fall, they will do no harm.

We've been invited out for Shabbat dinner. Should we take our own candlesticks?
It probably depends on your relationship with your hosts. If they invite you to bring along your own candlesticks, by all means do so (although to be strictly observant of Jewish law you will have to pick them up after Shabbat is over). Some families will offer extra candlesticks to guests who come for Shabbat dinner. If you sense that there will be no opportunity for you to light candles at the host's home, light your candles at home first.

What about my children who want to light candles?
There is a custom that families kindle one candle for each family member. Often, children are asked to kindle their own candle. When children reach the age of Bar/Bat Mitzvah, they take on adult Jewish obligations, and this includes the responsibility to have a Shabbat candle lit in their home. Younger (or older) children may wish to light their own candles. There is no reason they cannot do so. We do strongly suggest that children never be allowed to take over the adult's responsibility to light candles. Children should always see their parents lighting candles first. It is important that children realize that the Shabbat ritual is for the parents as well as for the children. Some parents will ask very young children to help light the candles by placing the child's hand on top of their own. Here are a few suggestions for children lighting candles:

1. If the children are lighting their own candles, use long fireplace or kitchen matches to avoid burning fingers. For some kids, this will be the first opportunity to learn to use matches safely.
2. There is a natural tendency among kids, reinforced by the birthday party ritual, to want to blow out candles. Since that is not allowed, let the kids blow out the match used to light the candles.
3. In all cases, encourage the children to imitate the candlelighting ritual motions and blessings. It is the best way for them to learn the Shabbat ritual.

What happens when other Jewish holidays fall on Shabbat? What is the candlelighting procedure then?

When the festivals of Passover, Shavuot, Rosh Hashanah, and Sukkot coincide with Shabbat, the blessing is slightly amended to

Barukh attah, Adonai, Eloheinu, melekh ha'olam, asher kideshanu be-mitzvotav vetzivanu lehadlik ner shel Shabbat veYom Tov.

Praised are You, Adonai, our God, Ruler of the universe, who made us holy through the commandments and commanded us to kindle the Shabbat and Festival lights.

On the first night of the festival, the *Sheheheyanu* prayer is also recited:

Barukh attah, Adonai, Eloheinu, melekh ha'olam, shehebeyanu vekiye-manu, vehigi'anu lazeman hazeh.

Praised are You, Adonai, our God, Ruler of the universe, who has kept us in life and has preserved us and enabled us to reach this season.

On the eve of Shabbat during Ḥanukkah, the Ḥanukkah candles are lit and blessed first, before the Shabbat candles, in order not to violate the prohibition against lighting fire on Shabbat.

When Yom Kippur falls on Shabbat, the candles are lit with the following blessing:

Barukh attah, Adonai, Eloheinu, melekh ha'olam, asher kideshanu be-mitzvotav vetzivanu lehakdlik ner shel Shabbat veYom Hakippurim.

Praised are You, Adonai, our God, Ruler of the universe, who made us holy through the commandments and commanded us to kindle the lights of Shabbat and the Day of Atonement.

Then, the *Sheheheyanu* is recited. By the way, when Yom Kippur coincides with Shabbat, there is no Shabbat Seder. The pre-fast meal is eaten on Friday afternoon, before candlelighting. At the official candlelighting time, this special candlelighting prayer is recited, along with the Blessing for the Children. However, since Shabbat does not begin until the candles are lit, and because of Yom Kippur, there is no Kiddush or eating after candlelighting.

Some Interesting Sources

Studying Jewish legal texts often teaches us more than just what we are supposed to do or not do. Legal texts often serve as vistas of Jewish values and concerns in action. These "laws" on the Shabbat candles were taken from the Law Code of Maimonides. Here, as in all his legal work, Maimonides fills his citations with all the nuances and details present in the Talmud, setting them in a way that makes them easily accessible.

In many of the interviews we conducted we heard a common theme. For people who were raised in traditional households, their encounter with Shabbat was often restrictive. As children, Shabbat often consisted of things they couldn't do. Only later did a new sense of celebration emerge. This same conflict between the strict observance of the prohibitions of labor and the desire to create an active celebration can be seen in these texts.

One clue to understanding these texts is a law called *muktzeh*. Not only was it forbidden to work on Shabbat, but to protect the law against labor, the Talmudic Rabbis added a "fence" around that law: they also forbade Jews to touch tools of labor on Shabbat. These things were in a category called *muktzeh*. In these texts, the concern over "tilting" the Shabbat light is a concern about touching something that is *muktzeh*.

1. The lighting of a lamp on Friday night is not a voluntary action. A person cannot choose to light it or leave it unlit. Lighting a lamp on the eve of the Shabbat is a *mitzvah* (an obligation).

   Both men and women are obligated to have a lamp burning in their house on Shabbat. Even if one has no food to eat, she or he must go begging in order to buy oil to light a lamp, for the lamp is an integral part of the Shabbat celebration.

2. It is permissible to make use of the light of Shabbat candles, provided that the objects to be looked at do not require close scrutiny. If, however, the objects require minute inspection, it may not be examined by the lamp's light. This prevents one from being tempted to tilt the lamp.

14. One does not read by lamplight on the Shabbat, even if the

lamp is situated twice a person's height above the ground. This prevents one from being tempted to tilt the lamp.

However, if two people read the same text together, they may do so by the light of the lamp, because each will remind the other should the other forget that it is Shabbat. But, the two of them may not do so if they are reading different texts. Each one may become too involved in his or her text to notice what the other is doing.

15. School children may read by lamplight on the Shabbat in the presence of their teacher, because the teacher will watch over them. But the teacher may not read. The teacher may, however, glance at the book by lamplight, to mark the beginning of the section which she or he wishes the children to read. Then the book is to be placed in the children's hands for them to read.

Can you explain the compromise these laws are trying to enact? Why do they make a special case for children? Can the ruling on school children serve as a model for decisions about your family's Shabbat practice?

5

שָׁלוֹם עֲלֵיכֶם

Shalom Aleikhem
Peace Be to You

We always sing at least one Shabbat song. Whether we sing more than that is highly dependent on when I come home, how stressed I am. If I'm in a good mood and relaxed, then we may sing for a while. If I'm stressed out, it's *Bim Bam* and "let's eat!"

LARRY NEINSTEIN

Angels aren't in vogue today. We don't believe in them any more. In the Jewish tradition, every stranger, every visitor, every guest was a potential angel. In chapter eighteen of Genesis, Abraham and Sarah, Israel's first family, welcome three strangers with hospitality. Before they leave, the visitors have blessed Sarah and Abraham, and we are left with the impression that they were angels. Jacob has the same kind of close encounter with a stranger, with whom he wrestles, and from whom he is blessed with the new name Israel. Visiting angels weren't only a biblical conception. The Talmud is filled with stories of rewards granted for showing hospitality to an unknown visitor. The stranger next door could be an angel, or Elijah in disguise, or even the Messiah. In Sephardi folktales, in Hasidic lore, families who welcomed the stranger in need to their Shabbat table or to their Passover Seder were often rewarded by heaven.

It was common Jewish practice to return home from the synagogue with a sojourner who had traveled as far as that town before Shabbat. It was common for even the best families to welcome the town poor to the Shabbat table. In most homes, an extra place was set because of the probability of a Shabbat guest. With this probability came the realistic expectation of visiting angels. When one entered the house, *Shalom Aleikhem* was sung, and with it, both the visiting Shabbat angels and the guests were made welcome.

For most of the families we interviewed, guests are a big part of celebrating Shabbat. In fact, many are almost missionary in their commitment to expose others to the joys of Shabbat. For them, *Shalom Aleikhem* is sung as a beautiful Shabbat anthem. (The *Billboard* charts show that *Shalom Aleikhem* is still a Top Ten Shabbat hit, ranking Number Two behind *Bim Bam*.) What seems to be missing is a realistic expectation of angels.

From the Ḥavurah

LARRY NEINSTEIN: We always sing at least one Shabbat song. Whether we sing more than that is highly dependent on when I come home, how stressed I am. If I'm in a good mood and relaxed, then we may sing for a while. If I'm stressed out, it's *Bim Bam* and "let's eat!"

JANICE REZNIK: We've been doing a lot of singing lately. Yoni (age three) loves music, and he has a lot of Shabbes songs that he loves performing. He loves to play *Ḥazzan*. He has his own siddur. He gets it out of the drawer, and he makes a whole ritual.

DEBRA NEINSTEIN: The kids love the singing, and we try to have a set ritual of doing the blessings with a song in each one. We do the candles, then sing a *niggun* (a wordless melody) and do the next blessing.

JANICE REZNIK: That's nice.

A Recollection

At *Shalom Aleikhem* time in our home, we surrounded our table ritual with mystery. We would tell the story of the bad and good angels visiting the home, and Havi and Michael would be wide-eyed. Once I pointed to the shadows flickering on the walls above the Shabbat candles and said, "See, there are the Shabbat angels coming to visit." The kids were enraptured, and to this day they playfully point out the shadow "angels" to guests.

Children love to play at being adults. An important way they learn is by imitating the actions of the grownups around them. Along with the standard airports and gas stations, our kids have built synagogues and Shabbat tables from kindergarten blocks. One Shabbat eve, the kids brought their favorite stuffed animals to the dinner table. Safely tucked into the sides of their chairs, their imaginary charges provided Havi and Michael the opportunity to play at being a Jewish adults. When we sang *Shalom Aleikhem*, Charlie and Arissa Wolfson joined in our circle. Of course, Charlie wears a kipah. After being blessed by us, both kids turned to their beloved toys, placing their hands upon stuffed heads, and pronounced a blessing for them. They don't participate at every one of our Shabbat dinners, but when they do, the Wolfson stuffed animals are welcome guests at our table.

Concepts

Angels

The hymn *Shalom Aleikhem* is the traditional song welcoming the Shabbat at the family table. It speaks of welcoming the "ministering angels," the messengers of God.

> A lovely legend is recorded in the Talmud (*Shabbat* 119a) about two angels that is said to have inspired the writing of Shalom Aleikhem:
> It was taught that Rabbi Jose ben Rabbi Judah said that on every Shabbat eve, two angels visit every Jewish home—the Angel of Good and the Angel of Evil. They approach the home and peer into the windows. If they see

that the house is messy, that the parents are unhappy, that the children are fighting, and that the table is not set for Shabbat, then the Angel of Evil rubs his hands with glee and says, "May all of your Shabbatot be just like this one." And the Angel of Good must say, "Amen. May it be so."

But if the angels see that the house is sparkling, that the candles are shining, and that the family is seated happily at the table, then the Angel of Good throws his arms into the air and says, "May all of your Shabbatot be just like this one." And the Angel of Evil has to say, "Amen. May it be so."

Hospitality

From the time Abraham and Sarah welcomed strangers into their tent, the principle of *hakhnasat orhim*—hospitality—has been a major theme in Jewish life. Throughout the centuries, Jews have welcomed family, friends, neighbors, and strangers into their homes, especially on Jewish holidays.

One expression of this valuing of hospitality is found in the prayer *Ha Lahma Anya*, which is recited at the beginning of the Passover Seder. It invites "all who are hungry" into our homes to join in our Seder celebration. *Hakhnasat orhim* has often been translated into action by Jewish families who open their homes to travelers, military personnel, college students away from home, and so on.

A second example of welcoming strangers regularly took place on Shabbat itself. Until very recently, Friday evening services were held before Shabbat dinner. Strangers would come to the *Beit Kenesset*—the House of Assembly—to seek fellow Jews. On Friday night, Jews without places to make Shabbat would be taken home from synagogue by members of the community. Some synagogues even had temporary guest quarters for those without a place to stay.

Shalom Aleikhem is really a hymn of hospitality. While using the metaphor of welcoming "ministering angels," the prayer also welcomes both the Shabbat and guests into the home.

Practice

Shalom Aleikhem is generally sung according to a traditional melody that is one of the best-known Jewish songs. Many families sit at the table when singing, although standing at the table is also appropriate. Some families sing each verse three times.

To enhance the singing, try joining hands or placing your arms around the shoulders of those sitting next to you and swaying to the music.

Practical Questions and Answers

Must we sing *Shalom Aleikhem*?
While *Shalom Aleikhem* has been the traditional hymn welcoming the Shabbat for generations, this does not preclude the addition of other Shabbat songs at this point in the Shabbat Seder. In fact, one family we spoke to told us that their children rapidly tire of the same song week after week, so they alternate a variety of Shabbat songs in its place.

Doesn't the Blessing of Children come before *Shalom Aleikhem*?
Traditionally, the children are blessed immediately after candles are lit, before the singing of *Shalom Aleikhem*. The father would bless the children immediately upon returning home from synagogue services and before sitting down at the table.

The outline of the Shabbat Seder presented here is based on what we have determined to be normative of American Jewish families today. This does not mean that the order of singing *Shalom Aleikhem* or blessing family members cannot be reversed if your family tradition differs from the suggested outline.

If we don't plan to attend Shabbat eve services in the synagogue, can we include those prayers at this point in the Shabbat Seder?
The Goodglick family does just that. Actually, they include several prayers and readings from the *Kabbalat Shabbat* ("Receiving the Shabbat") and the *Ma'ariv* ("Evening") services throughout their Shabbat Seder, beginning

just before *Shalom Aleikhem*. This is a wonderful way to broaden the Shabbat Seder experience later on in the development of your celebration.

SHALOM ALEIKHEM	PEACE BE TO YOU	
1. *Shalom aleikhem*	Peace to you,	שָׁלוֹם עֲלֵיכֶם, .1
2. *malakhei hasharet*	ministering angels,	מַלְאֲכֵי הַשָּׁרֵת, .2
3. *malakhei Elyon*	angels of the Most High,	מַלְאֲכֵי עֶלְיוֹן, .3
4. *mimelekh*	from the Ruler,	מִמֶּלֶךְ .4
5. *malkhei hamelakhim*	the Ruler of Rulers,	מַלְכֵי הַמְּלָכִים, .5
6. *Hakadosh barukh hu.*	the Holy One, praised is God.	הַקָּדוֹשׁ בָּרוּךְ הוּא: .6
7. *Bo'akhem leshalom*	Come in peace,	בּוֹאֲכֶם לְשָׁלוֹם, .7
8. *malakhei hashalom*	angels of peace,	מַלְאֲכֵי הַשָּׁלוֹם, .8
9. *malakhei Elyon*	angels of the Most High,	מַלְאֲכֵי עֶלְיוֹן, .9
10. *mimelekh*	from the Ruler,	מִמֶּלֶךְ .10
11. *malkhei hamelakhim*	the Ruler of Rulers,	מַלְכֵי הַמְּלָכִים, .11
12. *Hakadosh barukh hu.*	the Holy One, praised is God.	הַקָּדוֹשׁ בָּרוּךְ הוּא: .12
13. *Barkhuni leshalom*	Bless me with peace,	בָּרְכוּנִי לְשָׁלוֹם, .13
14. *malakhei hashalom*	angels of peace,	מַלְאֲכֵי הַשָּׁלוֹם, .14
15. *malakhei Elyon*	angels of the Most High,	מַלְאֲכֵי עֶלְיוֹן, .15
16. *mimelekh*	from the Ruler,	מִמֶּלֶךְ .16
17. *malkhei hamelakhim*	the Ruler of Rulers,	מַלְכֵי הַמְּלָכִים, .17
18. *Hakadosh barukh hu.*	the Holy One, praised is God.	הַקָּדוֹשׁ בָּרוּךְ הוּא: .18
19. *Tzeitkhem leshalom*	Go in peace,	צֵאתְכֶם לְשָׁלוֹם, .19
20. *malakhei hashalom*	angels of peace,	מַלְאֲכֵי הַשָּׁלוֹם, .20
21. *malakhei Elyon*	angels of the Most High,	מַלְאֲכֵי עֶלְיוֹן, .21
22. *mimelekh*	from the Ruler,	מִמֶּלֶךְ .22
23. *malkhei hamelakhim*	the Ruler of Rulers,	מַלְכֵי הַמְּלָכִים, .23
24. *Hakadosh barukh hu.*	the Holy One, praised is God.	הַקָּדוֹשׁ בָּרוּךְ הוּא: .24

Some Interesting Sources

Here are some rabbinic sources on hospitality. As you will see, they understand the mitzvah of *hakhnasat orḥim* as a form of outreach to those in need. Our very translation—hospitality—implies a shift in meaning and application. For us, opening our home on Shabbat tends to mean inviting friends and family. As you read these texts, see if you can find workable ways of implementing these values today.

> Let your house be open wide. How? We learn that one's house should have doors on the north, the south, the east, and the west, just like Job's house.
>
> Why did Job make his house with four doors? So that the poor would not be troubled to go all around the house. Someone coming from the north could enter directly, someone coming from the south could enter directly, and so on. This is why Job's house had four doors.
>
> Teach the members of your household humility. When a poor person comes and stands in the doorway and asks, "Is your father inside?" he [or she] should be answered, "Yes, come in; enter." Even before he [or she] has entered, a table is set for him [or her]. When he [or she] enters and eats and offers a blessing up to heaven, the master of the house has great joy.
>
> But when one is not humble and the members of his [or her] household are short tempered, the poor man [or woman] is rebuked and driven off in anger.
>
> *Avot deRabbi Natan A 7*

These practices may not be practical in our society, but the values they present are still important. What is a good modern equivalent for building a house with four doors? In what ways should members of the household be instructed to show hospitality today?

6

בִּרְכוֹת הַמִּשְׁפָּחָה

Birkhot Hamishpahah
Family Blessings

The best part of Shabbat for me is when I bless my children. I get to hug them and kiss them, and they have to stand there and take it whether they like it or not.

KAREN VINOCOR

Starting in the Middle Ages, it became traditional for parents to bless their children as part of the Shabbat Seder and for husbands to praise their wives through the recitation of *Eishet Ḥayil*, the chapter of the book of Proverbs beginning "A Woman of Valor." We've blended these practices into a section we've called *Birkhot Hamishpaḥah*: Family Blessings.

The Moment of Blessing

A head is bowed. Two hands rest on that head. A few words are whispered. A blessing is passed. Blessing is a difficult concept—most people are more comfortable making wishes. Intellectually, it is very hard to understand what it means to give someone a blessing. Usually, it's easier just to think of wishing someone well. The act of blessing another person is something we usually reserve for the Rabbi, and it's something he or she does before the *Aron haKodesh* in the synagogue.

Rabbinical blessings are something borrowed from the priestly tradition. In the days of the Jerusalem Temple, the priests would invoke the three-line, fifteen-word biblical formula known as the Priestly Benediction. Since the Temple was destroyed and as the synagogue has evolved, members of priestly families come to the *bima* at appointed times, pull their *tallitot* over their heads, spread their fingers into a ritual configuration, and bless the people with the ancient benediction. It is a moment of high religious drama.

The Jewish tradition brought this public blessing pageant into the home by providing a weekly moment wherein parents invoke a blessing for their children. When the Talmudic Rabbis came to discuss the Priestly Benediction, they centered on one question: "Who really does the blessing: God or the priests?" The question is never fully resolved, though one answer is found in *Midrash Tanḥuma*. There, God says: "Though I ordered the priests to bless you, I will stand with them and we will bless you together." Through quiet whispers in a child's ear and in the warm grasps of a family hug, religious abstraction becomes tangible. For many of the families with whom we talked, this moment of blessing was the weekly high point.

ELAINE ALBERT: I'll say something about this, and it always amazes me every Shabbat, because we come into it sometimes with not the best feelings for each other. But by the time I get to the blessing of the kids, there is never any reticence from them to me and not really from me to them, either. It seems like a very healing thing—it's a healing process that goes on when you take your child, and it's really on a one-to-one basis. There is something really very special that happens.

CARL ALBERT: I do it in English, and what I say is part of the traditional blessing, "May God make you like Ephraim and Menasseh," but then I say to each one of them that I hope when they're grown and married that one Friday night a month we will be at Elisa's house with her husband and her children, and I hope that David and his wife and children will be there, and Matthew and his wife and children will be there, and another Friday night we will be at David's house. I say this every week to each of them, that we hope to be in their homes having a Friday night service and a dinner when they are grown.

DAVID ALBERT: Elisa goes to my mom. Matthew goes to my father, and everybody sits on everybody's lap—and I'm all by myself. So they bless them and then they switch, and I'm still all alone by myself. Then I go to each one and get blessed, and they're sitting there all alone by themselves.

ASHER KELMAN: I put my hands on their heads, and I hold them, and I bless them, and I add in special things. I say it in Hebrew and English. Then I say things like: "Jeremiah, you've been a good boy and you've been good in school this week." "Emil, Shlemiel, man made of steel. You're going to grow up to be a strong boy. You're not to fight with your brothers. You should help the Jewish people with your strength. Play your music well, do your studies well." And this is a special time in which with each one I will try to pick out something that is important to them. "Ariel, you did well in school; your recital was good." Whatever is relevant for that particular day or week.

JEREMIAH KELMAN: It's fun, especially when he says good things about me. Sometimes when he puts his hands down on my face, I push them away and put them back on my head.

ARIEL KELMAN: He says it first in Hebrew, then in English, and then he says something like, "Good, you got an A on your test." I feel very good.

EMIL KELMAN: He says all these words I can't understand. Then he calls me "a man made of steel" and my brothers call me "a man made of cardboard."

WENDY KELMAN: I feel that my husband blessing the children is a wonderful thing to do, because I think that when you are in the humdrum of living, you don't think a lot about praising your children for the things that they've done and acknowledging that they are worthwhile, worthy, and have an innate goodness. You might feel this about your children, but you don't say it. I think it's a real good opportunity to remind your kids that you love them and that they are special.

SANDY GOODGLICK: Our children are now twenty-nine, twenty-seven, and twenty-five. They're not babies anymore.

YOUR AUTHOR: And you still bless them, even your twenty-nine-year-old?

BILL GOODGLICK: All three children, whenever they are here. And even telephonically—the one in Providence. And it seems to be important to them, which is very interesting to me, because I never thought it would be. Even when my Dad used to join my mother around the table not too many years ago, I insisted that he bless me—which he did rather willingly.

Blessing in Today's Families

We are used to talking about God with masculine language. Our ears anticipate masculine pronouns and masculine imagery describing God. Judaism, however, has a second, feminine image of the Divine: that of the *Shekhinah*, the close-dwelling presence of God. When the Rabbis talked of the portion of God people could experience, the language became feminine. Likewise, the Shabbat (herself) was spoken of as "Queen" or "Bride." In the Middle Ages, a portion of the Book of Proverbs (31:10–31), the *Eishet Ḥayil*, was introduced into the Shabbat Seder. Its original intent was as a hymn of praise to God (experienced as the *Shekhinah*) or to the Shabbat day—the Bride, the Queen, the "Woman of Valor."

It often happens that practices continue while understandings change. Looking across the table at their wives, husbands began to address their beloved spouses with this biblical description of the ideal woman. What was good enough for God and the Shabbat was what their wives deserved. As time passed, the practice continued while the understandings again changed. It became universally accepted that *Eishet Ḥayil* was the "wife's prayer."

Today, it is questionable whether women strive to be "a woman of valor" as defined by a biblical role model. New definitions and images are evolving; yet, as Jews, we are left with the heritage of a practice. In the households we visited, many new understandings of *Eishet Ḥayil* were in the process of coming to be. Husbands were joyful at the opportunity to formally verbalize their love and respect for their wives. Wives were often looking for ways of making peace with difficult images. Ironically, there seemed to be a pattern of *Eishset Ḥayil* being said in jest, with a true sense of appreciation lying just below the taunt of "many daughters have done excellently, but you excel them all." It seems clear that at the moment, *Eishet Ḥayil* provides us with a rare opportunity to witness tradition in transition.

WENDY KELMAN: I have mixed feelings about *Eishet Ḥayil*. I think it's somewhat male chauvinistic. However, it is traditional, and it basically has the right idea. Some of the things it says I don't know that I totally agree with, but again, it's a chance for your husband to say that he

115

appreciates you and you are special. He might not necessarily say that if you didn't have an organized way of doing it.

ASHER KELMAN: The *Eishet Ḥayil* is a link with many, many generations of celebrating Shabbes in which the woman was recognized for her central role in keeping the Jewish family going. My mother always considered it her reward. I start in Hebrew, say some words in English, some words I make a joke about—emphasizing some parts, like "She sneaks out and buys in the field." I think that's very good, because I would like some more property. And I like the part where it says, "She wakes up early and gets herself busy with the household." Things like that.

IRWIN WEINGARTEN: I love it when there are newcomers at the table and I recite it in English. Because it is an outdated prayer or blessing, whatever you want to call it, but when it's read and people start to listen to it, the comments are just precious. If it's another couple, typically the woman looks at the man and the man looks at the woman at certain parts and you hear this: "Oh, sure!"

DINAH WEINGARTEN: Once when Uncle Chuck came over, he goes, "Fairy tales." It says stuff like she goes out and makes her own fur coat from lambs and gives it to her children.

YOUR AUTHOR: You don't want a fur coat?

DINAH WEINGARTEN: We don't have any lambs.

SUZAN WEINGARTEN: I don't get it read to me every week. When I do, it's a special treat.

Concepts

A Complete Home

The Hebrew word שָׁלוֹם (Shalom) comes from the root *shalem*. While we translate one of its meanings as "peace," the vision expressed in the Hebrew is not the same as the Latin word *pax*, from which the English was taken. *Pax* literally means "quiet." *Shalom* means "whole" or "complete." This is a more dynamic conception of peace.

Shalom bayit—a complete home—is an ideal vision of a family at peace with itself. Yet, family harmony is not always the easiest goal to achieve. During the hectic work week, pressures build, tempers are frayed, and the opportunity to recognize and appreciate family members is often long in coming. The traditional Shabbat celebration brings us a way of actively building a dynamic sense of family *shalom*. The individual blessing of family members is a ritualized expression of this opportunity.

The Blessing of Children

The first of the family blessings are those for the children. The tradition of blessing children is quite old. The Bible itself records several parental blessings for children. We have Isaac's blessings of his sons and Jacob's blessing of his sons. The actual blessing formula still used for boys today refers to the blessing Jacob bestowed on his grandchildren Ephraim and Menasseh, Joseph's sons. We bless our sons with this formula: "May God make you like Ephraim and Menasseh." A modern midrash teaches that this benediction attests to their unique strength. These two boys were raised in Egypt, sons of an Egyptian nobleman; yet, they refused to give up their identity as Jews. Rather than assimilate into the dominant culture, they openly identified with their alien relatives, the nomadic Israelite immigrants. Ephraim and Menasseh are symbols of the loyalty of children to their parents and their faith.

The blessing formula we use for daughters refers to the shining examples of Jewish womanhood, the ancestral mothers: Sarah, Rebecca, Rachel, and Leah. We bless our daughters: "May God make you like Sarah, Rebecca, Rachel and Leah." Sarah was a woman of courage whose response to adversity was laughter. Rebecca, even more than Abraham, is the biblical model of hospitality and human concern. And Rachel and Leah are the two biblical characters who fully model being "their sibling's keeper," showing real sisterhood. These are the values we wish on any child.

The children's blessings are concluded with the ancient Priestly Benediction, the same formula as that recited by the high priests in the Temple.

This is the first of several echoes of the Temple service found in the Shabbat Seder. Parents preside over the Shabbat table as the priests presided over the altar in the Temple. The benediction itself asks God's blessing for protection, kindness, and peace.

The Blessing of the Wife; The Blessing of the Husband

The theme of *shelom bayit* continues with a second set of personal testimonials. It is traditional at this point in the Shabbat Seder for the husband to recite *Eishet Ḥayil,* a selection from Proverbs 31:10–31, which praises his wife as a "Woman of Valor." This text recognizes the contributions of the wife and mother to the family. Its definition of these contributions is rooted in a worldview in which the woman occupied specifically domestic and supportive roles. Although some women object to what they consider sexism in the

BIRKHOT HAMISHPAḤAH

For the Sons

1. *Y'simkha Elohim*
2. *k'Efrayim vekhiMenashe.*

For the Daughters

3. *Yesimekh Elohim*
4. *keSarah Rivka Raḥel veLeah.*

For all Children

5. *Yevarekhekha Adonai*
6. *veyishmerekha.*
7. *Ya'er Adonai panav elekha*
8. *viḥuneka.*
9. *Yisa Adonai panav elekha,*
10. *veyasem lekha shalom.*

FAMILY BLESSINGS

(May) God make you
like Ephraim and Menasseh.

(May) God make you
like Sarah, Rebecca, Rachel, and Leah.

(May) God bless you
and watch over you.
(May) God cause the Divine face to shine
upon you and be gracious to you.
(May) God lift up the Divine face toward you,
and (may) God give you peace.

Eishet Ḥayil, many find it quite meaningful. In some families, an additional text, Psalm 112, "Happy Is the Man," has been added. In other homes, the *Eishet Ḥayil* has been replaced with alternative texts of praise. In one family we know, the parents read selections from the Song of Songs together.

Surprisingly, in many of our interviews we found that the traditional text of *Eishet Ḥayil* has been retained, though it is treated as a playful moment. It is a moment for the husband to gently "mock" his wife through confronting her with a "traditional" role model. As with most humor, there is a truth lying just beneath the surface. While it is sometimes very difficult to tell a spouse just how much he or she is loved and appreciated, the play allows the interchange to happen. What we have learned is that these blessings offer an important opportunity for affirming and celebrating significant relationships. To that end, we have included a family blessing in our Shabbat Seder text as well.

1. יְשִׂימְךָ אֱלֹהִים
2. כְּאֶפְרַיִם וְכִמְנַשֶּׁה.

3. יְשִׂימֵךְ אֱלֹהִים
4. כְּשָׂרָה רִבְקָה רָחֵל וְלֵאָה.

5. יְבָרֶכְךָ יְיָ
6. וְיִשְׁמְרֶךָ.
7. יָאֵר יְיָ פָּנָיו אֵלֶיךָ
8. וִיחֻנֶּךָּ.
9. יִשָּׂא יְיָ פָּנָיו אֵלֶיךָ
10. וְיָשֵׂם לְךָ שָׁלוֹם.

EISHET HAYIL:	A WOMAN OF VALOR
(Proverbs 31:10–31)	(Proverbs 31:10–31)
1. Eishet hayil mi yimtza	A good wife, who can find?
2. verahok mipeninim mikhrah.	She is more precious than corals.
3. Batah ba lev ba'lah	The heart of her husband trusts in her,
4. veshalal lo yehsar.	And he has no lack of gain.
5. Gemalat'hu tov velo ra	She does him good and not harm
6. kol yemei hayeha.	All the days of her life.
7. Darsha tzemer ufishtim	She seeks out wool and flax
8. vata'as beheifetz kapeha.	And works it up as her hands will.
9. Hayta ka'oniyot soher	She is like the ships of the merchant;
10. mimerhak tavi lahmah.	From afar she brings her food.
11. Vatakom be'od lailah	She arises while it is yet night,
12. vatiten teref leveita	And gives food to her household,
13. vehok lena'aroteha.	And a portion to her maidens.
14. Zamema sadeh vatikaheihu	She examines a field and buys it;
15. mipri khapeha nat'ah karem.	With the fruit of her hands she plants a vineyard.
16. Hagrah ve'oz motneha	She girds herself with strength,
17. vate'ametz zero'oteha.	And braces her arms for work.
18. Ta'amah ki tov sahrah	She perceives that her profit is good;
19. lo yikhbeh valailah nerah.	Her lamp does not go out at night.
20. Yadeha shilhah vakishor	She lays her hands on the distaff;
21. vekhapeha tamkhu falekh.	Her palms grasp the spindle.
22. Kapah parsah le'ani	She opens her hand to the poor,
23. veyadeha shilhah la'evyon.	And extends her hands to the needy.
24. Lo tira leveita mishaleg	She does not fear snow for her household,
25. ki khol beitah lavush shanim.	For all her household are clad in warm garments.
26. Marvadim astah lah	Coverlets she makes for herself;
27. shesh ve'argaman levushah.	Her clothing is fine linen and purple.
28. Noda bashe'arim ba'lah	Her husband is distinguished in the council
29. beshivto im ziknei aretz.	When he sits among the elders of the land.

1. אֵשֶׁת חַיִל מִי יִמְצָא
2. וְרָחֹק מִפְּנִינִים מִכְרָהּ:
3. בָּטַח בָּהּ לֵב בַּעְלָהּ
4. וְשָׁלָל לֹא יֶחְסָר:
5. גְּמָלַתְהוּ טוֹב וְלֹא־רָע
6. כֹּל יְמֵי חַיֶּיהָ:
7. דָּרְשָׁה צֶמֶר וּפִשְׁתִּים
8. וַתַּעַשׂ בְּחֵפֶץ כַּפֶּיהָ:
9. הָיְתָה כָּאֳנִיּוֹת סוֹחֵר
10. מִמֶּרְחָק תָּבִיא לַחְמָהּ:
11. וַתָּקָם בְּעוֹד לַיְלָה
12. וַתִּתֵּן טֶרֶף לְבֵיתָהּ
13. וְחֹק לְנַעֲרֹתֶיהָ:
14. זָמְמָה שָׂדֶה וַתִּקָּחֵהוּ
15. מִפְּרִי כַפֶּיהָ נָטְעָה כָּרֶם:
16. חָגְרָה בְעוֹז מָתְנֶיהָ
17. וַתְּאַמֵּץ זְרוֹעֹתֶיהָ:
18. טָעֲמָה כִּי־טוֹב סַחְרָהּ
19. לֹא־יִכְבֶּה בַלַּיְלָה נֵרָהּ:
20. יָדֶיהָ שִׁלְּחָה בַכִּישׁוֹר
21. וְכַפֶּיהָ תָּמְכוּ פָלֶךְ:
22. כַּפָּהּ פָּרְשָׂה לֶעָנִי
23. וְיָדֶיהָ שִׁלְּחָה לָאֶבְיוֹן:
24. לֹא־תִירָא לְבֵיתָהּ מִשָּׁלֶג
25. כִּי כָל־בֵּיתָהּ לָבֻשׁ שָׁנִים:
26. מַרְבַדִּים עָשְׂתָה־לָּהּ
27. שֵׁשׁ וְאַרְגָּמָן לְבוּשָׁהּ:
28. נוֹדָע בַּשְּׁעָרִים בַּעְלָהּ
29. בְּשִׁבְתּוֹ עִם־זִקְנֵי־אָרֶץ:

121

30. *Sadin astah vatimkor*	She makes linen cloth and sells it;
31. *vahagor natnah lakena'ani.*	She delivers belts to the merchant.
32. *Oz vehadar levushah*	Strength and honor are her garb;
33. *vatishak leyom aharon.*	She smiles confidently at the future.
34. *Piha pathah vehokhmah*	She opens her mouth with wisdom,
35. *vetorat hesed al leshonah.*	And the teaching of kindness is on her tongue.
36. *Tzofiya halikhot beitah*	She looks well to the ways of her household;
37. *velehem atzlut lo tokhel.*	She eats not the bread of idleness.
38. *Kamu vaneha vayashruha*	Her children rise up and call her blessed,
39. *ba'lah vayehalelah:*	And her husband praises her:
40. *Rabot banot asu hayil*	"Many daughters have done excellently,
41. *ve'at alit al kulanah.*	But you excel them all."
42. *Sheker hahen vehevel hayofi*	Grace is deceptive and beauty is passing;
43. *isha yirat Adonai hi tit'halal.*	A woman revering Adonai, she shall be praised.
44. *Tenu la mipri yadeha*	Give her of the fruit of her hands,
45. *viyhaleluha vashe'arim ma'aseha.*	And let her own works praise her in the gates.

30. סָדִין עָשְׂתָה וַתִּמְכֹּר

31. וַחֲגוֹר נָתְנָה לַכְּנַעֲנִי:

32. עוֹז־וְהָדָר לְבוּשָׁהּ

33. וַתִּשְׂחַק לְיוֹם אַחֲרוֹן:

34. פִּיהָ פָּתְחָה בְחָכְמָה

35. וְתוֹרַת־חֶסֶד עַל־לְשׁוֹנָהּ:

36. צוֹפִיָּה הֲלִיכוֹת בֵּיתָהּ

37. וְלֶחֶם עַצְלוּת לֹא תֹאכֵל:

38. קָמוּ בָנֶיהָ וַיְאַשְּׁרוּהָ

39. בַּעְלָהּ וַיְהַלְלָהּ:

40. רַבּוֹת בָּנוֹת עָשׂוּ חָיִל

41. וְאַתְּ עָלִית עַל־כֻּלָּנָה:

42. שֶׁקֶר הַחֵן וְהֶבֶל הַיֹּפִי

43. אִשָּׁה יִרְאַת־יְיָ הִיא תִתְהַלָּל:

44. תְּנוּ־לָהּ מִפְּרִי יָדֶיהָ

45. וִיהַלְלוּהָ בַשְּׁעָרִים מַעֲשֶׂיהָ:

ASHREI ISH

(Psalm 112)

HAPPY IS THE MAN

1. *Haleluyah.*
2. *Ashrei ish yarei et Adonai*
3. *bemitzvotav hafetz me'od.*
4. *Gibor ba'aretz yihyeh zar'o*
5. *dor yesharim yevorakh.*
6. *Hon va'osher beveito*
7. *vetzidkato omedet la'ad.*
8. *Zarah bahoshekh or laysharim*
9. *Hanun verahum vetzadik....*
10. *Mishemu'ah ra'ah lo yira*
11. *Nakhon libo batu'ah bAdonai.*
12. *Samukh libo lo yira....*
13. *Pizar natan la'evyonim*
14. *tzidkato omedet la'ad.*
15. *Karno tarum bekhavod....*

Halleluya!

Happy is the man who reveres Adonai,

Who greatly delights in God's commandments.

His descendants will be honored in the land;

The generation of the upright will be praised.

His household prospers,

And his righteousness endures forever.

Light dawns in the darkness for the upright;

For the one who is gracious, compassionate and just...

He is not afraid of evil tidings;

His mind is firm, in Adonai trusting.

His heart is steady, he will not be afraid....

He has given to the poor.

His righteousness endures forever;

His life is exalted in honor....

אַשְׁרֵי־אִישׁ

1. הַלְלוּיָהּ

2. אַשְׁרֵי־אִישׁ יָרֵא אֶת־יְיָ

3. בְּמִצְוֹתָיו חָפֵץ מְאֹד:

4. גִּבּוֹר בָּאָרֶץ יִהְיֶה זַרְעוֹ

5. דּוֹר יְשָׁרִים יְבֹרָךְ:

6. הוֹן־וָעֹשֶׁר בְּבֵיתוֹ

7. וְצִדְקָתוֹ עֹמֶדֶת לָעַד:

8. זָרַח בַּחֹשֶׁךְ אוֹר לַיְשָׁרִים

9. חַנּוּן וְרַחוּם וְצַדִּיק:

10. מִשְּׁמוּעָה רָעָה לֹא יִירָא

11. נָכוֹן לִבּוֹ בָּטֻחַ בַּיְיָ:

12. סָמוּךְ לִבּוֹ לֹא יִירָא

13. פִּזַּר נָתַן לָאֶבְיוֹנִים

14. צִדְקָתוֹ עֹמֶדֶת לָעַד

15. קַרְנוֹ תָּרוּם בְּכָבוֹד:

BIRKHOT HAMISHPAHAH	FAMILY BLESSING	בִּרְכוֹת הַמִּשְׁפָּחָה
1. *Harahaman*	May the Merciful One	1. הָרַחֲמָן
2. *hu yevarekh*	bless	2. הוּא יְבָרֵךְ
3. *otanu kulanu yahad*	all of us together	3. אוֹתָנוּ כֻּלָנוּ יַחַד
4. *bevirkat shalom.*	with the blessing of peace.	4. בְּבִרְכַּת שָׁלוֹם.

Practical Questions and Answers

If the blessing for daughters refers to the ancestral mothers, why doesn't the blessing for sons refer to Abraham, Isaac, and Jacob?
The blessing for the sons is actually recorded in the Bible. When Jacob blesses Ephraim and Menasseh (Genesis 48:20), he states that future generations will use this very blessing.

Who is to be blessed first: the son(s) or the daughter(s)?
Since there are separate statements for sons and daughters, one necessarily has to be first. You may find that choosing a pattern and staying with it—for example, chronological order—may avoid weekly arguments. Or you might consider alternating the order by gender every week—one week daughters first, the next week sons first.

Do I recite the individual blessing for each child and then the Priestly Benediction for all the children, or should I repeat the Priestly Benediction for each child?
Although it will take a bit longer, reciting both the individual statement and the Priestly Benediction for each child gives that child your total attention. If the Hebrew is difficult for you, however, you might choose to recite the individual blessing for each child first, followed by the recitation of the

Priestly Benediction for all. Some of the families we interviewed enjoy a total family hug following the recitation of the priestly blessing.

What happens if I have more than one son or one daughter?
Again, several alternatives are available. You can bless each child separately with the entire blessing or with just the appropriate individual blessing. Or you might bless all the daughters individually, followed by a collective Priestly Benediction for the girls, and then turn to the sons (or vice versa). The main principle to keep in mind is to allow this part of the ritual to provide you with a private moment of closeness with each of your children.

Should my children get up and come to me, or do I get up and go to them?
Most parents spend a good part of the week going to their children, trying to meet their needs. Certainly, the parent(s) can stand up and go to their children to give them a blessing, particularly if they are very young or if having the children get up would be disruptive. Yet, there may be something important, though subtle, about having the children come to their parent(s) for this part of the ritual. As you think about this issue, consider this very early account of the Blessing of Children ceremony from *The Brautspiege*, a book by Moses Henochs, published in Basel, Switzerland, in 1602:

> Before children can walk, they should be carried on Shabbatot and festivals to the father and mother to be blessed; after they are able to walk, they shall go of their own accord with bowed head and shall incline their head and receive the blessing.

Who should bless the children: the father or the mother or both?
Although it is traditional for the father to bless the children upon returning from synagogue, the above quotation is just one of many indications that in some settings both parents joined in blessing the children. Certainly, having both parents bless the children is a powerful message to them. In a single-parent family, whoever is with the children would bless them, although it is certainly possible that the other parent would want to bless the children, perhaps in a pre-Shabbat call.

What if my children are not at home on Friday night?
In one interview we conducted, both parents individually telephone their twenty-five-year-old graduate student every Friday afternoon before Shabbat in order to perform this ritual. Talk about "reach out and touch someone"!

Do I really place my hands on the child's head while saying the blessing?
Many parents do just that, imitating the ancient practice of bestowing a blessing accompanied by physical touch. This is what Jacob did when he blessed his children. Young children tend to love this part of the ritual, while older kids may see it as corny and even refuse to let the parent do it. As an alternative to hands-on-head, try putting your hands on the child's shoulders or just hug the child after the blessing is said. Obviously, you do not want to embarrass the child to the point of his or her not wanting to participate. Some families even stand together in a circle, arms around shoulders, and recite the blessings together. Once again, use your judgment and do what feels right.

What about visiting grandparents? Should they bless me, the parent?
Nothing could be more impressive at a Shabbat table than to see grandparents blessing their adult children, followed immediately by the adult children— you, the parent(s)—blessing your own children. This modeling of behavior will reinforce what you are trying to establish in your own family ritual. However, if your parents have never participated in this ritual, prepare them for it in advance. As with any of the blessings, if the Hebrew is difficult, let them bless you using the English. Once they've blessed you, you'll probably see any resistance from your own children quickly disappear.

How can I make this moment special?
Try to personalize the ancient formulae with your own words and gestures. Some parents whisper a private wish or appreciation to each child after reciting the blessing. Other parents publicly pronounce their thoughts. On the other hand, if you feel uncomfortable embellishing the ritual form with personal remarks, especially as you begin this practice, don't feel you have somehow missed out. The whole point of the ritual formulation is to allow you to say things that you find difficult to say on your own. We have heard

of families where wishes are written out (before Shabbat) and placed in a "Shabbat Wishes Box," or others who use a special diary. In some families, parents give their children a small Shabbat gift; for others, the best gift is a hug and a kiss. Whatever you decide to do, make this a special private time for you and your children. This is the stuff of which memories are made.

Who recites the *Eishet Hayil*?

Traditionally, the husband recites the *Eishet Hayil* to his wife. In some families, the children join in as well; in others, everyone, including the mother, sings the prayer. Although the Hebrew is somewhat difficult to master, some of the families have learned a simple tune for singing *Eishet Hayil*. Usually the family remains seated during this part of the Shabbat Seder.

Can we include a parallel prayer for the husband?

Many families have added Psalm 112, "Happy is the Man," to their Shabbat Seder. Others have substituted a comprehensive family prayer for both of these prayers, an example of which we have included, entitled *Birkat Hamishpahah*.

Can we personalize this moment?

As with the blessing for children, this part of the Shabbat Seder invites the personal touch. After reciting the traditional formulations, consider exchanging a private word, glance, or hug with your spouse. A kiss would also be very appropriate and probably appreciated. Again, here is an opportunity for a harried couple to share a significant moment of closeness.

What if I am a single parent?

Since the traditional prayers are designed for saying to a spouse, you might consider three alternatives: (1) skipping this passage, (2) having your children recite this specific prayer for you, or (3) substituting a family blessing instead.

Some Interesting Sources

These two quotations from rabbinic sources point us toward the real purpose of Shabbat celebration.

> If a family is too poor to buy both candles for the Shabbat lights and wine for Kiddush on Friday night, the candles should be purchased. Light in the home brings peace, and the purpose of the Shabbat is peace and enjoyment.
>
> Ḥayye Adam, *Ḥullen Shabbat, Kelal 5*

> A simple vegetable meal on Shabbat in a home where there is love between husband, wife, and children is better than a fatted ox in a home where there is hatred. A man should not plan to honor the Shabbat with delicacies while he knows that he will quarrel with his wife, or father, or mother. Whether it be Shabbat or festival—"better a dry morsel and quietness there, than a house full of feasting with conflict" (Proverbs 17:1). One should honor the Shabbat by having no conflict on it.
>
> Judah He-Ḥasid, *Sefer Ḥasidim*

Both of these sources deal with choices that families have to make about their Shabbat celebrations. Compare them with some of the choices you have to make. How does the value of *shalom bayit* (family peace) fit into your decisions? Can Shabbat observance help you attain *shalom bayit*? How?

7

קִדּוּשׁ

Kiddush
Sanctification of the Day

The word that comes to both of our minds when we think of Shabbat is "yawn." Not because it is boring, but because the real sense of rest comes to me every time we say the blessing over the wine. We get to about "*attah*" and I yawn. It used to be something I was embarrassed about, but now I know it's true. That it is really greeting the Sabbath Queen. I mean—she's beautiful, and I yawn.

BOB SHAFTON

KAREN VINOCOR: I told Ari that he has to start singing with me because I want him to feel comfortable doing it before his Bar Mitzvah.

ARI VINOCOR: And I get to drink more.

KAREN VINOCOR: That's right. You say more, you drink more.

ERIN VINOCOR: What about me?

KAREN VINOCOR: Your time will come.

IRWIN WEINGARTEN: We're slowly weaning myself off the Kiddush. I think in another year or so, Dinah will be able to say the whole thing. She knows a little bit of the beginning and all of it after that. So maybe my responsibilities will come to just a directorship soon. And it will be passed down.

Kiddush seems to be the real test for Jewish adulthood. To make it as a successful Jewish child, it is common practice that you must survive the ordeal of the Four Questions on Passover. Just when you've learned how to say the words without stumbling, along comes some other kid, and you're not the youngest anymore. Our experience in the home has taught us that saying the Kiddush is the training ground for Jewish adulthood. Mastering the Kiddush is a way of preparing for the Bar/Bat Mitzvah—families make it an essential Jewish home skill.

Wine is a common symbol of celebration. You'll find toasts in virtually every human culture; yet, Kiddush stands alone, unique. The Shabbat Kid-

dush doesn't bless the wine; the beverage never becomes holy. The Shabbat day becomes holy, but our blessing of the day through the Kiddush over wine doesn't make the day holy. The wine doesn't change through the blessing. The day doesn't change. Only our perception changes. With the recitation of the Kiddush we acknowledge that we have entered into a realm of sacred time, into the day God set aside and sanctified as the Shabbat.

Simple things often have profound meanings. In the Jewish tradition, the drinking of wine provides the opportunity to consciously enter into a time of celebration. Kiddush makes a direct connection between the specific table at which we sit, the food, the utensils, the group with whom we've sat down, and the Jewish experience. The Shabbat Kiddush specifically recalls both the creation of the world and the Exodus from Egypt. In lifting our wine cups and blessing the Shabbat, we connect our family group, our moment of sitting down, with all human existence since creation and with the emergence of the Jewish people as a community. Blessing the wine makes the table into a symbolic time machine, transporting us through the entire Jewish time frame.

In the homes we visited, wine provides another source of historical connection. The most common pragmatic result of Kiddush is wine stains. Wonderfully, the size and shape of former spills serve as remembrances of other specific moments of family celebration. And the Kiddush cups from which the wine spills are among the proudest family heirlooms.

DEBRA NEINSTEIN: We have little Kiddush cups for all the children. They all have their own little Kiddush cups with their grape juice. I used to always give them cups that they made in school, but now I have little Kiddush cups that are just like Larry's, and that's what they want. They want the real thing. They don't want plastic cups.

SANDY GOODGLICK: When Todd turned twenty-five, he graduated from his Bar Mitzvah Kiddush cup to a really nice one. Bill got a special one when he turned fifty. Now, everyone including Mother Goodglick and me has a Kiddush cup. Then we started purchasing other Kiddush cups so that everyone at the table has one of their own now. That seemed to make it very finished. It seemed so unfinished with men having Kiddush cups and the ladies and guests, glasses.

WENDY KELMAN: We bought my husband's Kiddush cup together in Boston. He had another very small Kiddush cup that he got from Israel, from his brother. That one had little jewels around it. We went out for a walk one Shabbes eve, and I was very anxious about the candles, and I said, "I don't think we should go out while the candles are burning."

My husband said, "Never in the history of the Jewish people has there been a fire caused by Shabbes candles." When we came back, the whole tablecloth was completely burned, the rug was burned, the wallpaper was burned, and many of the jewels from the Kiddush cup had fallen off.

When Ariel was born, some friends of ours gave him a very large Kiddush cup with his name in Hebrew. That Kiddush cup somehow got into the garbage disposal, and it was all nicked. But my husband banged it out so it's at least usable, and we still use it because it has a lot of sentimental value.

JEREMIAH KELMAN: My grandparents got my Kiddush cup for me.

EMIL KELMAN: I got my wine cup, my Kiddush cup, from my Dad's brother—I like it really much and thank my Dad's brother.

ASHER KELMAN: We always use red wine for Kiddush, and I fill my cup to the top. The idea is that it's your life—you have a full cup, and you're brimming over. Also, if you're doing a mitzvah, don't be measly in doing it. And to me, it's symbolic of the fullness I would like in my family, and if it spills over, it spills over. You can always wash it off.

Concepts

Kiddush Sanctifies the Shabbat, Not the Wine

Kiddush is a form of the ubiquitous Hebrew word *kadosh*, "holy." Kiddush literally means "to make holy" or "to sanctify." But what is it we are sanctifying? Contrary to popular perception, we are not sanctifying the wine; few objects in Judaism are considered "holy." Rather, we are sanctifying the Shabbat. We are making time holy. As Abraham Joshua Heschel wrote in *The Sabbath*:

> Judaism is a religion of time, aiming at the sanctification of time. Unlike the space-minded man to whom time is unvaried, iterative, homogeneous, to whom all hours are alike, qualitiless, empty shells, the Bible senses the diversified character of time.... Judaism teaches us to be attached to holiness in time; to be attached to sacred events, to learn how to consecrate sanctuaries that emerge from the magnificent streams of a year. The Sabbaths

are our great cathedrals; and our Holy of Holies is a shrine that neither the Romans nor the Greeks were able to burn....

Why do we sanctify this time, this Shabbat, over a cup of wine? Because joy and happiness are synonymous with Shabbat, the weekly respite from the six days of labor. And our central symbol of joy is, of course, a full cup of wine. In the days of the Talmud, when the final formulation of the Kiddush was established, festive meals began with a cup of wine. So, too, the Shabbat evening meal, certainly the most festive of the week, began with wine. Thus, the juxtaposition of two blessings—one for wine and one for sanctifying Shabbat—became the core of the Kiddush prayer we recite today.

Shabbat in the Bible

The formula for sanctifying the Shabbat day contains within it the two biblical images of Shabbat. The Friday night Kiddush begins with the verses that tell the story of the first Shabbat (Genesis 2:1–3):

And there was evening and there was morning: the sixth day.

And the heavens were completed

and the earth and all its components (were completed).

And God completed on the seventh day

the work which God had been doing.

And God ceased on the seventh day

from all the work which God had done.

And God blessed the seventh day

and sanctified it,

because on it God

ceased from all the work

which God had created through doing.

This paragraph describes God finishing the work of creation and blessing the seventh day, declaring it to be holy. According to the Talmud, by reciting these words, it is as if we are ourselves at the moment of creation; the Kiddush becomes an echo of God's establishment of the seventh day as *kadosh:* unique and holy. The theme of creation is reiterated in the body of the Kiddush itself, where Shabbat is called זִכָּרוֹן לְמַעֲשֵׂה בְרֵאשִׁית *zikaron lema'aseh vereishit,* "a remembrance of the acts of creation." Thus, the sanctification of the seventh day becomes a tangible, living legacy of God's creation.

The second biblical reference in the Kiddush is to Shabbat as זֵכֶר לִיצִיאַת מִצְרָיִם *zeikher litziyat Mitzrayim,* "a remembrance of the Exodus from Egypt." Certainly, the liberation from bondage has close parallels to the liberation from the six days of labor.

In this way, Kiddush speaks of two creations: the cosmic first creation of all humanity, and the particular genesis of the Jewish people, who became a nation as they emerged from Egyptian bondage.

Kiddush Speaks of Chosenness

The Kiddush includes a reference to the chosenness of Israel: "You have chosen us and sanctified us from among all peoples." The idea of the Jews being a "chosen people" is not an elitist notion. Rather, God chose us for the purpose of observing the Law and for receiving and caring for the special gift of Shabbat. Likewise, the Jewish people chose to accept God's covenant, living up to the standards set by these laws. In the context of the biblical images of Shabbat—the Creation and the Exodus—the Rabbis remind us of the special relationship we have to God and the obligation we have assumed to "guard" the Shabbat.

Objects

The two items necessary for Kiddush are a cup and wine. The cup used for Kiddush has traditionally been among the most beautiful of vessels found in the home. Many families acquire silver Kiddush cups, but any material is suitable. The Kiddush cup, like the candlesticks, may well become a valued family heirloom, often featuring inscriptions or other decorative touches.

The wine used for Kiddush should be kosher and made from grapes—the fruit of the vine. It is traditional, although not required, to use red wine. Some families choose to use Israeli wine as a gesture of support for the Jewish state. Grape juice is a suitable alternative to wine.

Anatomy of the Shabbat Eve Kiddush

This is the traditional way to say Kiddush:

1. The Kiddush cup is raised. Some hold it in the palm of the hand, with fingers pointing up, as if God were pouring the wine into the cup.
2. The *Vaykhulu* is said. This introductory paragraph comes from Genesis (2:1–3) and is also found in the *Amidah* of the Friday evening synagogue service. It was probably added to the Kiddush at home to allow those who did not attend services to hear this passage, which recalls the creation of the Shabbat.

   Some say the first four words—*Vayehi erev vayehi voker*, "it was evening, it was morning"—in a whisper in order to emphasize the next words, *yom hashishi, vaykhulu hashamayim*, "the sixth day, the heavens were finished." This also highlights the symbolism of the first letters of these words: *yud* (Y), *hey* (H), *vav* (V), *hey* (H), which together spell YHVH—the four letters of the Tetragrammaton—the ineffable name of God.
3. Some people introduce the blessing for wine with the words *savri haverai*, "with the permission of friends." This is a formal announcement that a blessing is about to be said. By doing this, the leader is announcing that he or she is taking the responsibility for meeting everyone's obligation to say Kiddush.
4. *Borei peri hagafen*—the blessing over the wine is said. The Talmud explains that because the wine blessing is said at every meal where wine is served, this "regular" blessing is said before the "special" blessing for the Shabbat day. However, do not drink the wine until after reciting *Mekadesh Hashabbat*. The blessing for wine is linked to the Shabbat blessing; in fact, the wine is only a vehicle to enable

us to sanctify the Shabbat over something. Thus, we wait until the entire Kiddush is recited before drinking the wine.

5. *Mekadesh Hashabbat.* This is the blessing that sanctifies the Shabbat day. It contains the two major Shabbat themes, Creation and the Exodus, and a reference to God's choice of the Jewish people to sanctify the Shabbat. It is this blessing that directs our attention toward the sacred celebration of Shabbat time. Remember, you do not need to say "Amen" at the end of the blessing.

6. Drink the wine.

KIDDUSH   SANCTIFICATION OF THE DAY

VAYKHULU

1.	*Vayehi erev vayehi voker:*	And there was evening and there was morning:
2.	*yom hashishi.*	the sixth day.
3.	*Vaykhulu hashamayim*	And the heavens were completed
4.	*Veha'aretz vekhol tzeva'am.*	and the earth and all its components (were completed).
5.	*Vayekhal Elohim*	And God completed
6.	*bayom hashvi'i*	on the seventh day
7.	*melakhto asher asa;*	the work which God had been doing;
8.	*Vayishbot bayom hashvi'i*	and rested on the seventh day
9.	*mikol melakhto asher asa.*	from all the work which had been done.
10.	*Vayevarekh Elohim*	And God blessed
11.	*et yom hashvi'i*	the seventh day
12.	*vayekadesh oto*	and sanctified it,
13.	*ki vo shavat*	because on it, God rested
14.	*mikol melakhto*	from all the work
15.	*asher bara Elohim la'asot.*	which God had created through doing.

קִדּוּשׁ

1. וַיְהִי־עֶרֶב וַיְהִי־בֹקֶר

2. יוֹם הַשִּׁשִּׁי.

3. וַיְכֻלּוּ הַשָּׁמַיִם

4. וְהָאָרֶץ וְכָל־צְבָאָם.

5. וַיְכַל אֱלֹהִים בַּיּוֹם

6. הַשְּׁבִיעִי

7. מְלַאכְתּוֹ אֲשֶׁר עָשָׂה

8. וַיִּשְׁבֹּת בַּיּוֹם הַשְּׁבִיעִי

9. מִכָּל־מְלַאכְתּוֹ אֲשֶׁר עָשָׂה.

10. וַיְבָרֶךְ אֱלֹהִים

11. אֶת־יוֹם הַשְּׁבִיעִי

12. וַיְקַדֵּשׁ אֹתוֹ

13. כִּי בוֹ שָׁבַת

14. מִכָּל־מְלַאכְתּוֹ

15. אֲשֶׁר־בָּרָא אֱלֹהִים לַעֲשׂוֹת.

BOREI PERI HAGAFEN

1.	*Barukh attah Adonai*	Praised are You, Adonai,
2.	*Eloheinu melekh ha'olam*	our God, Ruler of the universe,
3.	*borei peri hagafen.*	Creator of the fruit of the vine.

MEKADESH HASHABBAT

4.	*Barukh attah Adonai*	Praised are You, Adonai,
5.	*Eloheinu melekh ha'olam*	our God, Ruler of the universe,
6.	*asher kidshanu bemitzvotav*	who made us holy through the commandments
7.	*veratza vanu.*	and who is pleased with us.
8.	*VeShabbat kodsho*	And the holy Shabbat,
9.	*b'ahava uvratzon*	with love and satisfaction,
10.	*hinhilanu—*	God gave us as an inheritance—
11.	*zikaron lema'asei vereishit.*	a remembrance of the work of Creation.
12.	*Ki hu yom tehilah*	For it was first
13.	*lemikra'ei kodesh—*	among the sacred days of assembly—
14.	*zeikher litziyat Mitzrayim.*	a remembrance of the Exodus from Egypt.
15.	*Ki vanu vaharta*	For You have chosen us
16.	*ve'otanu kidashta*	and You have sanctified us
17.	*mikol ha'amim;*	from (among) all the peoples;
18.	*veShabbat kodshekha*	and Your holy Shabbat
19.	*be'ahava uvratzon*	with love and satisfaction.
20.	*hinhaltanu.*	You gave us as an inheritance.
21.	*Barukh attah Adonai*	Praised are You, Adonai,
22.	*Mekadesh Hashabbat.*	Sanctifier of the Shabbat.

1. בָּרוּךְ אַתָּה יְיָ
2. אֱלֹהֵינוּ מֶלֶךְ הָעוֹלָם
3. בּוֹרֵא פְּרִי הַגָּפֶן.

4. בָּרוּךְ אַתָּה יְיָ
5. אֱלֹהֵינוּ מֶלֶךְ הָעוֹלָם
6. אֲשֶׁר קִדְּשָׁנוּ בְּמִצְוֹתָיו
7. וְרָצָה בָנוּ
8. וְשַׁבַּת קָדְשׁוֹ
9. בְּאַהֲבָה וּבְרָצוֹן
10. הִנְחִילָנוּ
11. זִכָּרוֹן לְמַעֲשֵׂה בְרֵאשִׁית
12. כִּי הוּא יוֹם תְּחִלָּה
13. לְמִקְרָאֵי קֹדֶשׁ
14. זֵכֶר לִיצִיאַת מִצְרָיִם
15. כִּי בָנוּ בָחַרְתָּ
16. וְאוֹתָנוּ קִדַּשְׁתָּ
17. מִכָּל הָעַמִּים
18. וְשַׁבַּת קָדְשְׁךָ
19. בְּאַהֲבָה וּבְרָצוֹן
20. הִנְחַלְתָּנוּ.
21. בָּרוּךְ אַתָּה יְיָ
22. מְקַדֵּשׁ הַשַּׁבָּת.

Practical Questions and Answers

Who recites the Kiddush?

While traditionally this role fell to the father, Jewish law states that both women and men are equally obligated to say the Kiddush. According to the *halakhah* (law), everyone who is duty bound to observe the prohibitions of Shabbat must also recite the Kiddush. Thus, a woman most certainly can recite the Kiddush on her own behalf or on behalf of any males present.

Nevertheless, in many families the father still recites the Kiddush. In some families, no matter who leads the Kiddush, everyone joins in at the phrase *ki vanu vaharta*. Other families ask all in attendance to sing the entire Kiddush together. Once again, you will choose a practice comfortable for your situation.

Is Kiddush recited while standing or sitting?

The Rabbis were undecided on this point. Some argued for sitting in order to establish those in attendance as a group, especially if one person led the blessing. Others pointed out that just standing around the table constituted a group. Many Rabbis compromised and taught their followers to stand during the blessing and then sit before drinking the wine.

So Kiddush may be recited while standing or sitting at the table. You may want to follow family tradition in this matter. Or, if you are just beginning your Shabbat observance, try standing for the Kiddush. Not only is it legally acceptable, but standing gives a certain honor to this central act of sanctifying the Shabbat.

Must the Kiddush cup be filled to the top?

Kiddush is to be recited over a *kos yayin malei*—a full cup of wine. Literally speaking, this means that a cup of wine from which someone has already taken a sip is unfit for Kiddush. Thus, the practice is to fill the cup to the brim, even if it slightly overflows, to ensure that no one has taken a sip. The full cup also becomes a symbol of our overflowing joy at welcoming the Shabbat and a sign of the fullness of the blessing.

Who should have a Kiddush cup?

Besides the leader's Kiddush cup, others at the table may have their own wine cups. Many families have a sacramental Kiddush cup for the leader and plain cups or glasses for the rest of the family and guests. Some families have acquired enough silver or crystal Kiddush cups for everyone. Some families provide cups filled with wine at every setting, while others place empty cups at each setting to be filled from the leader's cup after the Kiddush is recited. In some homes, the leader's Kiddush cup is passed around the table so that all may drink from it.

What happens if no wine is available or someone cannot drink it?
For ritual purposes, there is no difference between grape juice and wine—both are "fruit of the vine." Grape juice is one option, but the tradition provides others. Actually, this was an acute problem for Jews when wine was quite a luxury item. So, according to Jewish law, Kiddush may be recited over the two loaves of *hallah* bread. Recall that the Kiddush prayer sanctifies the day, not the wine. The blessing for bread *(Hamotzi)* is substituted for that of the wine *(Borei peri hagafen),* and the rest of the prayer remains the same. For those who cannot drink alcoholic beverages, substitute grape juice or use the *hallah* option.

Why do we say the Kiddush at home when it is also chanted at the synagogue on Friday night?
The origin of Kiddush in the synagogue is traced to Babylonia at a time when many travelers would seek food and shelter in special annexes to the sanctuary. Since these wayfarers could travel no farther on Shabbat, they would partake of the Shabbat meal in this synagogue hostel immediately after the conclusion of the Friday evening service. Thus, it became traditional to recite the Kiddush at the end of the service for their benefit. It remains part of our Friday night services in the Diaspora. However, since this custom never arose in Israel, Kiddush is not recited in Israeli synagogues on Friday night.

Some Interesting Sources

We've seen that Kiddush is a blessing that has to do with time. The recitation of Kiddush is an acknowledgment that the next period of time has been set aside (sanctified) for celebration. Compare the way two modern Jewish thinkers, Erich Fromm and Abraham Joshua Heschel, talk about the nature of Shabbat time.

ERICH FROMM

The Sabbath seems to have been an old Babylonian holy day, celebrated every seventh day *(Shapatu)*. But its meaning was quite different from that of the biblical Sabbath. The Babylonian Shapatu was a day of mourning and self-castigation. It was a somber day, dedicated to the planet Saturn (our "Saturday" is still, in its name, devoted to Saturn—Saturn's Day), whose wrath one wanted to placate by self-castigation and self-punishment.

Saturn (in the old astrological and metaphysical tradition) symbolizes time. He is the god of time and hence the god of death. Inasmuch as man is like God, gifted with a soul, with reason, love and freedom, he is not subject to time or death. But inasmuch as man is an animal, with a body subject to laws of nature, he is a slave to time and death. The Babylonians sought to appease the lord of time by self-castigation. The Bible in its Sabbath concepts makes an entirely new attempt to solve the problem: by stopping interference with nature for one day you eliminate time; where there is no change, no work, no human interference, there is no time. Instead of a Sabbath on which man bows down to the lord of time, the biblical Sabbath symbolizes man's victory over time; time is suspended, Saturn is dethroned on his very day, Saturn's Day.

The Forgotten Language

ABRAHAM JOSHUA HESCHEL

The higher goal of spiritual living is not to amass a wealth of information, but to face sacred moments. A religious experience, for example, is not a thing that imposes itself on a man, but a spiritual presence. A moment of insight is a fortune, transporting us beyond the confines of measured time.

We are all infatuated with the splendor of space, with the grandeur of the things of space. "Thing" is a category that lies heavy on our minds, tyrannizing all our thoughts. The result of our thingness is our blindness to all reality that fails to identify itself as a thing, as a matter of fact. This is obvious in our understanding of time, which being thingless and unsubstantial, appears to us as if it had no reality.

Judaism is a religion of time, aiming at the sanctification of time.

Unlike the space-minded man to whom time is unvaried, iterative, homogenous, to whom all hours are alike, qualitiless, empty shells, the Bible senses the diversified character of time. There are no two hours alike. Every hour is unique and the only one given at the moment, exclusive and endlessly precious.

Judaism teaches us to be attached to holiness in time; to be attached to sacred events, to learn how to consecrate sanctuaries that emerge from the magnificent streams of a year. The Sabbaths are our great cathedrals; and our Holy of Holies is a shrine that neither the Romans nor the Greeks were able to burn...

The meaning of the Sabbath is to celebrate time rather than space. Six days a week we live under the tyranny of things of space; on the Sabbath, we try to become attuned to the holiness of time. It is a day on which we are called to share in that which is eternal in time, to turn from the world of creation to the creation of the world.

The Sabbath

How can these two views help us to focus our thoughts when we say Kiddush?

8

נְטִילַת יָדְיִם

Netilat Yadayim
Washing the Hands

I like washing our hands in the kitchen because we don't say anything. Bill washes first. Then me, and then Todd. We say the blessing to ourselves. I usually get a little hug from Todd then. It's nice being surrounded by two men—a nice warm moment, away from everybody, relaxing, uninhibited. It feels free; that's why I like it.

SANDY GOODGLICK

The ritual washing of hands is a reminder of the Jerusalem Temple and its sacrifices. Cookouts we understand; sacrifices confuse us. People often have difficulty making peace with the sacrificial history of the Jewish people; they try to purge it from their Jewish understandings and practices. It seems primitive, pagan. It doesn't matter that the real process of the Temple cult was communal meals and a public acknowledgment that everything we grow, raise, or produce is as much a product of God's help as of our own efforts. One merely says the word "sacrifice" and people envision natives throwing things off the cliff to appease the god of the volcano. The Temple cult in Jerusalem was really much closer to being a tax bureau that offered a good stage show and held regular national barbecues. Most farmers came to the Temple one, two, or three times a year. Each trip involved bringing the tithe of their crops for both the priests and the poor. The Temple sacrifices were not attempts to feed a hungry God or bribe a capricious deity. Rather, they were tangible expressions of thanks for Divine involvement in the natural order, and physical expressions of the desire for high-quality interpersonal relations. The Jewish practice of sacrifice was not violent or mindless. It was just the opposite—reverent and communal.

While the Pharisaic Rabbis who created the Talmud were often alienated from the workings of the Temple cult, they found value in preserving remembrances of its operation in the day-to-day Jewish ritual they evolved. With the destruction of the Temple, Judaism lost the presence of a monolithic national focus. The religious hegemony moved from a single national cult to the emerging synagogue and into the home. The rabbinic leaders of this transition acted on the belief that there was significant value in preserving an active memory of the time when all Jews celebrated their relationship with God through a single national worship center. They seeded the daily practice of Judaism with echoes of the Temple. While facilitating the new centrality of the small worship community and the family, they never let the memory of a strong worship-connection common to all Jews slip from the collective memory. Today, the practices that are most directly rooted in the Temple are often those most difficult to understand.

In our society, washing is an act of hygiene. It has a physical outcome. The washing of already clean hands is something we leave to the surgical community. The notion of ritual cleanliness has no immediate context. It seems magical, primitive. Likewise for us, the act of eating is a physical process. Fuel is consumed, a certain amount of pleasure is experienced, and hunger is satisfied. The Jewish tradition has another view of eating, and this view is rooted in the sacrificial experience. In *Pirkei Avot*, the Rabbis teach, "When three people sit together and eat, and they don't discuss words of Torah, then it is as if they are eating dead bodies." The Rabbis weren't arguing for vegetarianism. Rather, they suggested that eating itself can be a religious experience. One can go beyond the mere physical acts of consuming fuel and satisfying hunger and reach an understanding that God was at work in the natural order that provided this food. Just eating can help us understand that all people are entitled to food, and that our temporary stewardship over any wealth comes with responsibility. This was the core message of the "primitive" sacrificial cult in Jerusalem.

To eat with spiritual intent takes focus and concentration. Therefore, every act of eating was framed with ritual. The washing of hands with a blessing is not a Shabbat action. It is an action tied to every formal Jewish meal, every act of eating bread.

In preparing this chapter on *Netilat Yadayim*, our experience with the families taught us that two things were important to share. First, that the ceremony of washing hands was not performed in every home we visited. For most of the families we interviewed, it was the hardest part of the Shabbat Seder in which to find meaning. Many did it anyway because it is a tradition. Second, it became clear that we were obligated to provide a clear vision of some of the values that can be encountered through this act.

JANICE REZNIK: My favorite Shabbat time is right after washing the hands. Yoni (age three) knows that he can't talk until he eats, so we take about three minutes to get to the bread, so we can have the silence.

SANDY GOODGLICK: I like washing our hands in the kitchen because we don't say anything. Bill washes first. Then me, and then Todd. We say the blessing to ourselves. I usually get a little hug from Todd then. It's nice being surrounded by two men—a nice warm moment, away from everybody, relaxing, uninhibited. It feels free; that's why I like it. If guests come in, then I don't get hugged or tickled. But they are certainly welcome. But usually it's just the three of us.

ELAINE ALBERT: I made a decision at some point.... I am now not sure that I still agree with. I'm sorry that I didn't include handwashing in our Shabbat ritual. It's an experience that my children don't have and they are not familiar with. For us, too, it is an experience that we have not had. But I just couldn't really understand it. I mean, I knew what the reason was, and I had studied and I understood what it was, but at that time I did not find that things having to do with the Temple were really relevant to me.

ERIN VINOCOR: We wash our hands, and while we're drying them we say a *berakhah*.

KAREN VINOCOR: Ari takes a glass or cup, anything that's around. I've shown him how to pour water three times over each hand and then pass the cup onto someone else; to take the towel and say the *berakhah*. Erin hasn't yet poured water over her hands. At that point, I am very hungry and cannot be bothered with taking time, so I pour water over both our hands and we say the *berakhah* together. She's just getting used to saying it. Then we sit down at the table as quietly as we possibly can, and we say a very quick *Hamotzi*.

Concepts

The Shabbat Table as Altar

The Talmudic Rabbis viewed the Shabbat table as a substitute for the altar in the Temple. For them, participants in the Shabbat Seder approached the meal as the high priests approached the altar. Thus, in the washing of hands and the breaking of bread, we see echoes of Temple times.

Netilat Yadayim, washing of hands, is not an act of cleanliness. It is a ritual preparation. Just as the priests ritually cleansed their hands before beginning their duties in the Temple (Exodus 30:20), we symbolically wash our hands before breaking bread. By doing so, we become celebrants in the holy act of eating.

Objects

A large cup or pitcher is required for *Netilat Yadayim*. Special pitchers with dual handles have been developed for this purpose. There are even *Netilat Yadayim* "sets" of a pitcher and basin made in Israel especially for this purpose. But any glass or cup and sink will do just fine. You will also need a towel for drying the hands. It is not appropriate to use the small pitcher and basin designed for *mayim aharonim*, the "after water" passed around the table in some families before *Birkat Hamazon*. The tradition prescribes that each person "cover his or her hands with water," and these "finger" pitchers don't hold enough water.

Practice

The first step in *Netilat Yadayim* is to remove any jewelry from your fingers. As in other ritual cleansing (e.g., the mikvah immersion), nothing should come between your hands and the water. Fill a cup or pitcher with water (or, a thoughtful person who precedes you will have refilled the cup after finishing). Take the cup in the left hand and pour some of the water over the right hand, letting the water cover the hand from the wrist down. Turn your hand under the water so it gets completely wet. Then switch the cup into the right hand and pour water over the left hand. (Actually, the order of hands is arbitrary.) Some repeat this procedure three times. When you are finished pouring, it is good etiquette to refill the cup for the next person. Then lift up your hands and begin reciting the blessing. Dry your hands after completing the blessing.

If you have left the table to perform this ritual at a sink, return to your place without talking. Since the handwashing is done in order to eat the bread, *Netilat Yadayim* and *Hamotzi* (the blessing for bread) are considered one act. As we learned earlier, a ritual is not complete until both the blessing is recited and the act is done. Nothing should interrupt this part of the ceremony until the blessing for bread is recited and the bread is actually eaten.

NETILAT YADAYIM	WASHING THE HANDS
1. *Barukh attah Adonai*	Praised are You, Adonai,
2. *Eloheinu melekh ha'olam*	our God, Ruler of the universe,
3. *asher kidshanu bemitzvotav*	who has made us holy through the commandments
4. *vetzivanu*	and commanded us
5. *al netilat yadayim.*	concerning the washing of hands.

The Blessing

There is an interesting point to make about the use of the word *netilat* in the *berakhah* for washing hands. If you recall the Passover Seder, the leader symbolically washes hands at the beginning of the service. This is called *rohtzah*—the Hebrew word for "washing." We might expect, then, that the blessing for washing hands would read *al rehitzat yadayim*, not *al netilat yadayim*. *Netilat* literally means "take" or "lift up." The use of this term indicates that the hands are in fact "lifted up" to a higher level by this symbolic cleansing, ready to participate in the breaking of bread.

Practical Questions and Answers

Can we wash hands at a sink, or must we use a special pitcher and basin?
Either way is fine. Washing at the table can be somewhat cumbersome, with the chance of spilling significant amounts of liquid in the process. On the other hand, using a kitchen or bathroom sink requires everyone to get up from the table to perform the ritual. Do what seems comfortable in your situation.

Who washes first?
In some homes there is a weekly race to the sink to see who will wash first. Of course, whoever washes first has the longest time to stay quiet before the *Hamotzi* is recited. Some families establish a regular order of washing to avoid arguments.

נְטִילַת יָדַיִם

1. בָּרוּךְ אַתָּה יְיָ
2. אֱלֹהֵינוּ מֶלֶךְ הָעוֹלָם
3. אֲשֶׁר קִדְּשָׁנוּ בְּמִצְוֹתָיו
4. וְצִוָּנוּ
5. עַל נְטִילַת יָדַיִם.

Is there absolutely no talking once the washing is completed?
Since the act of washing the hands is preparation for the breaking of bread, no talking is to interrupt what is considered to be one complete ritual act. There are some interesting dynamics to this process. Because not everyone can wash simultaneously, some will have completed washing while others are waiting in line. Those waiting to wash can, of course, talk, while those who have finished must wait silently. Some families have taken to humming a niggun, a melody without words, during this waiting time. Try humming the tune for *Shabbat Shalom* or any of your other favorite Shabbat songs. It will help reduce the temptation to talk.

By the way, since there is no talking before the actual tasting of the *hallah,* you will have to establish who is to do the various actions associated with the *Hamotzi* before you wash hands. Decisions about who will uncover the *hallot,* who will say the blessing, who will break the bread, and who will pass the bread around should be made before *Netilat Yadayim.* Otherwise, you'll find a lot of people trying to give directions with hand motions.

What should we do if guests are at the table who have never seen this ritual?
As with any of the steps of the Shabbat Seder, guests may be invited to participate in your ritual. The chances of their doing so are much greater if you take the time to explain the reasons why you do these actions. It also helps to demonstrate the ritual for them. In the case of *Netilat Yadayim,* some even consider it a sign of friendship to pour the water over another's hands. For young children in the family, you will certainly want to do the pouring. It is

also a good idea to warn your guests about the "no talking" rule and the reasons for it before someone is embarrassed by talking at the wrong time.

What if I can't get my rings off?
Go ahead and wash. For those who can get their jewelry off, be careful where you put the valuables. We spoke to one person who nearly lost a wedding ring when it fell into a kitchen sink!

Some Interesting Sources

As we've seen, the practice of *Netilat Yadayim* is rooted in the Temple ritual, in the practice of sacrifice. Here is a rabbinic text that tries to explain the real purpose of sacrifice by eliminating some misconceptions. Once the false understandings are stripped away, what do you think it sees as the "true" purpose of the sacrifices?

> God said: "I do not need sacrifices, for all the world is Mine, and the animals which you offer I created, as it teaches in the Bible, 'If I am hungry, I would not tell you, for the world is Mine and its fullness' (Psalm 50:12). I do not eat or drink."
>
> Rabbi Simon said: "Thirteen stages of compassion are ascribed to God. Would a compassionate Being assign that Being's feeding to one who is cruel (as people can be cruel)?"
>
> Rabbi Ḥiyya ben Abba said: "God says, 'My creatures do not need My creatures.' Have you ever heard of a person who says: 'Give this vine wine to drink, that it may give much more wine,' or 'drench this olive tree with oil, that it may give much oil?' If My creations do not need My creations, why should I need My creations?'"
>
> *Numbers Rabbah, Pinḥas,* 21:16–17

Here is a text about "washing hands." It makes a great deal out of the practice. Why do you think the transmitters of this legend found such value in this ritual action?

When Rabbi Akiba was in prison (incarcerated by the Romans for teaching Torah), Rabbi Joshua ha-Garsi used to attend him. Every day he would bring him a certain amount of water. Once the prison guard met him and said, "You have too much water today. Do you want to flood the prison?" He poured out half the water. When Rabbi Joshua came to Rabbi Akiba, Akiba said, "Joshua, do you not know that I am old, my life depends on you, why have you brought me so little water?" Joshua told him what had happened. Then Rabbi Akiba said to him, "Give me the water to wash my hands." Joshua said, "You don't even have enough drinking water, why wash?" Akiba said, "The Rabbis have made washing an important act. How can I go against the words of my colleagues?"

9

הַמּוֹצִיא

Hamotzi
The Blessing over Bread

There's something sensual about that. Tearing off and feeling the warmth and putting warm *hallah* to the lips. It really carries warmth.

SALLY SHAFTON

SALLY SHAFTON: With just two of us eating now, the menu is not that ornate any more. We're very diet conscious during the week. I eat no bread during the week—so that first bite into the warm _hallah_ is very exciting.

BOB SHAFTON: The _hallah_ is in the oven until the last minute. It's not on the table until after the Kiddush, because the _hallah_ in our family's tradition must burn the fingers on the first tear. It must be hot throughout.

SALLY SHAFTON: There's something sensual about that. Tearing off and feeling the warmth and putting warm _hallah_ to the lips. It really carries warmth.

ANONYMOUS: On Shabbat we went to my in-laws, and when we were passing the _hallah_ around, my father-in-law said to my mother-in-law, "It's a little cold in the middle," and she says, "I had it in the freezer and it just didn't get defrosted in time." Then he says, "But you went to the store and bought a fresh one today." She says, "Yes, but I put the fresh one in the freezer because I didn't want this one to get too old." She sat for a moment with this blank look on her face, and then this look of knowledge came over my mother-in-law.

ASHER KELMAN: When you cut the bread, there are different traditions. There are "cutters" and "pullers." The kids want me to rip the _hallah,_ especially if there is a braided _hallah._ Then the kids think that I have a duty to rip it apart. But if my mother-in-law is there, she'll think we should be cutting it. If we have a square _hallah,_ I do cut it. Next, the kids look at me to see if I am going to mix up the salt and pepper shakers. The kids make this whole big fuss, and Ariel thinks that I should have learned by now which shaker the salt comes out of...the shaker with the large holes or the small holes.

ARIEL KELMAN: Then he just puts a little on the table so we don't get high sodium, which is very bad.

Hallah is the most tangible part of Shabbat. It is real. It is not a symbolic expression or a transformation of time and cognition. It is bread, basic. You can even bake it yourself. Of all the parts of the Shabbat Seder, *hallah* is the most real. It is the one Shabbat symbol you get by taking a ticket at the bakery, the one that comes out of the oven, the freezer, or the microwave.

The Judaism we know emerged from the farm. The most basic rhythms and insights of Jewish celebrations weren't intellectual; they came from people who worked the soil. They were profoundly simple. When each harvest was ready, the people came together. Success was celebrated, food was shared with those in need, and a unity of purpose was solidified. This was the practice of the three pilgrimage festivals: Sukkot, Pesa*h*, and Shavuot. Farmers worked from just after dawn till just before dusk. A brief, simple meal was eaten, and darkness brought sleep. Once a week, dusk brought the time to kindle lights and to celebrate a day of rest—this was Shabbat. Then, the warm loaf of bread freshly baked from the oven was the direct result of a week's worth of work in the field. It brought a very specific lesson.

The Torah carefully regulated the farm. As farmers, Jews were never allowed to imagine that they fully owned their land or anything it produced. Always, there were the tithes. Portions of everything raised and everything grown had to be shared. Part went as an offering to God—an acknowledgment that without Divine help, nothing would grow or mature. Part went to the Temple, manifesting in every individual act of work a common connection to the national vision of the future and the communal relationship with God. And part was left for the widow, the poor, the orphan, and the stranger. Ownership (even ownership of only a little) brought the responsibility to share with those in need that which God allowed us to produce.

For the biblical farmer, the warm loaf of bread on Shabbat eve wasn't *hallah*. For that farmer, the *hallah* had already been taken. Like every other step in the cultivation of food, a tithe had to be taken when dough was made. In baking the bread from grain raised in their own field, the biblical family took a portion of the dough as a "gift to the Lord" (Numbers 15:19–20). This dough was given to the priests who worked in the Temple and was called the *hallah* portion. Later on, the loaves themselves were called *hallot*. In the dim light of a Shabbat lamp, the taste of warm new bread brought the satisfaction of accomplishment and a practical reminder of a covenantal partnership.

If it is possible to talk about a best-loved Shabbat symbol, it would have to be *ḥallah*. People rip into it with joy. They excavate caves in it, removing the soft center and leaving the crust. Others take great delight in slicing it into neat, even slices. *Ḥallah* is a hands-on experience. This simple egg bread—braided, round, or square; homemade or on standing bakery order, with its raisins or sesame seeds—is the catalyst that breaks the formality of the Shabbat Seder service and lets the meal begin.

Concepts

Manna and the Exodus from Egypt

Ḥallah, the special bread for Shabbat, is a remembrance of the manna God provided for the Israelites during their forty years of wandering in the desert. *Ḥallah* is therefore another reminder of the Exodus theme. It also symbolizes God's bounty through nature, focusing on bread, which is the "staff of life."

Objects

Ḥallot

The *ḥallah* bread is, of course, special. The word *ḥallah* means a round loaf or cake. Our *ḥallah* is a remembrance of the share of bread given to the priests during the days of the ancient Temple. After the destruction of the Temple, the taking of a portion of a dough became a fixed ritual, expressed as the *ḥallah,* the egg bread made for Shabbat.

It is traditional to place two *ḥallot* (plural of *ḥallah*) on the Shabbat table. They remind us of the double share of manna that God caused to fall every Friday while the children of Israel were in the wilderness. This double portion on Friday was necessary because no manna fell on Shabbat (see

Exodus 16:22–30). Even if the manna had fallen on Shabbat, the gathering of food would still have been prohibited as an act of labor.

Today, *ḥallah* bread is usually braided. This makes it a bit more festive than the weekly loaves of bread. Some have seen the braids as being symbolic of each person's multifaceted personality; others interpret it as the intertwining of the Jewish people. Actually, Jewish bakers have felt free to experiment with a variety of creative shapes for the *ḥallah* loaves. The only requirement is that the *ḥallah* must be whole, not sliced, before blessing it.

Plates

The *ḥallot* can be placed on any plate, although beautiful decorative *ḥallah* plates are available in a variety of materials. Special *ḥallah* knives are also crafted for slicing the *ḥallah*. Although not required, these objects enhance the status of the *ḥallot* on the table.

Covers

You will need a covering for the *ḥallot*; it can be plain or decorative. The *ḥallot* are covered by a cloth during the entire Shabbat Seder until their use. This, too, is explained as a remembrance of the Exodus. The manna in the desert was covered with a special (white) dew in order to preserve its freshness (see Exodus 16:23f).

There is a second explanation for covering the *ḥallah*. Before blessing the *ḥallah*, we light candles and say Kiddush. Some might think that those ceremonies are more important than *Hamotzi*. But by covering the *ḥallot* we give proper recognition to this part of the ritual. A popular explanation for children is that the loaves are covered so the *ḥallot* won't get jealous while we bless the lights and say Kiddush over wine.

HAMOTZI	BLESSING OVER BREAD
1. *Barukh attah Adonai*	Praised are You, Adonai,
2. *Eloheinu melekh ha'olam*	our God, Ruler of the universe,
3. *hamotzi leḥem min ha'aretz.*	who brings forth bread from the earth.

Practice

The *Hamotzi* sequence is as follows:

1. Uncover the *ḥallot*.
2. Hold the *ḥallah*. (Optional: nick the "chosen" *ḥallah* with a knife.) Say the blessing.
3. Tear or slice off a piece of *ḥallah*.
4. Sprinkle salt on that piece of *ḥallah*.
5. Eat the *ḥallah*.
6. Share the salted *ḥallah* with the rest of the family and guests.
7. Now you can talk!

Practical Questions and Answers

Why is salt sprinkled on the *ḥallah*?
It is traditional to sprinkle salt on the first piece of *ḥallah* immediately after the *Hamotzi* is recited. This act is an additional reminder of the Temple service. In Jewish tradition, the act of eating is likened to a Divine service. After all, according to the script, we say a blessing before the meal and a series of blessings afterwards. Salt is sprinkled on the bread to be eaten just as it was used on the sacrifices in the Temple. Thus, the meal is transformed into a sacred ritual; the ordinary is transformed into the extraordinary

Is there a proper way to "break" the *ḥallah*?
No. There seem to be three major approaches among families to *ḥallah*

הַמוֹצִיא

1. בָּרוּךְ אַתָּה יְיָ,
2. אֱלֹהֵינוּ מֶלֶךְ הָעוֹלָם
3. הַמוֹצִיא לֶחֶם מִן הָאָרֶץ.

"breaking": the slicers, the tearers, and the pullers. The slicers prefer to cut the *hallah* with a knife. The tearers like to tear off a single large piece of the bread. The pullers are a subcategory of the tearers; they have everyone stand, place their hands on the *hallah*, and pull it apart, all at the same time.

Why do some people place one *hallah* on top of the other and nick the top *hallah* with a knife before slicing it?

According to custom, when the *Hamotzi* is recited, the section of bread to be to eaten first is to be marked off by a slight circular incision on the loaf. Because the Shabbat *hallot* must be whole, this is impossible. As a compromise, a small nick can be made to indicate where the *hallah* will be cut once the *Hamotzi* is recited. To demonstrate that both *hallah* loaves are equally capable of being chosen the object of this mitzvah, some people place the loaves on top of each other.

How is the *hallah* to be distributed to those at the table?

Some authorities suggest that once the *hallah* is broken, the pieces should be placed on a tray and passed around the table rather than given to each person by the leader or another person. The reasoning is that God, not humanity, is the provider of the *hallah*. By acceptance of the piece of *hallah* from a human hand, this fact might be lost. Others are not as concerned with this and simply pass the pieces of *hallah* around by hand. Of course, the "pullers" get their *hallah* as soon as the blessing is recited.

Some families told us that they even have a particular order of distribution of the *hallah*. In one family, guests are always served first. In another, the most senior member of the group has the honor of the first piece. A third family serves the parents first and then the children in chronological order.

Can we break the second _hallah_ on Friday night?

Certainly, if you wish, although some families save the second _hallah_ for Shabbat lunch when, once again, two complete _hallot_ are required for _Hamotzi_.

Is there any size requirement for _hallah_ loaves?

Not really. The _hallah_ loaves can be large or small. Some families bake two loaves of uniform size. Those who buy _hallah_ at the bakery often get one large _hallah_ and one small "Kiddush" _hallah_ as the second required loaf.

Why must the _hallot_ be whole and not sliced?

The _hallot_ are symbolic of the manna given to the Israelites in the desert. The whole _hallah_ represents the completeness of the portion of manna delivered by God.

Are raisins and sesame seeds permissible in _hallah_?

Absolutely! The addition of raisins or sesame seeds embellishes the festive bread. In fact, _hallah_ made of different flours, such as whole wheat, is also permissible.

What should I do if I forget to bake or buy _hallah_?

One way to avoid this situation is to put an extra _hallah_ or two in the freezer just in case this happens. If necessary, any whole roll can do for saying the _Hamotzi_.

A couple of years ago, Passover began on Saturday night, and I didn't know what to do about _hallah_ on the preceding Friday night. Since my kitchen was already made kosher for Passover, I didn't want to bring in _hallah_. What should I have done?

This situation does occur with some regularity. In order not to bring _hallah_ into the Passover-ready kitchen, substitute egg matzah instead, and recite the regular _berakhah_.

Some Interesting Sources

By following these three selections—one from the Torah, one from the *Mishnah*, and one from the *Shulhan Arukh*—you can trace the history of *hallah*. See how many "lessons" you can find as to what can be learned from the ritual of *hallah*.

Speak to the Children of Israel and say to them,
"When you come into the land where I will bring you,
When you eat from the bread of the land,
you shall separate a gift-portion for Adonai.
Of the first of your dough, you shall take *hallah* as a gift-offering.
Separate this, just like the gift-offering which is separated
from your threshing floor.
From the first of your dough, you shall give Adonai a gift-offering
throughout your generation."

Numbers 15:18–21

From five kinds of grain one is obligated to take *hallah*. These are wheat, barley, spelt, oats, and rye.

Mishnah Hallah 1:1

From the dough made of one of the five species of grain, the *hallah* portion must be separated. Immediately before separating the *hallah*, the following benediction is recited: "Praised are You, O Lord our God, Ruler of the universe, who has sanctified us with the commandments, and has commanded us to separate *hallah*." Then a portion of dough no less than the size of an olive is separated and burned. The custom is to burn it in the oven where the bread is being baked.

Yoreh De'ah 328:1

10

סְעוּדַת שַׁבָּת

Se'udat Shabbat
The Shabbat Meal

You see, while we're eating, my Dad talks about things. Sometimes he tells us what it was like when he was a kid, or lots of Jewish questions, stuff about Pharaoh and things like that. In the middle we enjoy our food. I like the food that my Mom makes. I especially like cow tongue.

ARIEL KELMAN

Fast food is a mentality. It rapidly becomes a way of life. Endless fifteen-second and thirty-second commercial spots have trained us to eat to the beat of a drum-machine (with dancers gyrating and spinning in our mental background). Afterwards, we dump the paper in the trash container and stack our trays. At home, the eating pattern is often equally rushed. After all, what else can you do on a TV tray?

Dining is a whole different activity. Think cloth napkins, and everything slows down. From television, we've learned to dance our way from winning the big game to fast eating. Dining takes dressing up, going to a special setting, and changing the rhythm. While good food is important, the essence of fine dining is conversation, communication, and connection. A real dinner isn't merely a moment of human grazing; it is an event, an occasion, an experience. It's not the formality, the lavishness, the two forks and three spoons that make a difference. Those are merely props that help to cue the time signature. Dining is when we go beyond "grabbing a bite" (or even "taking" a lunch) to breaking bread together. A quick meal is a pause, a momentary replenishment, a few shared remarks. Dining is when there is time to talk, to savor, to spend a period of significant time together around the table.

The Talmudic Rabbis introduced the concept of a *se'udat mitzvah,* a ritual meal that accompanies the performance of a mitzvah. Every caterer will confirm that it is the dinner that makes the Bar/Bat Mitzvah, the wedding, the *simha* (happy occasion) special. There is something about the collective focus of a table and the shared experience of eating that almost automatically allows people to create their own good time. Yet, the rabbinic concept of *se'udat mitzvah* was not stressed merely to produce nice affairs. It started with their view of mitzvot.

Mitzvot are more than commandments. They are opportunities, potential moments of linkage. The performance of a mitzvah can take a Jew far beyond mere compliance with Jewish law. When done with intention and conscious direction, simple actions (often focused through a blessing) can become spiritual encounters. On one level, the Jew is obligated to perform certain acts because of a legal covenant made with God accepting the Torah and its way of life. On a second level, the mitzvah becomes a personal way of experiencing a whole national historical tradition. Standing at the *bima* publicly reading the Torah for the first time is an act that has the potential to create a profound experience of membership and continuity for the Bar/Bat Mitzvah child. The glow of the Ḥanukkah menorah can inspire a family with the knowledge that it is worth struggling to preserve the difference and uniqueness of Jewish life. Mitzvot provide us with the opportunity to make Jewish values, Jewish lessons, and Jewish experiences part of our life rhythm.

Mitzvot aren't fast-food experiences. They work best with reflection. The twofold message of Shabbat—the wonder of creation and the joy of liberation—takes reflection. The Rabbis knew that reflection takes a catalyst, time for the experiential to mix with the symbolic. That's the essence of a *se'udat mitzvah* (a mitzvah-meal). The ritual serves as a metronome for the dinner, while the dinner process allows the symbols to become personal and interactive—part of the family's experience of being a family. Family traditions, with their private jokes and impromptu rituals, are the building blocks that actualize the Jewish tradition. The Shabbat Seder and *Se'udat Shabbat* work together. They are interwoven. The Shabbat Seder is not a meal preceded by a short service, nor is it a service followed by dining. Rather, the Rabbis evolved it as a whole table evening: a celebration that lets us dance to a different drum-machine.

BOB SHAFTON: In our family we've done something that Sally pushed from before the kids were born, and that was to make the dinner hour important. We may be busy and be home now only one or two nights a week. But as a couple, we have always tried to be home for dinner, no matter what was going on in the rest of the world. Friday night was a terrific time to talk and to be together with the kids—there was always a lot of family discussion around the table.

SALLY SHAFTON: We would be at the table, and someone would have a *farkrimt* (pouting) face. Of three kids, it would generally happen with one. It was no problem; you could be excused; you could leave. We had a rather strong philosophy that we wanted them to understand. Shabbat was going on in our home whether they participated or not. If they were there, we loved it, and we welcomed their participation. But if they were *farkrimt* and they felt a little sour, they also had the right to excuse themselves because we needed to go on with Shabbat.

BOB SHAFTON: In Palm Springs we once had a family gathering with all three generations: grandparents, us, and our children. I remember one Friday night when Randy, our youngest, just didn't want to be around the Shabbes table at all—and she wasn't. However, the friend she had invited said to her, "I don't care what you do, I am going to stay. This is a great conversation." Randy went "Oy vay." She was really upset.

WENDY KELMAN: I usually make some kind of first course we normally don't have, such as my husband's favorite, Israeli-style baked eggplant, which the kids don't like. They usually get a piece of melon or sometimes fruit salad. Everybody's favorite is artichokes. And usually in the winter I make soup, *matzah* ball, chicken soup, or mushroom barley soup. And then we often have chicken. That seems to be a traditional Friday night dinner, although I do vary it with veal; and everybody loves tongue in this family, so I make sweet and sour tongue. Brisket sometimes. If I don't have time, I go to the bakery and get some kind of special dessert.

ARIEL KELMAN: You see, while we're eating, my Dad talks about things. Sometimes he tells us what it was like when he was a kid, or lots of Jewish questions, stuff about Pharaoh and things like that. In the middle we enjoy our food. I like the food that my Mom makes. I especially like cow tongue.

SANDY GOODGLICK: Sometimes it's hard to break away from sitting at the table after the meal.

BILL GOODGLICK: We are usually at the table for a minimum of two hours. We'll sit at the table with friends, with family, and we will carry on any kind of conversation for as long as we can stand the sitting position. We don't leave the table and go into the living room.

SANDY GOODGLICK: Although my parents could never understand why we were doing all this and couldn't make head nor tail of it, they always loved Friday night. They looked forward to it. And there wasn't a Friday night that they were here that my mother didn't come into the kitchen and give me a hug and a kiss before dinner.

Concepts

Se'udat Mitzvah

The Shabbat dinner meal is itself an integral part of the holiday celebration. Food has long been an important element of Jewish ritual, and the Rabbis urged Jews to mesh the performance of significant mitzvot with festive meals. This they called *se'udat mitzvah*, the meal in celebration of a mitzvah.

On Shabbat, we are commanded to eat three meals of this kind: Shabbat dinner, Shabbat lunch, and the third meal, *se'udah shlishit*, on Shabbat afternoon. Of the three, Friday night dinner is clearly the most elaborate. It involves special foods, special songs, and a special tone that makes it unlike any other meal of the week.

Objects

Shabbat dinner is a time for traditional favorite foods. Among the traditional dishes are gefilte fish, chicken soup, kugel, and a meat dish. Why fish? Because it reminds us that God promised that the Children of Israel would multiply like the stars in heaven (and there are lots of fish in the sea). Why kugel? Because kugel is a corruption of the Hebrew *ke'ugal*, "having a round shape." The manna given in the desert was said to be *ke'ugal*—round in shape.

For families today, Shabbat dinner can be a time when favorite as well as traditional foods can be enjoyed. In our hectic-paced week, it is unusual to have a formal meal complete with appetizers, main course, and dessert. Choose foods you and your children especially enjoy.

The most important object to acquire for the meal is, of course, a book of Jewish recipes. There are literally hundreds available. We have listed a few of the better ones in the Selected Bibliography.

Practice

The Shabbat meal should be enjoyed at a leisurely pace. Unless you are running off to late Friday night services at the synagogue, there will be plenty of time to spend more than the usual fifteen minutes eating dinner. The practice of including several courses, with the singing of Shabbat *Zemirot*—"table songs"—in between, and sharing stories and words of Torah are all ways to enhance the Shabbat meal.

Practical Questions and Answers

Must I serve the "traditional" Shabbat foods?
While gefilte fish, chicken soup, and meat are the most common foods found on Shabbat tables, many families vary the fare, depending on several factors. Families with young children often feature foods that they know are favorites with the kids. Parents without much time to prepare elaborate meals often use foods that can be quickly cooked in the microwave before Shabbat. Vegetarians make special meals for Shabbat without meat. Other families rely on the traditional standard menu week after week. Here, again, your "artistry" as a Shabbat maker can excel.

During the summer months when Shabbat begins so late, is it proper to eat the meal first and then light the candles and do the rest of the Shabbat ritual?
Not really. Most of the Shabbat Seder is designed as preface to the *se'udat mitzvah*, the Shabbat meal. It would be better to light the candles and begin Shabbat early, even if it is several hours before the official candlelighting

time. You may begin Shabbat any time after noon on Friday. Remember, though, that all of the Shabbat rules apply once you begin it.

What other kinds of things can we do at the table besides singing to interest our children and guests?
This will depend in large measure on the ages of both. For older children and adult guests, informal discussions centering on the Jewish issues of the day or interpretations of the weekly Torah portion are excellent things to try. For families with young children, consult the Shabbat Gallery chapter for a variety of ideas.

So, when our kids grow up and leave the house, how can we make Shabbat interesting for us?
Since the first edition of *Shabbat—The Art of Jewish Living* was published, our children Havi and Michael have left our home and set off on their own. We discovered that Shabbat dinner alone can be wonderful, but it is often quite lonely. We also discovered that a number of our friends have experienced the same feelings. We agreed to take action. So, along with six other couples from our congregation, we have created a monthly "Empty Nesters' Shabbat" experience. We gather together for a "potluck" Shabbat dinner that rotates between our homes. No kids—or grandkids—allowed, just adults enjoying each other's company and Shabbat. It's a great evening and we all enjoy celebrating together.

Some Interesting Sources

In making the Friday night meal a *se'udat mitzvah,* the Talmudic Rabbis were trying to prescribe an experience for families. Look at these rabbinic texts and see if you can isolate some of the elements of this *se'udah* experience.

Rabbi Yehuda ha-Nassi once invited the Roman emperor Antoninous for two meals. The first was during the week, and Rabbi Yehuda served hot food. Because the second was on Saturday, Rabbi Yehuda served the Emperor a cold dish. The Emperor said that the Shabbat meal tasted much better, even if it was cold. Rabbi Yehuda explained that there was one spice missing from the weekday meal. Then the Emperor asked, "Does the king's pantry lack anything?" Rabbi Yehuda answered, "It is the Sabbath which is missing."

This story, found in Genesis Rabbah 11:2, is a variation on the more famous Shabbat spice story told about Rabbi Joshua ben Hananyah, found in *Shabbat* 119a. See the Shabbat Gallery and compare the differences.

One of the Rabbis told this story: "Once I was invited by a man in Laodicea to dine with him. The food was served on silver plates and in costly vessels. Twenty-four people were in attendance. Two children were standing—one on each side of my host. One child recited the biblical verse 'The earth is the Lord's and the fullness thereof.' The other child recited 'Mine is the silver, and mine is the gold, said the Lord of Hosts.' This was done to remind my host that he should not think too much of himself.

"I asked him, 'My son, how do you come by all of these honors?' He replied, 'My master, I used to be a butcher. Whenever I would find a fat animal during the week, I would keep it for the Shabbat.' I said, 'It is not for nothing that you have come by all these blessings.'"

Pesikta Rabbati 23, cf. Genesis Rabbah 11:4

Rabbi Hiyya ben Abba: The Shabbat was given for enjoyment. Rabbi Shmuel ben Nahmani: The Shabbat was given for studying the Torah.

One saying does not contradict the other. Rabbi Hiyya was speaking about scholars who spend the week studying the Torah and use the Shabbat to enjoy themselves. Rabbi Shmuel was talking about workers who are busy with their work all week, and on Shabbat they come and study Torah.

Pesikta Rabbati 121a

One who makes the Shabbat a delight shall have the wishes of one's heart fulfilled. Here "delight" must mean special food. Even a little is regarded as "Shabbat delight," if it is prepared to honor the Shabbat.

Shabbat 118b

זְמִירוֹת

Zemirot
Shabbat Songs

I think it is the out-loud singing that helps me make the transition [from the weekday to Shabbat], and I have encouraged others around the table to please try and sing out loud, because I find when you are singing out loud that it's hard to be very caught up in an argument you have just had with a client or an attorney.

BILL GOODGLICK

You can't sing *Ufaratztah* and not have a little bit of spirit.

BOB SHAFTON

BILL GOODGLICK: I have spoken to my family and friends of the pain in the transition from the weekday to the Shabbes. It is a very difficult transition because I come directly from work. I rush home and change my clothes. I'll never come to the Shabbes table with the same clothes on that I've worn during the day. I'll change clothes hurriedly, coming into the Shabbes having just come from a business meeting that could have been rather traumatic, and that discipline of getting into a *Shabbesdik* [appropriate for Shabbat] mood is very difficult. Now that I've thought about it, I think it is the out-loud singing that helps me make the transition, and I have encouraged others around the table to please try and sing out loud, because I find when you are singing out loud that it's hard to be very caught up in an argument you have just had with a client or an attorney. You have to concentrate your mentality on singing, which is so different than what you do on an everyday basis. It's the vocalizing that tends to sweep me into what I know I have to do—which is to make a little different pace for Shabbes.

SALLY SHAFTON: When we have a group, we really sing—lots and lots of singing. When the kids are here—lots and lots of singing. When Jill was in New York, she met some gal named Judy Flumenbaum who works in one of the Federation groups. She put together that blue and green songbook, and Jill bought us about thirty of them. We have them all over the house, and they are really terrific. We sing a lot.

BOB SHAFTON: It's a great icebreaker. If you have people who are a little uncomfortable, especially people who don't know each other, singing is a great way. You can't sing *Ufaratztah* and not have a little bit of spirit.

SALLY SHAFTON: We have a lot of clapping of hands and beating on the table, and it is a very spirited songfest. The other thing I love happened just three months ago. Our youngest daughter just moved out of the house eight or nine months ago. She came over, and I found her taking about fifteen of those *Zemirot* books out of the house. That's wonderful. I'll get some more.

A midrash: Every night when King David slept, he hung his harp over his head. At midnight, winds from the four corners of the earth would blow, vibrate the strings, and caress melodies from the harp. At midnight, King David would rise and join in singing praise to the Creator. These songs became the Psalms.

A legend: The Baal Shem Tov would often wander the fields, looking at nature and gaining inner peace. Once, during such a walk, he heard the sound of a shepherd boy's flute carried on the wind. As he hummed the tune he was suddenly filled with a great joy. Soon he realized that the melody had been passed on from shepherd to shepherd—that its original author was King David.

Later, when working as an assistant to the town teacher, the Baal Shem Tov had to lead the school children through a dark and scary forest. All the children refused to go until the Baal Shem taught them this melody. Upon learning the melody, the children followed the Baal Shem Tov, dancing their way through the forest.

A folk teaching: Often, it is impossible for one person to raise up his or her voice and sing with joy. But when another comes along and joins in, often the two of them can lift up their voices and sing with joy together. Song forms a connection between souls.

Fun is riding a rollercoaster. Joy is something different. Fun is laughing at a good joke, watching TV, family vacations, winning a game. Joy has something to do with warmth. Fun is momentary; it has to do with pleasure, having a good time. Joy involves a longer view. Joy involves reaching a certain point in your life; joy is realizing the nature of your family or community; joy is appreciating that which you have. Shabbat is not a fun holiday (though it does have its moments). Purim is fun; Shabbat centers on *oneg* (joy). Joy is the long sigh at the end of a great meal, the look around the table at family and friends, the spirit of *Zemirot*—a good Shabbat songfest.

Concepts

Oneg Shabbat

To increase the enjoyment of the Shabbat experience, singing, good conversation, and even dancing are encouraged during the meal. *Oneg Shabbat*—the joy of Shabbat—is a concept that Jews have taken very seriously throughout the ages. Many poets and Rabbis created special hymns of praise to honor the Shabbat.

These Shabbat table songs are known as *Zemirot*, which literally means "songs," but the term has come to mean the special songs about God and Shabbat that have been sung at Shabbat table celebrations for centuries.

Many of the traditional *Zemirot* date back to the Middle Ages. Some, like *Tzur Mishelo,* speak of God who feeds the world. Others, like *Lekha Dodi*, welcome the Shabbat day. Some are universal—*Hinei mah tov umah na'im*, "Behold, how good it is for brethren to dwell together"—while others are particular: *Eretz zavat ḥalav udvash*, "[Israel,] a land flowing with milk and honey."

Modern Hebrew and English songs have their place in this attempt to enhance the Shabbat spirit in the home. Only songs that speak of work and toil would not be considered *Shabbesdik.*

Oneg Shabbat can also mean the opportunity to share good conversation at the table. During the hurried weekday schedule, we rarely have time to discuss matters of consequence with our family. The leisurely pace of the Shabbat meal allows for the sharing of information and feelings that goes beyond "How was your day?"

Objects

Collections of *Zemirot*, called *benschers* or *shironim*—"songbooks"—are often found in homes where Shabbat is celebrated. Coming from the Yiddish word for "blessings," *benschers* (a.k.a. *Birkat Hamazon* booklets) usually contain traditional Shabbat table songs as well as the *Birkat Hamazon.*

Some families collect the *benschers* that are distributed at weddings and Bar/Bat Mitzvah celebrations. These are lovely reminders of a past *simha* of which you have been a part.

The only problem with using different *benschers* is that the *Zemirot* are often found on different pages. If you are just beginning your Shabbat observance, we recommend that you use uniform song booklets. Of course, you may wish to start with the songs included in this book.

Practice

Singing *Zemirot* is often a spontaneous round of songs, with each person suggesting the next selection by simply beginning. If, however, you are just starting to include *Zemirot*, have one person lead the singing by choosing the songs that are most familiar. Or you may want to go around the table, asking each person to pick a favorite song. Try to learn one song at a time and slowly build up a repertoire of favorites. One caution: it is difficult to force joyousness. End the singing before people get bored or restless. Start with a couple of songs and steadily increase the number you sing. When you make it truly fun, *Zemirot* can be an eagerly awaited part of your Shabbat celebration.

As for good conversation, this is a bit more difficult to program. Try to focus on issues of substance rather than the trivial aspects of everyday life. You could include discussions of current events, politics, or a serious concern of the day.

Some families have experimented with including discussions of the weekly Torah portion at the table. This can take the form of a serious presentation of information and insights about the biblical reading or, in younger families, a puppet show acting out the biblical story.

Another activity to try is to share the feelings and appreciations of family members. A simple exercise of this type is to ask each person around the table, "What was your favorite time this past week?" Other things to share might be "Something Jewish I have learned...," "Someone I helped...," or "A famous Jew with whom I would like to spend a day is..."

An old standby activity is reading aloud a Jewish story. There are many sources to choose from; some are listed in the Selected Bibliography. (See page 281.) You may want to read a short selection at the table or save a long story for after *Birkat Hamazon*.

One final note. Beware of dragging out this part of the Shabbat Seder. Depending on the ages of your children and/or guests, timing is crucial to maintain an atmosphere of joy. Remember, Friday night is the end of a long work week for adults and for children. People may well be tired and have only limited patience. A good short song session is far better than one that has gone on too long.

ZEMIROT   **SHABBAT SONGS**

SHABBAT SHALOM

1. *Bim bam, bim bim bim bam,*
   Bim bim bim bim bim bam.
2. *Shabbat shalom,*
   Shabbat shalom,
   Shabbat, Shabbat, Shabbat,
   Shabbat shalom.

HINEI MAH TOV

1. *Hinei mah tov umah na'im*   Behold, how good and pleasant it is
2. *shevet ahim gam yahad.*   For brethren to dwell together in unity.

DAVID MELEKH YISRA'EL

1. *David, Melekh Yisra'el,*   David, King of Israel,
2. *Hai, hai, vekayam!*   lives forever!

LO YISA GOY

1. *Lo yisa goy el goy herev,*   Nation shall not lift up sword against nation,
2. *Lo yilmedu od milhamah.*   Neither shall they learn war any more.

1. בִּים בָּם

בִּים בָּם

2. שַׁבָּת שָׁלוֹם

שַׁבָּת שָׁלוֹם.

1. הִנֵּה מַה־טּוֹב וּמַה־נָּעִים

2. שֶׁבֶת אַחִים גַּם־יָחַד.

1. דָּוִד מֶלֶךְ יִשְׂרָאֵל

2. חַי וְקַיָּם.

1. לֹא־יִשָּׂא גוֹי אֶל־גּוֹי חֶרֶב

2. לֹא־יִלְמְדוּ עוֹד מִלְחָמָה:

LEKHA DODI

1. *Lekha dodi likrat kallah*	Come, my friend, to greet the Bride.
2. *Penei Shabbat nekablah.*	Let's encounter the presence of Shabbat.
3. *Shamor vezakhor bedibur ehad.*	"Observe" and "Remember" in one word.
4. *Hishmi'anu El hamyuhad.*	The One God who caused us to hear.
5. *Adonai ehad ushmo ehad.*	Adonai is One and the Divine Name is One.
6. *Leshem ultiferet velit'hilah.*	To the Divine Name is the glory and the fame.
(Lekha dodi...)	
7. *Likrat Shabbat lekhu venelkhah!*	To greet the Shabbat, let us go!
8. *Ki hi mekor haberakhah,*	Because it is the source of blessing,
9. *Meirosh mikedem nesukhah,*	Conceived before life on earth began,
10. *Sof ma'aseh bemahshavah*	Last in God's work, first in God's thought.
tehilah. (Lekha dodi...)	
11. *Hit'oreri hit'oreri,*	Arise, arise, for your light has risen,
12. *Ki va orekh kumi ori.*	For the dawn has broken, the light has come.
13. *Uri uri shir daberi;*	Awake, awake, and joyously sing;
14. *Kevod Adonai alayikh niglah.*	The honor of Adonai is upon you and revealed.
(Lekha dodi...)	
15. *Yamin usmol tifrotzi;*	From the right to the left, you will prosper;
16. *Ve'et Adonai ta'aritzi.*	And you will always revere Adonai.
17. *Al yad ish ben Partzi,*	Through the person descended from Peretz [King David],
18. *Venismha venagilah.*	We will rejoice and exult.
(Lekha dodi...)	
19. *Bo'i veshalom ateret ba'lah,*	Come in peace, crown of her husband,
20. *Gam besimhah uvtzoholah.*	Come in happiness and with good cheer.
21. *Tokh emunei am segulah,*	Amidst the faithful of the treasured people,
22. *Bo'i khallah; bo'i khallah!*	Come, Bride; Come, Bride!
(Lekha dodi...)	

1. לְכָה דוֹדִי לִקְרַאת כַּלָּה
2. פְּנֵי שַׁבָּת נְקַבְּלָה:

3. שָׁמוֹר וְזָכוֹר בְּדִבּוּר אֶחָד
4. הִשְׁמִיעָנוּ אֵל הַמְיֻחָד
5. יְיָ אֶחָד וּשְׁמוֹ אֶחָד
6. לְשֵׁם וּלְתִפְאֶרֶת וְלִתְהִלָּה:

7. לִקְרַאת שַׁבָּת לְכוּ וְנֵלְכָה
8. כִּי הִיא מְקוֹר הַבְּרָכָה
9. מֵרֹאשׁ מִקֶּדֶם נְסוּכָה
10. סוֹף מַעֲשֶׂה בְּמַחֲשָׁבָה תְּחִלָּה:

11. הִתְעוֹרְרִי הִתְעוֹרְרִי
12. כִּי בָא אוֹרֵךְ קוּמִי אוֹרִי
13. עוּרִי עוּרִי שִׁיר דַּבֵּרִי
14. כְּבוֹד יְיָ עָלַיִךְ נִגְלָה:

15. יָמִין וּשְׂמֹאל תִּפְרוֹצִי
16. וְאֶת־יְיָ תַּעֲרִיצִי
17. עַל יַד אִישׁ בֶּן פַּרְצִי
18. וְנִשְׂמְחָה וְנָגִילָה:

19. בּוֹאִי בְשָׁלוֹם עֲטֶרֶת בַּעְלָהּ
20. גַּם בְּשִׂמְחָה וּבְצָהֳלָה
21. תּוֹךְ אֱמוּנֵי עַם סְגֻלָּה
22. בּוֹאִי כַלָּה, בּוֹאִי כַלָּה:

TZUR MISHELO

1.	*Tzur mishelo akhalnu*	Our Rock, from whose goodness we have eaten,
2.	*Barkhu emunai*	Let us praise our God, my faithful ones.
3.	*Sava'nu vehotarnu*	We have satisfied ourselves and we have left over (food)
4.	*Kidvar Adonai.*	According to the word of Adonai.

5.	*Hazan et olamo*	You feed the world,
6.	*Ro'einu avinu*	Our Shepherd, Our Parent.
7.	*Akhalnu et lahmo*	We eat of God's bread,
8.	*Veyeino shatinu.*	Of Your wine we drink.
9.	*Al ken nodeh lishmo*	For this, we give thanks to God
10.	*Unehalelo befinu.*	And praise God with our mouths.
11.	*Amarnu ve'aninu;*	We say and we answer:
12.	*Ein kadosh kAdonai.*	None is as holy as Adonai.
	(Tzur mishelo…)	
13.	*Beshir vekol todah*	With song and a voice of thanks,
14.	*Nevarekh leloheinu.*	We praise our God,
15.	*Al eretz hemdah*	For the good and spacious land,
16.	*Shehinhil la'avoteinu.*	Which is the inheritance of our ancestors.
17.	*Mazon vetzeidah*	Food and sustenance
18.	*Hisbi'a lenafsheinu.*	is rich reward to our souls.
19.	*Hasdo gavar aleinu*	God's gracious love determines all,
20.	*Ve'emet Adonai. (Tzur mishelo…)*	And the truth of Adonai.

YISMEHU BEMALAKHUTEKHA

1.	*Yismehu bemalakhutekha*	Rejoice in Your reign.
2.	*Shomrei, shomrei, shomrei Shabbat,*	Observe the Shabbat.
3.	*vekorei oneg Shabbat.*	Call the Shabbat a delight.

EILEH HAMDAH LIBI

1.	*Eileh hamda libi*	Be merciful, my beloved, and pray,
2.	*Husa na v'al na titalem.*	Do not hide from us.

1. צוּר מִשֶּׁלוֹ אָכַלְנוּ
2. בָּרְכוּ אֱמוּנַי
3. שָׂבַעְנוּ וְהוֹתַרְנוּ
4. כִּדְבַר יְיָ.

5. הַזָּן אֶת־עוֹלָמוֹ
6. רוֹעֵנוּ אָבִינוּ
7. אָכַלְנוּ אֶת־לַחְמוֹ
8. וְיֵינוֹ שָׁתִינוּ
9. עַל כֵּן נוֹדֶה לִשְׁמוֹ
10. וּנְהַלְלוֹ בְּפִינוּ
11. אָמַרְנוּ וְעָנִינוּ
12. אֵין קָדוֹשׁ כַּיְיָ.

13. בְּשִׁיר וְקוֹל תּוֹדָה
14. נְבָרֵךְ לֵאלֹהֵינוּ
15. עַל אֶרֶץ חֶמְדָּה טוֹבָה
16. שֶׁהִנְחִיל לַאֲבוֹתֵינוּ
17. מָזוֹן וְצֵידָה
18. הִשְׂבִּיעַ לְנַפְשֵׁנוּ
19. חַסְדּוֹ גָּבַר עָלֵינוּ
20. וֶאֱמֶת יְיָ.

1. יִשְׂמְחוּ בְמַלְכוּתְךָ
2. שׁוֹמְרֵי שַׁבָּת
3. וְקוֹרְאֵי עֹנֶג שַׁבָּת.

1. אֵלֶּה חָמְדָה לִבִּי
2. חוּסָה נָא וְאַל נָא תִּתְעַלֵּם.

Practical Questions and Answers

What's the best way to learn to sing *Zemirot*?

By singing *Zemirot!* Begin with songs you already know or songs your children have learned in religious school. The more you sing them, the easier it will be to add them to your repertoire. Try acquiring records or tapes of traditional Shabbat *Zemirot*. You might be able to find some in your synagogue gift store or library. Visit with families who know some *Zemirot*, and ask them to teach you one or two when you are their guests for Shabbat. Even if you only sing one, singing *Zemirot* is a wonderful way to enhance the Shabbat table experience.

What's so important about singing out loud?

Bill Goodglick said it best. Singing takes your mind off whatever mundane thoughts may have carried over with you into Shabbat. It is also very much like laughter. When you sing, your whole body physiology goes to work. Your lungs and diaphragm expand; even your muscles are sent into motion. Singing is great exercise for your mind and body

What if our guests don't know the songs?

Teach them one or two. It is very helpful to have uniform *benschers* or *shironim* for each of your table participants. Several good songbooks are listed in the Selected Bibliography. (See page 283.) In addition to having enough Shabbat Seder booklets containing the basic steps of the table service, invest in these songbooks, and you may be repaid with many evenings of great singing.

12

בִּרְכַּת הַמָּזוֹן

Birkat Hamazon
Blessing after Food

After the meal, we usually have a song, a little *Birkat Hamazon* with Dinah doing the *bensching* with a little song and a dance at the end.

7

187

Question: What's in a *berakhah?* Answer: A moment of insight and a chance for connection. *Berakhot* are designed to work like directional arrows, helping us to focus both our attention and intention. They seem to be a series of magic formulae that, when incanted, can change what is. There is a folk belief (one that goes back to grade school) that prayers are supposed to change God. "Please God, if only You let me pass this test, I promise that I will never again..." The truth, however, is that Jewish prayers and blessings are designed to change people. Time doesn't shift when we light the Shabbat candles; rather, our perception of time changes weekday into Shabbat through saying a *berakhah.* The beginning of Shabbat isn't a physical change, it is a perceptual change. When the Kiddush is said, the wine doesn't change—the Jewish tradition doesn't have a notion of transubstantiation. Sanctification comes through our perception. Shabbat has a holiness; it is there, ready for us to recognize. The drinking of wine is a mundane act, one that normally leads to physiological change. Yet, on Friday night, a single glass can link us to the moment of creation and to the seminal experience of liberation. Our reality changes with the making of a *berakhah. Mekadesh Hashabbat* and fermented grape juice become a symbol, and Friday night becomes the emulation of God's rest period.

Linkage is the second purpose of *berakhot.* We see a rainbow, and the tradition prescribes a *berakhah: asher zokher et brito im Noah* ("Praise God, who remembers the covenant with Noah.") Right after the flood, God makes a covenant with Noah: "Never again will waters become a flood and destroy the earth." Every rainbow we encounter becomes an opportunity to re-experience that promise, that responsibility to be like Noah. The *berakhah* points the way; it lets us link our moment, our experience, to that primal Jewish moment. In the same way, the Kiddush becomes "a remembrance of the work of creation...a remembrance of the Exodus from Egypt." *Berakhot* create moments of connection.

The *midrash* roots the tradition of *Birkat Hamazon* with Abraham. In the Jewish tradition, Abraham, with his four-doored tent open to welcome all who passed his way, has been the host par excellence. Abraham would welcome, feed, shelter, clothe, support, and totally provide for the needs of any who passed his way. In return, Abraham asked only one thing: that all who had shared his hospitality join him in blessing the One God, the source of all food (and everything else). This was Abraham's one teaching moment, his chance to have those he met share his recognition that all people are siblings, that the one God unites us all.

In general, *berakhot* are designed to precede an action. They are a way of making the act meaningful, because the intention has been focused through the blessing. *Birkat Hamazon* is an exception. It is a culmination. The Rabbis rooted the placement of "grace" after the meal in a verse from Deuteronomy (8:10), which says, in essence, first *eat and be satisfied*, then *bless Adonai your God for the good land*. This is Abraham's teaching style: use the experience of having our needs satisfied to create a moment when our appreciation for God's support is tangible. Because of that moment, *Birkat Hamazon* has evolved into a series of *berakhot* that lead us through the entire Jewish experience, that review our total relationship with God, and that direct us toward a full sense of Jewish mission.

That's the theory of *Birkat Hamazon*. Sometimes theory works better than its application. *Birkat Hamazon* is often a difficult process, with families finding themselves dragging kids back to the table, trying to re-energize guests, and working to refocus their own attention. The real culprit here is probably the rhythm of electronic lives. We've learned to go from the table to the television (though it started with the radio). We find our entertainment elsewhere. We're just not used to "long meals." *Birkat Hamazon* (like much of the Shabbat Seder) was part of the rabbinic reworking of the formal Greco-Roman meal. After dinner there was entertainment, and then, finally, parting toasts to the host. For the Rabbis, words of Torah became our entertainment, and *Birkat Hamazon* became praise for the host. *Birkat Hamazon* has sometimes become a test of attention spans, another sign of the tension of agricultural life rhythms being expressed in a technological age. It also serves as an opportunity for closure, being the grand finale to the experience that is the *Seder Leil Shabbat*—the Friday night Shabbat experience. Through its linkages, the Exodus is completed, the Promised Land has been entered, and the redemption awaits in the near future. This "Ultimate Shabbat" stands as the potential climax to every Shabbat experience. This is the final message of *Birkat Hamazon*: to point us toward the future that can be created through our sitting down to a Shabbat meal.

189

IRWIN WEINGARTEN: After the meal we usually have a song, a little *Birkat Hamazon* with Dinah doing the *bensching* with a little song and a dance at the end.

YOUR AUTHOR: How does that go?

DINAH WEINGARTEN: No, no, no…

YOUR AUTHOR: But I'd love to see the dance.

SUZAN WEINGARTEN: It's just something. It's personal.

IRWIN WEINGARTEN: Dinah, Suzan, and I do the *Birkat Hamazon*. Sometimes we harmonize. We do it until *Hazan et hakol*, and Dinah has an abridged version of the prayers afterwards that she's got from school.

DINAH WEINGARTEN: I have *Kakatuv* and I go to the end of that, then I go to *Uvnei Yerushalayim*, do two *Harahamans*, and end with *Migdol Yeshu'ot*.

EMIL KELMAN: Whenever I go, "Am I excused?" my brother goes, "You're not excused!" and sometimes I just leave. My Daddy goes, "Why are you standing?" "How did you get there?" and I go, "I walked there." And he goes, "You're supposed to be sitting down and ask me to leave." Well, I don't like that. I wish we could just leave.

ASHER KELMAN: They're getting their chance to report me as a tough Daddy. After the meal, the kids' attention span is usually gone, and we don't have a *mezuman* (three adults needed to say *Birkat Hamazon* out loud), so I will *bensch* while Wendy is picking up things. At the moment, the kids do not have the attentiveness to sit through that. When we have guests, they will stay put pretty well. Actually, I think that Friday night starts out with a very big bang, with lots of things to do, but toward the end I allow the kids to vanish. The difficult thing is not to allow the whole Friday night to become a burden for the kids.

SALLY SHAFTON: We are not great on the *Birkat*. We should be—that's another place where we can grow. The thing is, Friday night is a long process, and by the time we get to the end of the Torah discussion, we're ready for a short *Birkat*.

BOB SHAFTON: There's no question that the Hebrew in the *Birkat* is the hardest for me.

KAREN VINOCOR: Our *bensching* routine is a very traditional *bensching*. It is from beginning to end. I don't have a *mayim aḥaronim* thing (people have these little toys with the hanging pitchers...); we have a water glass to stick fingers in. *Birkat Hamazon* takes us fourteen minutes—we have a fourteen-minute *Birkat Hamazon*. And the reason it takes fourteen minutes and not nine is because Erin is just learning to say it, so I say it slowly so she can follow along. She's already very good at it. Ari knows the whole thing by heart already.

Concepts

The Blessing *after* Food

In common English, the invocation asking that a meal be a special experience is called grace. It is hoped that the participants experience a "state of grace" through the invocation and the meal. Christian traditions follow the logical pattern: "grace" is said before the meal—God is thanked "for what we are about to receive." Although Jews do praise God with the *Hamotzi*, before the meal, the Jewish parallel to "grace" takes place after eating.

In the book of Deuteronomy, just after Moses recalls the Exodus, the years in the wilderness, and the giving of the Ten Commandments, he tells the people of Israel that God will bring them into a new land. This is a land where they will eat bread without shortage, a land of milk and honey. Then the Torah says: "When you have eaten and are satisfied, you shall bless Adonai your God for the good land which God has given you. Beware, lest you forget Adonai your God and fail to keep God's commandments...lest when you will eat and be sated...you then forget Adonai your God." (Deuteronomy 8:10–14). This passage is the source of *Birkat Hamazon*, the reason why the major blessing takes place after eating. First we *eat* and are *satisfied*, then we *bless*. We *eat* and are *sated*, and we *remember not* to *forget* the Lord.

The blessings after eating are a safeguard; they direct us toward the Ultimate Source of sustenance, not letting us imagine that "my power and the might of my hand has won this wealth for me" (Deuteronomy 8:17). We are instructed to say the blessings after the meal to articulate gratitude to the true source of nourishment.

Four Themes

Four major blessings constitute the *Birkat Hamazon* (literally, "the blessing for the sustenance"). As in every *berakhah*, the final line of each (the closing *Barukh*) stresses the specific theme. The first three of these blessings were biblically commanded; the fourth was added on later rabbinic authority.

ONE: THE BLESSING FOR FOOD

Closing with the line *Barukh attah, Adonai, Hazan et hakol,* "Praised are You, Adonai, who provides food for all," this blessing acknowledges God as the Great Provider. It makes the point that God not only sustains all flesh but provides food for every living creature. This is a universalistic expression, the foundation of *Birkat Hamazon.*

TWO: THE BLESSING FOR THE LAND

Culminating with the phrase *Barukh attah, Adonai, al ha'aretz ve'al hamazon,* "Praised are You, Adonai, for the Land and for the sustenance," this blessing fulfills the biblical command to bless God for "the good land which God has given you." In this context, the "land" means "the Land of Israel." We bless God, linking ourselves to the experience of entering the Promised Land, the ultimate destination of the Jewish people. This is the Land that sustained the growth of a band of refugee slaves into a great people, the Land that fostered our relationship with God. Even if we do not live in Israel, we recognize the importance of God's gift of the Land to the development of the Jewish nation.

THREE: THE BLESSING FOR JERUSALEM

Originally the *Birkat Hamazon* contained a prayer of thanks for Jerusalem and the Temple. After the Temple was destroyed, the wording was changed to emphasize the rebuilding of the holy city. The signature to this blessing, *Barukh attah, Adonai, boneh verahamav Yerushalayim, Amen,* "Praised are You, Adonai, who in compassion rebuilds Jerusalem, Amen," focuses this aspiration. Jerusalem has long been synonymous with the desire for national sovereignty. As referred to in the preceding paragraph, Jerusalem is the seat of "the royal House of David, Your anointed," a clear reference to the messianic aspirations that are associated with Jerusalem and Zion. Thus, the spiritual hopes of the Jewish people are inexorably tied to the national hopes, and both are reflected in this third blessing of the *Birkat Hamazon.*

FOUR: THE BLESSING OF GOODNESS

Shortly after the destruction of the Second Temple, the rabbinic sages added this final blessing to *Birkat Hamazon.* It begins *Barukh attah,*

Adonai, Eloheinu melekh ha'olam hamelekh hatov veha-metiv lakol, "Praised are You, Adonai, Our God, Ruler of the universe, the Ruler who is good and does good for all." Certainly, the people's faith in God was severely tested when their holy Temple was savagely destroyed. Yet, the unending belief that God is good was reinforced by the inclusion of this blessing in the *Birkat Hamazon.* Today, it attests to the hope that God will continue to show kindness and mercy to the Jewish people.

The four sections of *Birkat Hamazon* form a "salvation history" of the Jewish people. Starting with a universal appreciation of God's role in nature, we follow the Jewish people into the Land of Israel, through the destruction of the Temple, and stand waiting for the redemption. Our final expectation is *Oseh shalom bimromav, hu ya'aseh shalom aleinu,* "The One who makes peace in the heavens above will make peace for all of us." We end by affirming our belief and involvement in the positive outcome of history: the final redemption.

Objects

The only object required for *Birkat Hamazon* is the text of the blessings. There is an advantage in having uniform copies of the text in Hebrew, transliteration, and English to facilitate everyone's participation. However, many families prefer to collect *benschers* as a remembrance of particular celebrations in which they have participated.

The Anatomy of Birkat Hamazon

While *Birkat Hamazon* consists of the four *berakhot* described above, the full Shabbat rendition surrounds these blessings with other elements. Here is the complete outline:

Shir Hama'alot: A Song of Ascents

Psalm 126 serves as the Shabbat introduction to *Birkat Hamazon*. This psalm speaks of the dreamlike joy that will be experienced when Adonai returns us to Zion, the context being a future return from exile. Likewise, it teaches that "those who sow in tears will reap with joyous song." This is a parable, teaching that the present struggles of the Jewish people will ultimately result in a full redemption. Shabbat is seen as a foretaste of the world to come, an anticipation of the messianic era. The optimism of this Song of Ascents expresses the hope Shabbat brings, introducing it to *Birkat Hamazon*.

Zimmun: Invitation to Bless

Judaism is partial to communal prayer. While it is permissible to say *Birkat Hamazon* silently and/or individually, the tradition has a preference for communal renditions. To express this preference, two legal terms were introduced: having a *mezuman*, a minimum of three adults eating together, and having a *minyan*, a minimum of ten adults eating together. Achieving each of these minimum numbers allows the group to voice the *Birkat Hamazon* differently.

With a *mezuman* (a quorum of three), the group adds a responsive reading/chanting introduction called the *Zimmun*, the "invitation to bless." This is done by a leader and responded to by all others who are present.

With a *minyan*, the word *Eloheinu*, "our God," is added to the *Zimmun* formula. In the *Mishnah* there are other additions that come for groups of one hundred, one thousand, and so on, but these are generally not used now.

Hazan et Hakol: The Blessing for Food

The first of the four core *berakhot* that make up *Birkat Hamazon*, this is a universal blessing expressing thanks to God for providing sustenance for all living things.

195

Al Ha'aretz Ve'al Hamazon—Birkat Ha'aretz: Blessing for the Land

The second of the four core *berakhot*, this blessing thanks God for the gift of *Eretz Yisra'el*.

Retzei: The Blessing for Shabbat

This blessing, which is a Shabbat addition to the weekday *Birkat Hamazon*, begins *Retzei vehahalitzeinu*, "May it please You to strengthen us." It asks God to help us to observe the commandments, especially the mitzvah of Shabbat as a "day of rest, free from trouble, sorrow, or sighing."

Uvnei Yerushalayim—Birkat Yerushalayim: The Blessing for Jerusalem

This is the third of the core *berakhot*, which asks God to speedily rebuild Jerusalem. This is another blessing that expresses messianic anticipation.

Hu Hetiv, Hu Metiv—Birkat Hatovah: The Blessing of Goodness

The fourth and final core *berakhah*, this is a rabbinic addition, affirming God's goodness.

The *Harahaman* Prayers

These are a series of short petitions recited by the leader to which the table group responds, "Amen." They ask the "Merciful One" to give us an honorable livelihood, to lead us in dignity to our land, to send blessing to our household, and so on. In recent years, additional petitions have been created to bless the State of Israel and to bless all our people who suffer and to bring them "out of darkness and into light."

These short statements provide a moment for individuals to offer specific prayers of petition. Some, such as a guest asking blessing on his or her hosts and their household, are included in most renditions of *Birkat Hamazon*. Others may be spontaneously created. A special Shabbat petition expands this section.

Migdol—Tefillat Hayeshu'ah: The Prayer for Redemption

This portion of *Birkat Hamazon* is a series of wishes for future salvation and for peace and prosperity. While not among the four core *berakhot*, these final aspirations close both the weekday and the Shabbat texts. A single word change, *magdil* into *migdol,* is made for Shabbat. Included in this section are the words *Na'ar hayiti:* "I have been young and now I am old, yet I have not seen the righteous forsaken, nor their children begging for bread." Through the centuries many people have had trouble reciting these words in all good conscience. Some choose to say them silently or not at all.

BIRKAT HAMAZON: GRACE AFTER MEALS

SHIR HAMA'ALOT

1. *Shir Hama'alot:*	A song of ascents:
2. *Beshuv Adonai*	When Adonai restores
3. *et shivat Tzion*	the fortunes of Zion,
4. *hayinu keholmim.*	we will be as in a dream.
5. *Az yimalei sehok pinu*	Then our mouths will be filled with laughter
6. *ulshoneinu rina.*	and our tongues (filled with) songs of joy.
7. *Az yomru vagoyim:*	Then they will say among the nations:
8. *"Higdil Adonai la'asot*	"Adonai did great things
9. *im eileh."*	for them."
10. *Higdil Adonai la'asot imanu;*	Adonai will do great things for us;
11. *hayinu semeihim.*	we will be happy.
12. *Shuva Adonai et sheviteinu*	The Lord will restore our fortune
13. *ka'afikim baNegev.*	like streams in the Negev.
14. *Hazor'im bedim'a*	Those who sow in tears,
15. *berina yiktzoru;*	with songs they shall reap;
16. *Halokh yeleikh uvakho*	One who walks along and weeps,
17. *nosei meshekh hazara—*	carrying a sack of seeds—
18. *bo yavo verina,*	that one will come back with song,
19. *nosei alumotav.*	carrying sheaves.

1. שִׁיר הַמַּעֲלוֹת
2. בְּשׁוּב יְיָ
3. אֶת־שִׁיבַת צִיּוֹן
4. הָיִינוּ כְּחֹלְמִים:
5. אָז יִמָּלֵא שְׂחוֹק פִּינוּ
6. וּלְשׁוֹנֵנוּ רִנָּה
7. אָז יֹאמְרוּ בַגּוֹיִם
8. הִגְדִּיל יְיָ לַעֲשׂוֹת
9. עִם־אֵלֶּה:
10. הִגְדִּיל יְיָ לַעֲשׂוֹת עִמָּנוּ
11. הָיִינוּ שְׂמֵחִים:
12. שׁוּבָה יְיָ אֶת־שְׁבִיתֵנוּ
13. כַּאֲפִיקִים בַּנֶּגֶב:
14. הַזֹּרְעִים בְּדִמְעָה
15. בְּרִנָּה יִקְצֹרוּ:
16. הָלוֹךְ יֵלֵךְ וּבָכֹה
17. נֹשֵׂא מֶשֶׁךְ־הַזָּרַע
18. בֹּא־יָבוֹא בְרִנָּה
19. נֹשֵׂא אֲלֻמֹּתָיו:

199

ZIMMUN

Leader:

1. _H_averai nevarekh.   My friends, let us praise.

Everyone:

2. Yehi shem Adonai mevorakh   May Adonai's name be praised

3. me'attah ve'ad olam.   from now and until forever.

Leader:

4. Yehi shem Adonai mevorakh   May Adonai's name be praised

5. me'attah ve'ad olam.   from now and until forever.

6. Birshut _h_averai,   With the consent of my friends,

7. nevarekh (Eloheinu)   let us praise (our God) the One

8. she'akhalnu mishelo.   whose food we have eaten.

Everyone:

9. Barukh (Eloheinu)   Praised is (our God) the One

10. she'akhalnu mishelo   whose (food) we have eaten,

11. uvtuvo _h_ayinu.   and by whose goodness we live.

Leader:

12. Barukh (Eloheinu)   Praised is (our God) the One

13. she'akhalnu mishelo   whose (food) we have eaten,

14. uvtuvo _h_ayinu.   and by whose goodness we live.

Everyone:

15. Barukh hu uvarukh shemo.   Praised be God and praised be God's name.

1. חֲבֵרַי נְבָרֵךְ:

2. יְהִי שֵׁם יְיָ מְבֹרָךְ
3. מֵעַתָּה וְעַד עוֹלָם:

4. יְהִי שֵׁם יְיָ מְבֹרָךְ
5. מֵעַתָּה וְעַד עוֹלָם:
6. בִּרְשׁוּת חֲבֵרַי
7. נְבָרֵךְ (אֱלֹהֵינוּ)
8. שֶׁאָכַלְנוּ מִשֶּׁלּוֹ.

9. בָּרוּךְ (אֱלֹהֵינוּ)
10. שֶׁאָכַלְנוּ מִשֶּׁלּוֹ
11. וּבְטוּבוֹ חָיִינוּ.

12. בָּרוּךְ (אֱלֹהֵינוּ)
13. שֶׁאָכַלְנוּ מִשֶּׁלּוֹ
14. וּבְטוּבוֹ חָיִינוּ.

15. בָּרוּךְ הוּא וּבָרוּךְ שְׁמוֹ:

HAZAN ET HAKOL

1.	*Barukh attah Adonai*	Praised are You, Adonai,
2.	*Eloheinu melekh ha'olam*	Our God, Ruler of the universe,
3.	*hazan et ha'olam*	who feeds the world,
4.	*kulo betuvo*	all of it with goodness,
5.	*behen behesed uvrahamim.*	with graciousness, with love, and with compassion.
6.	*Hu notein lehem lekhol basar*	God provides food to every creature
7.	*ki le'olam hasdo.*	because divine love (endures) forever.
8.	*Uvtuvo hagadol tamid*	And through it, God's great goodness
9.	*lo hasar lanu*	has never failed us,
10.	*ve'al yehsar lanu mazon*	and food will not fail us
11.	*le'olam va'ed*	ever,
12.	*ba'avur shemo hagadol.*	for the sake of God's great name.
13.	*Ki hu El zan umfarnes lakol*	Because God who feeds and provides for all,
14.	*umetiv lakol*	and does good for all,
15.	*umekhin mazon*	and prepares food
16.	*lekhol beriyotav asher bara.*	for all creatures that God created.
17.	*Barukh attah Adonai*	Praised are You, Adonai,
18.	*Hazan et hakol.*	the Provider of food for all.

1. בָּרוּךְ אַתָּה יְיָ
2. אֱלֹהֵינוּ מֶלֶךְ הָעוֹלָם
3. הַזָּן אֶת־הָעוֹלָם
4. כֻּלּוֹ בְּטוּבוֹ
5. בְּחֵן בְּחֶסֶד וּבְרַחֲמִים.
6. הוּא נוֹתֵן לֶחֶם לְכָל־בָּשָׂר
7. כִּי לְעוֹלָם חַסְדּוֹ
8. וּבְטוּבוֹ הַגָּדוֹל
9. תָּמִיד לֹא חָסַר לָנוּ
10. וְאַל יֶחְסַר לָנוּ מָזוֹן
11. לְעוֹלָם וָעֶד
12. בַּעֲבוּר שְׁמוֹ הַגָּדוֹל
13. כִּי הוּא אֵל זָן וּמְפַרְנֵס לַכֹּל
14. וּמֵטִיב לַכֹּל
15. וּמֵכִין מָזוֹן
16. לְכָל־בְּרִיּוֹתָיו אֲשֶׁר בָּרָא:
17. בָּרוּךְ אַתָּה יְיָ
18. הַזָּן אֶת הַכֹּל:

AL HA'ARETZ VE'AL HAMAZON

1.	Nodeh lekha, Adonai, Eloheinu,	We thank You, Adonai, Our God,
2.	al shehin<u>h</u>alta la'avoteinu:	for Your inheritance to our ancestors:
3.	eretz <u>h</u>emda tovah, ur<u>h</u>avah,	a land—desirable, good, and spacious,
4.	berit veTorah, <u>h</u>ayim umazon.	the covenant and the Torah, life and food.
5.	Yitbarakh shimkha	May Your name be praised
6.	befi khol <u>h</u>ai	by the mouth of every living thing,
7.	tamid le'olam va'ed.	always and forever.
8.	Kakatuv:	As it is written:
9.	"ve'akhalta vesavata	"and (when) you have eaten, and are satisfied,
10.	uverakhta et Adonai Elohekha	you shall praise Adonai, Your God,
11.	al ha'aretz hatovah	for the good land
12.	asher natan lakh."	which God gave to you."
13.	Barukh attah Adonai	Praised are You, Adonai,
14.	al ha'aretz ve'al hamazon.	for the land and for the sustenance.

BIRKAT YERUSHALAYIM

1.	Uvnei Yerushalayim	Rebuild Jerusalem,
2.	ir hakodesh	the Holy City,
3.	bimherah veyameinu.	soon, and in our days.
4.	Barukh attah, Adonai,	Praised are You, Adonai,
5.	boneih vera<u>h</u>amav Yerushalayim,	who with compassion rebuilds Jerusalem,
6.	Amen.	Amen.

1. נוֹדֶה לְךָ יְיָ אֱלֹהֵינוּ
2. עַל שֶׁהִנְחַלְתָּ לַאֲבוֹתֵינוּ
3. אֶרֶץ חֶמְדָּה טוֹבָה וּרְחָבָה
4. בְּרִית וְתוֹרָה, חַיִּים וּמָזוֹן.
5. יִתְבָּרַךְ שִׁמְךָ
6. בְּפִי כָל־חַי
7. תָּמִיד לְעוֹלָם וָעֶד.
8. כַּכָּתוּב,
9. וְאָכַלְתָּ וְשָׂבָעְתָּ
10. וּבֵרַכְתָּ אֶת יְיָ אֱלֹהֶיךָ
11. עַל הָאָרֶץ הַטֹּבָה
12. אֲשֶׁר נָתַן לָךְ.
13. בָּרוּךְ אַתָּה יְיָ
14. עַל הָאָרֶץ וְעַל הַמָּזוֹן:

1. וּבְנֵה יְרוּשָׁלַיִם
2. עִיר הַקֹּדֶשׁ
3. בִּמְהֵרָה בְיָמֵינוּ.
4. בָּרוּךְ אַתָּה יְיָ
5. בּוֹנֶה בְרַחֲמָיו יְרוּשָׁלָיִם.
6. אָמֵן:

BIRKAT HATOVAH

1. *Barukh attah Adonai*	Praised are You, Adonai,
2. *Eloheinu melekh ha'olam*	Our God, Ruler of the universe,
3. *hamelekh hatov*	the Ruler who is good
4. *vehametiv lakol.*	and does good for all.
5. *Hu hetiv hu metiv*	God has been good, God is good,
6. *hu yeitiv lanu.*	God will be good to us.
7. *Hu gemalanu*	God bestowed upon us,
8. *hu gomleinu*	God bestows upon us,
9. *hu yigmeleinu la'ad*	God will bestow upon us forever,
10. *hen vahesed verahamim*	grace, kindness, and compassion,
11. *vizakeinu limot hamashiah.*	and gain for us the days of the Messiah.

HARAHAMAN

1. *Harahaman hu yanhileinu*	(May) the Merciful One give us as an inheritance
2. *yom shekulo Shabbat*	a day that is completely Shabbat,
3. *umnuha lehayei ha'olamim.*	and rest in life everlasting in the world to come.

OSEH SHALOM

1. *Venisa verakhah*	Then shall we receive blessing
2. *me'et Adonai*	from Adonai
3. *utzedakah me'Elohei yish'einu.*	and justice from the God of our deliverance.
4. *Venimtza hen*	And may we find favor
5. *veseikhel tov*	and good understanding
6. *be'einei Elohim ve'adam.*	in the eyes of God and people.
7. *Oseh shalom bimromav*	The One who makes peace in the heavens,
8. *hu ya'aseh shalom aleinu*	(May) God make peace for us
9. *ve'al kol Yisra'el*	and for all Israel,
10. *ve'imru, Amen.*	and let us say, Amen.

1. בָּרוּךְ אַתָּה יְיָ
2. אֱלֹהֵינוּ מֶלֶךְ הָעוֹלָם,
3. הַמֶּלֶךְ הַטּוֹב
4. וְהַמֵּטִיב לַכֹּל
5. הוּא הֵטִיב, הוּא מֵטִיב
6. הוּא יֵיטִיב לָנוּ
7. הוּא גְמָלָנוּ
8. הוּא גוֹמְלֵנוּ
9. הוּא יִגְמְלֵנוּ לָעַד
10. חֵן וָחֶסֶד וְרַחֲמִים
11. וִיזַכֵּנוּ לִימוֹת הַמָּשִׁיחַ.

1. הָרַחֲמָן הוּא יַנְחִילֵנוּ
2. יוֹם שֶׁכֻּלּוֹ שַׁבָּת
3. וּמְנוּחָה לְחַיֵּי הָעוֹלָמִים.

1. וְנִשָּׂא בְרָכָה
2. מֵאֵת יְיָ
3. וּצְדָקָה מֵאֱלֹהֵי יִשְׁעֵנוּ
4. וְנִמְצָא חֵן
5. וְשֵׂכֶל טוֹב
6. בְּעֵינֵי אֱלֹהִים וְאָדָם:
7. עֹשֶׂה שָׁלוֹם בִּמְרוֹמָיו
8. הוּא יַעֲשֶׂה שָׁלוֹם
9. עָלֵינוּ וְעַל כָּל יִשְׂרָאֵל
10. וְאִמְרוּ אָמֵן:

The preceding "short" version of the *Birkat Hamazon* is officially sanctioned by all arms of the Conservative movement. For teaching purposes, we have included it here. The "complete" version of the *Birkat Hamazon* can be found in the Appendix.

Practical Questions and Answers

When is *Birkat Hamazon* recited?

The *Birkat Hamazon* is recited at the conclusion of the Shabbat Seder. Generally, this means that dessert has been eaten and all the *Zemirot* and table talk are over.

Why do some people remove knives from the table before reciting the *Birkat Hamazon*?

As we have learned, the table is compared to an altar. In Deuteronomy 27:5 it is written: "You shall not lift up any iron upon [the altar]." Iron is an instrument of violence that shortens human life, while the table and its offerings sustain life.

How can I include *Birkat Hamazon* when my young children are squirming at the table?

As the last and by far the longest prayer in the Shabbat Seder, the *Birkat Hamazon* is often recited hurriedly. To counteract the problem, families have devised interesting solutions. Some families choose to recite *Birkat Hamazon* immediately after dessert and before a long round of *Zemirot* so the children can be excused. (Note the similarity to the Passover Seder, when the hymns such as *Had Gadya* are sung after *Birkat Hamazon*.) This allows "the young and the restless" the opportunity to excuse themselves to play. In other families, the children are excused after eating the main part of the meal and are called back to the table for dessert, *Zemirot*, and *Birkat Hamazon*. Other families choose the short version of the *Birkat Hamazon*, concentrating on the key phrases of the four major blessings.

Another great help is to learn the tunes for the recitation of the *Birkat Hamazon*. They are easy to pick up, and as the children hear them repeated every Shabbat they, too, will soon know the tunes. Again, you can learn the melodies from friends who know them, from tapes, or perhaps from your children!

Should I let the kids leave the table and then ask them back for the *Birkat Hamazon*?

Depending on the ages of the children, once they leave the table it can be difficult to get them back, particularly if they resent it as interference in their play. Some families are successful with this approach; others maintain that saying the *Birkat Hamazon* as soon as possible after eating is the only way to have their involvement.

Some Interesting Sources

Look at these two rabbinic selections about *berakhot*. How do they explain the importance of a blessing "after" a meal? What is their moral impact?

A person is forbidden to enjoy anything of this world without saying a *berakhah*. Whoever does so commits an act of theft against God.

Berakhot 35a

A person should not taste anything without first saying a *berakhah*, because it teaches in the Psalms (24:1), "The earth is the Lord's and the fullness thereof." Someone who gets enjoyment out of this world without a *berakhah* has defrauded the Lord.

Tosefta, Berakhot 4:1

In saying *Birkhat Hamazon*, we adopt the focus of two moments in Jewish history. The first comes before the Israelites enter the land of Canaan after forty years in the wilderness. Look at these two texts, and explore what can be gained from understanding and reliving these two moments in the Jewish experience.

For Adonai your God is bringing you into a good land,
a land with streams and springs,
and lakes coming from plain and hill;
a land of wheat and barley,
of vines, figs, and pomegranates,
a land of olive oil and of honey;
a land where you may eat food without worry,

where you will lack for nothing;
a land whose rocks are iron
and from whose hills you can mine copper.

When you have eaten and are full,
give thanks to Adonai your God
for the good land which God has given you.
Take care not to forget Adonai your God
and fail to keep the commandments,
the statutes and the laws
which I command you today.

When you have eaten your fill,
and have built the houses to live in,
and your herds and flocks have multiplied,
and your silver and gold have increased,
and everything you own has prospered,
beware not to let your heart grow proud
and you forget Adonai your God
who freed you from the Land of Egypt,
the House of Bondage; who led you through the
great and terrible wilderness with its seraphs,
serpents, and scorpions,
a parched land with no water in it,
who brought forth water for you from the flint rocks;
who fed you in the wilderness with manna
which your fathers had never known,
in order to test you in the end;
and you say to yourselves, "My own power and the
might of my own hand
have won this wealth for me."

Deuteronomy 8:7–17

A song of ascents:
We will be as in a dream.
When Adonai restores the fortunes of Zion,
Then our mouths will be filled with laughter,
our tongues with songs of joy.
Then shall they say among the nations,
"Adonai did great things for them!"
Adonai will do great things for us;
and we will be happy.
Adonai will restore our fortune
like streams in the Negev.
Those who sow in tears, with songs they shall reap;
He who walks and weeps
carrying his sack of seeds—
he will come back with song,
carrying his sheaves.

Psalm 126

Both of these settings are moments of expectation rather than fulfillment. Why do you think that *Birkat Hamazon* is set in moments of hope (waiting to go into Israel, waiting to return from Babylon) rather than moments of success (the conquest of the Land, the return from Exile)? What is the lesson?

13

The Sabbath Day

Shabbat does not end on Friday night. In fact, Shabbat is a twenty-five-hour "island in time" that affords a complete day of rest and rejuvenation. In the first edition of *Shabbat—The Art of Jewish Living*, we limited ourselves to describing the Friday evening table ritual in the home. In this second edition, we add this chapter as an overview of the rest of the Sabbath day.

A Recollection

While Friday night was the most important Jewish event in our home each week, the Shabbat day was far more complicated. My father, Alan, who committed to being home from the grocery store every Friday night, had to work every Saturday, one of the busiest days of the week in the food business. So he rarely went to shul Shabbat morning. Mom also worked during the week; her weekly time in synagogue was Friday night when she sang in the volunteer choir. But my parents wanted me to go to shul Saturday morning. In fact, they had moved to a home within six blocks of the synagogue so I could walk there easily.

I am not sure what compelled me to go to shul almost every Saturday morning. Most of my friends were happy to sleep late or watch the endless parade of cartoons on television. But go to shul I did. There were some attractions, to be sure. For many years I participated in junior congregation. We met in the basement social hall for an abbreviated service, conducted entirely by the kids in Hebrew school. This was a kind of "basic training" for the big Bar and Bat Mitzvah performance we all had known was coming from the time we were eight years old. Each of us was given a prayer to lead in Hebrew, and we took our turns standing in front of a portable ark, leading the twenty or so regulars in "junior cong," as we liked to call it.

At 11:30 A.M. or so, we were marched up the stairs to the main sanctuary to take our places in the front row of the congregation. I always found the place to be quite intimidating, but endlessly interesting. I would count the number of chandeliers, round circles containing the outline of a *Magen David*, a Jewish star. I would look through the prayerbooks, always wondering about the people who were listed on the dedicatory bookplate. I would stare at the memorial tablets, calculating how long the person had lived. Occasionally I would even try to pray, mimicking the adult "regulars," the people who were always in shul, always sitting in their same seats. There were the Estradas, a lovely couple who sat three rows from the back on the aisle. There were the Ermans, parents of my best friend, Milt; they sat on the right side of the shul toward the front. There was Mr. Epstein, Yak's Dad; he was the *shammes*, the head usher, constantly running around the congregation, tapping people for *aliyot* (honors), instructing the Bar Mitzvah family where to sit, handing out *ḥumashim* (Bibles) when it came time for the Torah reading.

In the fifth row on the left side, situated directly in front of the rabbi's podium on the *bima* (pulpit), sat Mrs. Kripke, the *rebbetzin* (rabbi's spouse). No one sat with her, hardly ever. As a child I wondered why; as a young adult I understood that most of the congregants were so in awe of her brilliance. Dorothy Kripke was the most famous author of Jewish children's books in the 1950s and 1960s. Her first book, *Let's Talk about God*, is a classic of Jewish children's literature. I loved that book and I felt it totally wrong that the rabbi's wife didn't have anyone to sit with in synagogue. After all, the rabbi was busy, her own children were grown up, my parents weren't there and the congregants were intimidated. So whenever I could I sat with Dorothy, thus beginning a lifelong friendship.

Then there was "the Bunch." For some inexplicable reason, a whole group of parents who were interested in synagogue life all had boys in the same year. Richard Green, Ricky Chudacoff, Milt Erman, David Bloch, Mark Zalkin, Sanford Friedman, Jimmy Fried, Jon Whitman, Ronnie Wolfson—in junior high we called ourselves the Bunch. At Beth El Synagogue we all sang in the Junior Choir and we all learned how to *daven* (pray) and read Torah. What a group! To this day, the old-timers at Beth El say there was never a group like it, before or after. We loved being together, performing together, and carousing together.

It was in high school that I learned how to celebrate the rest of the Shabbat day. The Bunch had made it through the Bar Mitzvah year and entered the synagogue youth group, United Synagogue Youth. A new Jewish educator, Jack Molad, had come to Omaha from Israel, and he immediately recognized the potential in our group. "Mar Molad," as we affectionately called him, was full of *ru'aḥ*, spirit. With typical Israeli enthusiasm he quickly recruited us boys to be the core of his teenage program. Jack had an unusual strategy to keep us involved. Each Saturday afternoon, at 2:00 P.M., he invited us to his home for a game of football or basketball, depending on the season. But before we played, Jack insisted that we study Jewish texts with him. We loved the text study, we loved the games, and we loved Jack! It was a great way to spend Shabbat afternoon.

I learned about the "third meal" of Shabbat, the *se'udah shelishit*, and *Havdalah*, the ceremony demarcating the conclusion of Shabbat from the beginning of the new week, at USY camp. Each summer during high school, kids from the USY chapters in EMTZA (Midwest) Region would gather at Camp Esther K. Newman outside of Omaha for a ten-day encampment. The highlight of camp was always Shabbat. In the waning hours of the day, we would enjoy a light meal between *Minḥah* and *Ma'ariv*, and sing the Shabbat afternoon *Zemirot* (songs) at the top of our lungs. The Shabbat day was always so magical; we hated to see it go. *Havdalah*, the sensual ceremony of separation, held special meaning. Of course the old joke among Jewish educators is that you can't make *Havdalah* without a lake. (Most Jewish summer camps had a lake.) We didn't have a lake at USY camp, but we loved the short *Havdalah* service anyway.

When my wife, Susie, and I established our own home, the challenges of observing Shabbat day fully were considerable, especially during the long summer months in Southern California. We resisted the temptation to shop, to travel, and to engage in other forms of business and entertainment. Oh, we allowed the television to be turned on, something we never did on Friday night. We went to synagogue in the morning. But those long afternoons were another story. For many years we devised a way to gather our Shabbat-observant neighbors together. After lunch, we would meet in a nearby schoolyard or even out in the side street for a spirited game of football or basketball. We called ourselves "The SFL," "The Shabbat Football League." Or, "The SBL," "The Shabbat Basketball League." Everyone played—parents, kids, even grandparents. We all looked forward to these friendly competitions and they certainly helped us pass the hours of a long Shabbat day.

Of course the other time-honored Shabbat afternoon activity is a "Shabbes nap." Some would call this truly "sacred time"! On a day dedicated to rest, what better way to spend the afternoon than restoring the body and the soul through a good, long nap?

The Shabbat day has its own rhythm, and as we shall see, its own themes. It is a day of gathering, a day of rest, a day of prayer and study, and a day of re-creation. It can be a "palace in time," a phenomenal gift to body, to soul and to community. In a way, Shabbat is among the greatest gifts of the Jews to human civilization—the notion that if God rested from the work of creation, so, too, must we human beings, made in the image of God, cease and desist from our busy lives and enjoy the respite Shabbat offers us.

Shabbat Morning

Concepts

Revelation

If the theme of Friday night is creation, then the theme of Shabbat morning is revelation. The centerpiece of the Shabbat service is the reading of the Torah, God's word to humankind.

Surrounding the reading of Torah are three distinct prayer services:

Birkhot HaShachar/P'sukei D'zimrah—Blessings of the Morning
Shaharit—The Morning Prayers
Musaf—The "Additional" Prayers

In many synagogues there is a Bar or Bat Mitzvah celebration during the Torah service. The young person is welcomed into the adult community by leading the service and reading from the Torah and/or Haftarah portions for the week.

A recent development reflecting the variety of approaches to Jewish prayer is the emergence of "multiple *minyanim*," several different prayer services conducted simultaneously in the same synagogue. In some larger congregations there can be a number of "alternative" services in addition to the "main sanctuary" service. Each has a particular style or purpose: a "learner's *minyan*" where the Shabbat morning service is explained and practiced; a family service designed for families with young children; a Carlebach-style service using the melodies of Shlomo Carlebach, a Hasidic rabbi and performer; a *minyan* conducted completely in Hebrew with no Bar/Bat Mitzvah celebrations; a "One Shabbat Morning"-style service, popularized by Craig Taubman, which uses musical instrumentation and combines traditional Shabbat *nusah* (chants) and the new "American *Nusah*" of Taubman, Debbie Friedman, Danny Maseng, and others. This welcome development has opened new opportunities for engaging in communal prayer on Shabbat morning.

After services, many congregations sponsor a Kiddush or *Oneg Shabbat*, a light luncheon featuring traditional Shabbat foods—gefilte fish, herring, kugel, lox and bagels, brownies, and *kiḥel*, an airy pastry confection. Whether enjoying a congregational Kiddush or eating at home with the family, the ritual around Shabbat lunch is simple and straightforward:

1. Kiddush
   The Shabbat luncheon Kiddush has three parts:
   A. *V'shamru*—a selection from Exodus 31:16–17 that describes the keeping of the Shabbat as a sign of the covenant between God and the children of Israel and a reminder of the fact that God ceased from the work of creation on the seventh day.
   B. *Al kein*—the conclusion of Exodus 20:11, the fourth commandment, which calls on us to "remember the Shabbat to keep it holy." Some recite the entire paragraph Exodus 20:8–11.
   C. *Borei peri hagafen*—the blessing over the fruit of the vine.
2. *Netilat Yadayim*
   Before breaking bread we symbolically wash our hands as part of the act of eating and say the blessing *Netilat Yadayim*.
3. *Hamotzi*
   The blessing over bread. Two *ḥallot* (or two "complete" breads—small kiddush *ḥallot* will do) should be used, the minimum required for each meal of Shabbat.
4. The Meal
   Meat or dairy may be served, although many prefer the lighter dairy meal.
5. *Zemirot*
   Shabbat table songs.
6. *Birkat Hamazon*
   Blessings after food (the same as Friday night).

Steps 2–6 have been detailed and explained in the chapters describing the Friday night meal. Let us then look at the text of the Kiddush for Shabbat lunch:

1. *V'shamru v'nei Yisra'el* — The children of Israel shall observe — ‎1. וְשָׁמְרוּ בְנֵי יִשְׂרָאֵל

2. *Et Hashabbat* — the Shabbat — ‎2. אֶת הַשַּׁבָּת,

3. *La'asot et Hashabbat* — making Shabbat — ‎3. לַעֲשׂוֹת אֶת הַשַּׁבָּת

4. *L'dorotam* — throughout their generations — ‎4. לְדֹרֹתָם

5. *B'rit olam.* — as an everlasting covenant. — ‎5. בְּרִית עוֹלָם:

6. *Beini uvein* — Between Me — ‎6. בֵּינִי וּבֵין

7. *B'nei Yisra'el* — and the children of Israel, — ‎7. בְּנֵי יִשְׂרָאֵל

9. *Oat hee l'olam* — it is a sign forever — ‎8. אוֹת הִיא לְעוֹלָם,

9. *Ki sheishet yamim* — that in six days — ‎9. כִּי שֵׁשֶׁת יָמִים

10. *Asah Adonai* — God made — ‎10. עָשָׂה יְיָ

11. *Et hashamayim* — the heavens — ‎11. אֶת הַשָּׁמַיִם

12. *Ve'et ha'aretz.* — And the earth. — ‎12. וְאֶת הָאָרֶץ,

13. *Uvayom hashvi'i* — And on the seventh day — ‎13. וּבַיּוֹם הַשְּׁבִיעִי

14. *Shavat vayinafash.* — God ceased from work and rested. — ‎14. שָׁבַת וַיִּנָּפַשׁ.

15. *Al kein beirakh Adonai* — Therefore, God blessed — ‎15. עַל כֵּן בֵּרַךְ יְיָ

16. *Et yom Hashabbat* — the Shabbat day — ‎16. אֶת יוֹם הַשַּׁבָּת

17. *Vayekadsheihu.* — And made it holy. — ‎17. וַיְקַדְּשֵׁהוּ.

18. *Barukh attah Adonai* — Praised are You, Adonai, — ‎18. בָּרוּךְ אַתָּה יְיָ

19. *Eloheinu melekh ha'olam* — our God, Ruler of the universe, — ‎19. אֱלֹהֵינוּ מֶלֶךְ הָעוֹלָם,

20. *Borei peri hagafen.* — Creator of the fruit of the vine. — ‎20. בּוֹרֵא פְּרִי הַגָּפֶן.

As with Friday night Kiddush, the blessing can be made over wine or grape juice.

The meal of Shabbat luncheon can often be just as long and luxurious as Friday night. Extended song sessions, even some Torah study, can mark the meal. However, some prefer a shorter meal, heading immediately to a restful Shabbat afternoon.

Favorite activities of Shabbat afternoon include the cherished "Shabbes nap," taking walks, visiting friends and studying Torah. It is traditional in some communities to recite Psalms 104 and 120–134, the "Songs of Ascent," beginning with the first Shabbat after Sukkot and ending with the Shabbat before Pesach. Then, on the Shabbat after Pesach until the Shabbat before Rosh Hashanah, we study *Pirkei Avot*, a popular series of *Mishnah* texts emphasizing ethical conduct. The texts of the Psalms and *Pirke Avot* can be found in many prayerbooks.

The Final Hours

Toward the end of Shabbat afternoon, many people return to the synagogue for the afternoon *(Minḥah)* and evening *(Ma'ariv)* prayer services. Some prefer to *daven* at home. Either way, the final hours of Shabbat have their own distinctive theme. If Friday night celebrates creation and Saturday morning centers on revelation, then the third major idea of Shabbat is redemption. These three ideas form the foundation of Judaism: God created the world, God revealed the divine word and God will redeem us always.

There is a beautiful flow to these final, fleeting hours of Shabbat, infused with a kind of melancholy that the precious gift of this day is fast coming to a close.

Minḥah

The afternoon service is held every day, but Shabbat *Minḥah* has its own special flavor. The Torah reading for the coming week is read for the first time—just the first few verses but enough to foreshadow the week to come.

(The same reading will be recited on Monday and Thursday morning, traditional market days in the ancient world, when a maximum number of people would hear the words of Torah.) The emphasis in the prayers is on God as Redeemer: "You are One." And, as the words of the *Aleinu* attest, "On that day [in the messianic time]—when all shall recognize God as One—God will be One and God's name One."

Shabbat is a "taste" of the world to come—a messianic moment. At *Minhah*, we begin to feel grateful for the treasure of the Shabbat we have just enjoyed, complete with good food, family and friends, prayer and study and rest. This is what life could be like every day, not just on Shabbat. So *Minhah* is a time of dreaming, dreaming of that day when true redemption will be upon us, when there will be peace and completion, when every day will be Shabbes.

Se'udah Shelishit—The Third Meal

There are three meals during Shabbat: Friday night dinner, Shabbat lunch and this, the "Third Meal," *Se'udah Shelishit*. (Shabbat breakfast does not count as a meal; in fact, many do not eat much at all before *davening* and certainly not a meal with bread, a distinctive characteristic of a Jewish meal.) Typically, the third meal itself is not very substantial. Most people are still full from lunch. Once again, *hallot* begin the meal, along with the blessing of *Hamotzi* and the preliminary *Netilat Yadayim*. The food itself is often quite light: herring, light salads, cakes, and cookies. It is not surprising to see a bottle of Schnapps or Slivovitz, dessert wines, and brandies.

The highlight of *Se'udah Shelishit* is singing. Special *Zemirot* are chosen, often with the messianic theme of redemption. Often, the singing sways in mood—from nostalgic to rambunctious, the participants giddy with the fullness of a complete Shabbat observance. Sometimes a story is told; a *devar Torah* is offered. The meal is taken around a table, a convenient instrument for pounding out the rhythm of the songs.

The singing can last well past darkness, but eventually, someone calls an end to the *Se'udah Shelishit* and announces *Birkat Hamazon* and *Ma'ariv*. The Shabbat is nearly over, but no one wants to let go.

221

Ma'ariv

The *Ma'ariv* (evening) service is technically the beginning service of the next day, *Yom Rishon* (Day One or First Day) in the Jewish week. But we have not yet bid Shabbat farewell. The evening service is recited, and some additional Psalms are included. But the climax of the day is yet to come.

Havdalah

Havdalah (literally, "separation") is one of the most beautiful and inspiring of all Jewish rituals. The purpose of *Havdalah* is to distinguish between the sacred and the regular, between Shabbat and the workdays to come in the new week, between a time when we have celebrated the very act of Creation and a time of returning to the business of creating.

There are two competing theories as to the origin of *Havdalah*. One holds that *Havdalah* began as a synagogue ritual (*Berakhot* 33a). Since God created light on the first day of Creation, we kindle a light in the synagogue at the very moment the first day of the new week begins. The second theory holds that *Havdalah* most likely emerged as a home ceremony at the end of the Shabbat afternoon meal. The *Birkat Hamazon* was traditionally recited over a cup of wine, the *Ma'ariv* service was prayed, a light would be kindled to brighten the darkness of the evening, and spices were often placed on burning coals in the home. Since the laws of Shabbat prohibited the kindling of lights and the use of spices, the first opportunity to do so was at the end of the Shabbat "third meal." As with most Jewish rituals, *Havdalah* has been embellished over the centuries with a variety of interpretations, actions and meanings.

The ritual is conducted in four parts:

1. *Hinei El Yeshu'ati*—the theme of redemption is sounded immediately: "Behold, God is my deliverance!"
2. A series of blessings over wine, spices, light, and praising God who makes a distinction between the sacred and the regular. A simple mnemonic helps to remember the order: "YaVNeH"—*yud* (*yayin*, wine); *vet* (*vesamim*, spices); *nun* (*ner*, light); and *hey* (*havdalah*, distinction).
3. Songs to celebrate the coming week and a prayer for the messianic time.

HOW TO CELEBRATE *HAVDALAH*

You'll need:

A twisted candle with multiple wicks (most synagogue gift shops have these special candles)

A cup of wine or grape juice

A selection of spices, often kept in a special spice box

A text of the blessings

Steps of the ceremony:

1. Light the special *Havdalah* candle. Hold it high.

2. Pour a cup of wine to overflowing. Hold it in your hand.

3. Have the spice box nearby.

4. Recite *Hinei El Yeshu'ati* (except in the synagogue where the ceremony begins with the blessing over the wine).

5. Recite the *Borei peri hagafen* but *do not* drink the wine. Put the wine cup down.

6. Recite the *Borei minay vesamim* and smell the spices. Pass the spice box to others joining in the ceremony so they may smell the spices.

7. Recite the *Bori M'orei ha'aish,* hold your hand up to the candlelight, palm toward you, fingers slightly bent, and look at your fingertips to see the reflected light of the candle on your fingernails.

8. Take the wine in hand and recite the final paragraph of the *Havdalah.* Sip the wine.

9. Extinguish the candle in the overflow of the wine.

10. Sing *Hamavdil bein kodesh, A Good Week,* and *Eliyahu Hanavi.*

11. Wish each other *Shavua Tov* (a good week) with hugs and kisses!

THE TEXTS OF *HAVDALAH*

1. *Hinei El Yeshu'ati*	Behold, God is my deliverance
2. *Evtach velo ef<u>h</u>ad*	I am confident and unafraid.
3. *Ki ozi vezimrat Ya Adonai*	Adonai is my strength, my might
4. *Vayehi li lishu'ah.*	And my deliverance.
5. *Ush'avtem mayim besason*	With joy shall you draw water
6. *Mima'aynei hayeshu'ah*	from the wells of deliverance.
7. *L'Adonai hayeshu'ah;*	Deliverance is Adonai's;
8. *Al amkha virkhatekha selah.*	God will bless God's people.
9. *Adonai tzeva'ot imanu*	Adonai of hosts is with us
10. *Misgav lanu Elohei Ya'akov selah.*	the God of Jacob is our fortress.
11. *Adonai tzeva'ot,*	Adonai of hosts,
12. *Ashrei adam botei'a<u>h</u> bakh.*	Blessed is the one who trusts in You.
13. *Adonai hoshi'a*	Help us, Adonai
14. *Hamelekh ya'aneinu,*	answer us, O Ruler,
15. *Veyom koreinu.*	When we call.
16. *Layehudim hayetah ora vesim<u>h</u>a*	Grant us the blessings of light and happiness
17. *Vesason vikar, kein tiheyeh lanu.*	gladness and honor,
18. *Kos yeshu'ot esah*	I lift the cup of deliverance
19. *Uvesheim Adonai ekra.*	And call upon the name of Adonai.

BLESSING OVER THE WINE

1. *Barukh attah Adonai*	Praised are You, Adonai,
2. *Eloheinu melekh ha'olam*	our God, Ruler of the universe,
3. *borei peri hagafen.*	Creator of the fruit of the vine.

BLESSING OVER THE SPICES

1. *Barukh attah Adonai*	Praised are You, Adonai,
2. *Eloheinu melekh ha'olam*	our God, Ruler of the universe,
3. *borei minei vesamim.*	Creator of fragrant spices.

1. הִנֵּה אֵל יְשׁוּעָתִי,
2. אֶבְטַח וְלֹא אֶפְחָד,
3. כִּי עָזִּי וְזִמְרָת יָהּ יְיָ,
4. וַיְהִי לִי לִישׁוּעָה:
5. וּשְׁאַבְתֶּם מַיִם בְּשָׂשׂוֹן
6. מִמַּעַיְנֵי הַיְשׁוּעָה:
7. לַיְיָ הַיְשׁוּעָה
8. עַל עַמְּךָ בִרְכָתֶךָ סֶּלָה:
9. יְיָ צְבָאוֹת עִמָּנוּ
10. מִשְׂגָּב לָנוּ אֱלֹהֵי יַעֲקֹב סֶּלָה:
11. יְיָ צְבָאוֹת
12. אַשְׁרֵי אָדָם בֹּטֵחַ בָּךְ:
13. יְיָ הוֹשִׁיעָה
14. הַמֶּלֶךְ יַעֲנֵנוּ
15. בְיוֹם קָרְאֵנוּ:
16. לַיְּהוּדִים הָיְתָה אוֹרָה וְשִׂמְחָה
17. וְשָׂשׂוֹן וִיקָר: כֵּן תִּהְיֶה לָּנוּ,
18. כּוֹס יְשׁוּעוֹת אֶשָּׂא.
19. וּבְשֵׁם יְיָ אֶקְרָא:

1. בָּרוּךְ אַתָּה יְיָ
2. אֱלֹהֵינוּ מֶלֶךְ הָעוֹלָם,
3. בּוֹרֵא פְּרִי הַגָּפֶן.

1. בָּרוּךְ אַתָּה יְיָ,
2. אֱלֹהֵינוּ מֶלֶךְ הָעוֹלָם,
3. בּוֹרֵא מִינֵי בְשָׂמִים:

BLESSING OVER THE FLAMES OF THE CANDLE

1. *Barukh attah Adonai*   Praised are You, Adonai,

2. *Eloheinu melekh ha'olam,*   our God, Ruler of the universe,

3. *borei m'orei ha'aish.*   Creator of the lights of fire.

BLESSING OF DISTINCTION

1. *Barukh attah Adonai*   Praised are You, Adonai,

2. *Eloheinu melekh ha'olam,*   our God, Ruler of the universe,

3. *hamavdil bein*   who distinguishes between

4. *kodesh lehol,*   sacred and secular time,

5. *bein or lehoshekh,*   between light and darkness,

6. *bein Yisrael la'amim,*   between the people Israel and other people,

7. *bein yom hashevi'i,*   between the seventh day,

8. *lesheishet yemei hama'aseh.* and the six working days of the week.

9. *Barukh attah Adonai*   Praised are You, Adonai,

10. *Hamavdil bein*   Who distinguishes between

11. *kodesh lehol.*   sacred and secular time.

SONGS OF PRAISE:

1. *Hamavdil bein*   God distinguishes between

2. *kodesh lehol*   sacred and secular time

3. *Hatoteinu hu yimhol.*   May God forgive our sins from on high.

4. *Zareinu vekhaspeinu*   Our families and means

5. *Yarbeh kahol*   May God increase

6. *Vekhakokhavim balailah* like (grains of sand and) stars in the night.

7. *Shavua tov!*   A good week!

8. *Ah gutte voch!*   A good week!

1. בָּרוּךְ אַתָּה יְיָ,
2. אֱלֹהֵינוּ מֶלֶךְ הָעוֹלָם,
3. בּוֹרֵא מְאוֹרֵי הָאֵשׁ:

1. בָּרוּךְ אַתָּה יְיָ,
2. אֱלֹהֵינוּ מֶלֶךְ הָעוֹלָם,
3. הַמַּבְדִּיל בֵּין
4. קֹדֶשׁ לְחוֹל,
5. בֵּין אוֹר לְחֹשֶׁךְ,
6. בֵּין יִשְׂרָאֵל לָעַמִּים,
7. בֵּין יוֹם הַשְּׁבִיעִי,
8. לְשֵׁשֶׁת יְמֵי הַמַּעֲשֶׂה:
9. בָּרוּךְ אַתָּה יְיָ,
10. הַמַּבְדִּיל בֵּין
11. קֹדֶשׁ לְחוֹל:

1. הַמַּבְדִּיל בֵּין
2. קֹדֶשׁ לְחֹל,
3. חַטֹּאתֵינוּ הוּא יִמְחֹל.
4. זַרְעֵנוּ וְכַסְפֵּנוּ
5. יַרְבֶּה כַּחוֹל,
6. וְכַכּוֹכָבִים בַּלָּיְלָה.
7. שָׁבוּעַ טוֹב!
8. אַ גוטע וואָך!

227

ANOTHER POPULAR SONG

Shavua tov!

A good week, a week of peace,

May happiness and joy increase!

A good week, a week of peace,

May gladness reign and joy increase!

1. *Eliyahu hanavi,* — Elijah the prophet

2. *Eliyahu haTishbi!* — Elijah the Tishbite!

3. *Eliyahu, Eliyahu,* — Elijah, Elijah,

4. *Eliyah haGiladi.* — Elijah from Gilad.

5. *Bimheira veyameinu* — Quickly in our day

6. *Yavo eileinu!* — Come to us!

7. *Im mashiach ben David,* — With the Messiah, descendant of David,

8. *Im mashiach ben David!* — With the Messiah, descendant of David!

1. אֵלִיָּהוּ הַנָּבִיא,
2. אֵלִיָּהוּ הַתִּשְׁבִּי
3. אֵלִיָּהוּ אֵלִיָּהוּ
4. אֵלִיָּהוּ אֵלִיָּהוּ

5. בִּמְהֵרָה בְיָמֵינוּ
6. יָבוֹא אֵלֵינוּ
7. עִם מָשִׁיחַ בֶּן דָּוִד,
8. עם משיח בן דוד!

Practical Questions and Answers

Why must we have two _ḥallot_ on the table for Shabbat lunch and _Se'udah Shelishit_?

A formal Jewish meal begins with the blessing _Hamotzi_. To remember that God sent a double portion of manna in the desert to the Israelites, enabling our ancestors to survive, we offer two whole loaves of bread at each of the three meals of Shabbat. "Whole loaf" can be defined as a complete piece of bread or roll. This is what a Kiddush _ḥallah_ was invented for! Many households bake or purchase one or two large _ḥallot_ and several Kiddush _ḥallot_ to use as the second loaf at these meals.

I often see the old-timers in our synagogue drinking liquor instead of wine for Kiddush. Is that permitted?

Yes, indeed. However, the blessing changes since hard liquor is not "fruit of the vine." It is fermented grain. So, the _Veshamru_ is recited, then the blessing is: _"Barukh attah Adonai, Eloheinu melekh ha'olam, shehakol nihiyeh bidvaro"_—"Praised are You, Adonai, Ruler of the universe, at whose word all things come into being."

When is the _Minḥah_ service held?

Typically, synagogues schedule _Minḥah_, _Ma'ariv_ and _Havdalah_ about an hour before sundown on Saturday afternoon.

Is there a precise time when _Havdalah_ is said?

The rabbis determined the end of Shabbat by when they could see three stars in the sky. A wonderful tradition is to go outside and look for three stars in order to tell whether it is time to say _Havdalah_. Through the inspiration of our good friend Harlene Appelman, we often pulled out our trusty telescope to view the stars. One of Harlene's most famous Jewish family education programs is held at the planetarium in Detroit, where families gather to look at the stars and then celebrate _Havdalah_ together.

Havdalah is recited one hour after the candlelighting time of the previous Friday night—forty-two minutes after sundown.

How late can _Havdalah_ be recited?

Just as Shabbat can begin early if the candles are lit and blessed eighteen minutes or more before sunset, so, too, *Havdalah* can be said well after darkness sets in on Saturday night. In fact, among some authorities, *Havdalah* can be recited until *mitvoch* (midweek), literally Tuesday! This is a rare occurrence, and if *Havdalah* is recited later than Saturday night, the spices and the candle are omitted. Typically, *Havdalah* is recited at or near the end of the *Ma'ariv* service in the synagogue, just after returning from synagogue at home or forty-two minutes after sunset or later.

How can we light a candle if Shabbat is not over until *Havdalah* is said?
Technically, Shabbat ends at forty-two minutes after sundown, whether *Havdalah* is said or not. We light the *Havdalah* candle in preparation for the *Havdalah* ceremony, which marks the distinctions between sacred and secular time.

Why are there multiple wicks in the *Havdalah* candle?
Unlike Shabbat candles, the *Havdalah* candle symbolizes the workweek to come. So, the rabbis prescribed a "torch" consisting of two or more wicks. A braided candle, usually created from four or more wicks, is specifically made for *Havdalah*. If you do not have a special *Havdalah* candle, you can hold two Shabbat candles together to make up the "torch."

What color is the *Havdalah* candle?
Any color will do. While Shabbat candles are usually white, *Havdalah* candles come in all shades—blue, red, yellow, multicolored.

I have heard that the person who holds the *Havdalah* candle should hold it as high as possible. Why?
There is a tradition that one should hold the *Havdalah* candle as high as you wish your *beshert* (intended spouse) to be tall!

What is the significance of the spices?
The spices symbolize the *neshama yeteira*, the "extra soul," that is given to us on Shabbat. The Rabbis imagined that each of us is imbued with this extra measure of "soulfulness" in order to take in the spirituality of the day. When Shabbat is over, the extra soul leaves us and the remaining soul is saddened. The spices of *Havdalah* are said to soothe the soul (Maimonides, *Hilkhot Shabbat* 29:29).

What kind of spices can be used?

Anything will do. Pick an assortment of your favorite fragrant spices—cinnamon, sage, rosemary, etc.

What is a "*besamim* box?"

As with most Jewish rituals, artisans have developed holders for various objects. Spices are no exception. Elaborate *besamim* boxes have been shaped from silver, including windmills reminiscent of the famous windmill in Yemin Moshe, a Jerusalem neighborhood; musical instruments; and even a train! Or a selection of spices can be held in a simple, handmade box or container. Often children in religious school will craft "spice boxes" for *Havdalah*. Another favorite way to create *besamim* is to insert cloves into the *etrog* (citron) at the conclusion of the Sukkot festival. Or cloves in an orange or lemon will work. If all else fails, keep a box of spice tea in your cupboard!

Why do people hold up their hands to the light of the *Havdalah* candle?

We drink the wine of Kiddush, we smell the spices, so we must use the light of the *Havdalah* candle. A simple way to "use the light" is to look at the palms of your hands while reciting the blessing. Some turn the hands over, cupping the fingers towards the palms, extending the fingers to look at them. Why? Some say the *neshama yeteira* will leave our bodies through the fingertips. Others say that by looking at the fingernails we see how much we've grown over the past week!

How do I handle all these objects; I only have two hands!?

That's why it is wonderful to celebrate *Havdalah* with family and friends. Give one person, usually a young person, the task of holding the *Havdalah* candle high. Be careful of the falling wax; it is helpful to put the candle in a specially designed holder, or wrap the base of the *Havdalah* candle with aluminum foil to catch the drippings. Some candles come advertised as "no drip," but I have yet to find one that keeps that promise! Do be careful—hot wax is painful to the skin and impossible to get out of carpeting!

The "leader" can hold the Kiddush cup in the right hand and the *besamim* box in the left. Or just hold the Kiddush cup and give the *besamim* box to another to hold.

Do we pass the *besamim* box around to each person?

If there is one *besamim* box, then certainly pass it around to each of the people participating in the ritual. Or have enough sachets, tea bags or *besamim* boxes for each person.

I have seen beautiful *Havdalah* ceremonies done in a circle. Is that a requirement?

No, but it is certainly wonderful to ask everyone who will celebrate the ritual to join together in a circle for *Havdalah*. This adds to the sense of community and family coming together to mark the conclusion of Shabbat. *Havdalah* is recited while standing. Many people enjoy putting arms around each other to sing *Shavua Tov* and *Eliyahu Hanavi*. Of course, don't forget those *Shavua Tov* hugs and kisses!

Is there special music for *Havdalah*?

There is a traditional melody for *Hinei El Yeshu'ati*. Debbie Friedman has written a lovely *niggun* that is quite popular for singing the blessings. The traditional *Eliyahu Hanavi* is often the very last song of the ceremony, reminding us of the messianic time yet to come.

Why is the wine drunk at the very end of the blessings and not directly after reciting *borei peri hagafen*?

A great question. Usually in Jewish ritual, we do the act immediately following the blessing. However, in the *Havdalah* ceremony, we begin with the blessing over wine, but the most important part of the ceremony is actually the concluding paragraph, the blessing that details God's desire for us to distinguish between the sacred and the secular, between the seventh day and the rest of the week, between the children of Israel and other people. The *ḥatimah* (seal) of the blessing is "Praised are You, Adonai, Who distinguishes between sacred and secular time." At the conclusion of this paragraph, we drink the wine, indicating the completion of the formal part of the ritual.

Why is the *Havdalah* candle extinguished in the wine?

This is a tradition that probably emerged out of the folk practice of *Havdalah*. It is customary to pour some of the wine onto a plate or into another container and then extinguish the light. It has no real significance, except perhaps that since we do not blow out Shabbat candles, we do not blow out the *Havdalah* candle.

Are there other such customs?

Yes. Some people dip their fingers into the wine and touch their eyes. This recalls the line in Psalm 19:9, "The commandment of Adonai is pure, enlightening the eyes." Some touch their hands with the wine and put them in their pockets, hoping for a week of prosperity (Isaac Klein, *A Guide to Jewish Religious Practice*).

Are there parallels between the beginning of Shabbat and the conclusion of Shabbat?

There are such parallels, indeed. We begin Shabbat with kindling of lights; we conclude Shabbat with light. We begin Shabbat with a blessing over wine; we conclude Shabbat with a blessing over wine. We begin Shabbat by praising God, who makes the time of Shabbat sacred; we conclude Shabbat by praising God, who makes distinctions between sacred and secular time.

Why do we omit the use of spices when a festival immediately follows after Shabbat?

The soul is rejoicing over Shabbat, and it will continue to rejoice during the holiday. So the spices are not needed to "revive" the remaining soul as is usual at the conclusion of Shabbat followed by a regular workday.

Why is there a special *Havdalah* when Passover, Shavuot, Sukkot, or Simhat Torah falls on Saturday night?

Since we are moving from the sacred time of Shabbat to the sacred time of a holiday, we alter the *Havdalah*. There are two blessings—one for light (we don't use the *Havdalah* candle since we have already lit the *yom tov* holiday candles) and one for distinction. But the distinction blessing is different. Instead of *bein kodesh lehol*, between sacred time and secular time, the blessing is *bein kodesh lekodesh*, "between sacred time and sacred time."

14

The Shabbat Gallery

ACTIVITIES FOR SHABBAT ENJOYMENT

When Yael was in nursery school, the teacher composed a recipe book where the children would give their favorite food that their mom cooks and how their mom makes it. And, of course, being in nursery school these kids had no conception. "You take two pounds of water and you take a handful of salt and you mix it until it's hard and you put it in the oven." My favorite was to make pizza: "Take it out of the freezer and put it in the oven." Yael's entries were chicken soup and *lukshen kugel*.

DEBRA NEINSTEIN

One of the challenges of creating an enjoyable Shabbat experience is to develop a set of activities for family involvement. Traditionally, the singing of Shabbat *Zemirot* would last for hours, occupying most of the evening after the completion of the Shabbat dinner and Shabbat lunch. Today, families often do not spend much time at the table, even on Shabbat, hence the need to expand the celebration of Shabbat into the rest of the evening.

In this Shabbat Gallery we present a variety of activities for Shabbat enjoyment. All of them fall within the spirit of *Oneg Shabbat;* none requires actions that violate the letter or spirit of Jewish laws concerning Shabbat. We offer them as a selection of possibilities, and we encourage you to develop your own creative expressions of Shabbat enjoyment.

Torah Discussion

Many children study the weekly Torah portion in Jewish schools. Open a Bible with your child, and read a passage or two together. Use a text that is age appropriate. Some newer editions such as *Being Torah* have discussion questions listed in the text. Discuss the text. Ask questions that put you into the action; e.g., "What would you have done if you were Esau and your brother stole something important of yours?" Create a midrash, an interpretation of the story, using your own imaginations. Young children will especially like to act out the Torah story. Older teenagers can engage in some serious discussion and study.

Read Aloud

Reading aloud is one of the best things a family can do together. By sharing a story out loud, everyone experiences the same story simultaneously, yet differently. There is an ever-improving selection of Jewish children's literature that is ideal for reading aloud. Try some of the books by Barbara Cohen, Sydney Taylor's *All-of-a-Kind Family* stories, and tales told by Isaac Bashevis Singer for elementary school children. There are new picture books for preschoolers and collections of all-time favorites, such as the Chelm stories. A recent addition to read aloud for older children is *Elijah's*

Violin, a collection of Jewish fairy tales edited and translated by Howard Schwartz. Look for the book reviews of children's literature in *Moment* Magazine or *Melton Gleanings* (from the Melton Research Center, 3080 Broadway, New York, NY 10027). Contact the Jewish Book Council (15 E. 26th Street, New York, NY 10010) for current book lists. Consult your synagogue librarian or local Jewish bookstore for ideas. For tips on how to read aloud in the family setting, read *The Read Aloud Handbook* by Jim Trelease.

Singing

We have already discussed the importance of singing *Zemirot* at the table. In addition to the traditional Shabbat songs, try asking your children to sing songs they have learned at religious school. Ask them to teach the songs to you so you can join in.

Dancing

It can be quite fun to get up from the table and join in Israeli dancing around the dining room or wherever there is adequate space. Besides the exercise it affords after a big meal, the dancing can be a wonderful physical release for the children. Try some simple *hora* steps to *Hava Nagila* or other easy dances, such as *Mayim.* If you don't know the steps, the kids might. Let them teach you.

Tefillot: Worship Services

Of course, it is nice to go to late Friday night services at the synagogue at the conclusion of your home Shabbat Seder. If you have young children, that will not be possible most of the time. However, your kids might love to "play synagogue" by constructing their own congregation in the living room. When our son Michael was in preschool, he used to love to build a synagogue out of kindergarten blocks, complete with pulpit, pews, and, of course, a parking lot. He would dress up as the "Rabbi" by donning a *kipah* and his father's old Pierre Cardin scarf as a *tallit* (prayer shawl). Holding a siddur and announcing pages, Michael, with the assistance of his older sister Havi as <u>H</u>azzan, would lead us in a prayer service that was among the most meaningful his parents have ever attended!

You could make creation of a Shabbat worship service a major project. During the week you might construct a cardboard Torah ark and a simple podium. Create your own prayer services, with songs and readings. Encourage the kids to build or construct Torahs and other Jewish ritual items. As they "play" at being Jewish, they are internalizing important Jewish values.

Show Time

Most children love to perform in front of an audience. Shabbat eve is an ideal time for your aspiring actors and actresses to present their latest achievements in singing, dancing, gymnastics, skits, and other skills. Just after you have completed dinner or *Birkat Hamazon,* let the kids create a "stage" and put on their performance. Parents could get into the act, too, making it a family talent show. Be careful not to force a reluctant child into performing against his or her will. But if they enjoy it, your Shabbat shows can be among the happiest times for the family.

Puppets

If you have puppets and a puppet stage in the house, there is no better time for the children to create a puppet show for the family to enjoy. Often they will give the puppets Jewish names or develop Jewish or biblical story lines. Encourage this activity. You could take a turn at presenting a biblical story using puppets. You will never have more complete attention of young children than when the story is presented by "Bert and Ernaleh."

Games

A whole variety of games can be played on Shabbat that do not require writing or other non-*Shabbesdik* activities. Favorites we know of are: UNO, Candyland, Trivial Pursuit (a great game for Shabbat), and Scrabble (Devoted Shabbat-observant Scrabble players use bookmarks to mark the pages of books corresponding to their scores.)

Reading

Several families we spoke to told us that Friday night was reading night in their home. In an effort to stay away from the television set, everyone chooses a favorite book to read on his or her own. This quiet activity can be a welcome antidote to the sometimes frenetic pace of Fridays.

Walking

A cherished tradition in many families is the Shabbat walk after dinner. Even if it is just around the block, it is a great idea to take a walk after the meal is completed.

Visiting

Some families we spoke to told us that part of their Shabbat walk included stopping in to say "Shabbat Shalom" to friends or relatives in the neighborhood. Depending on the situation, you may want to let the prospective hosts know that you are coming in advance of Shabbat. Often, families are invited to friends' homes for Shabbat dessert and *Zemirot*.

Sharing Oral Histories

Shabbat is a wonderful time to share family histories. Especially if grandparents or other relatives are with you, ask them to share their family stories with you and your children.

Shabbat Photo Albums

One family told us that they save photo albums of special family vacations and important events for sharing only on Shabbat eve. This becomes a highly anticipated activity for family members.

Shabbat Gifts

Some families have created "Shabbat treasure boxes" for their children. Each week, each child receives a small Shabbat gift in his or her treasure box. Sometimes the gift is an object; sometimes it is a kiss. It can also be a written blessing from the parents that can be kept in a scrapbook.

Shabbat Orchestra

Some families allow young children to bring percussion instruments such as triangles and cymbals to the Shabbat table for playing during *Zemirot*. The added motivation seems to help their involvement.

Stuffed Guests for Shabbat

When our children were young, two welcome guests at our home most Friday nights were named Arissa and Charlie Wolfson. Yes, they were stuffed animals who took their place right next to their "adopting parents," Havi and Michael. They even joined hands with the human beings for *Shalom Aleikhem*. And, of course, Havi and Michael bestowed a "pretend" blessing upon them immediately after Susie and I blessed them "for real." This type of play is also important for children.

Attend Synagogue Services

Late Friday night services present families with a terrible dilemma. On the one hand, Shabbat eve has traditionally been a time for a relaxing dinner, with plenty of time for Shabbat talk and singing. On the other hand, it is wonderful to be able to join with the community to celebrate Shabbat in the synagogue. If your children are old enough to stay up through late Friday services and enjoy them, by all means go to shul. If the children are too young, watch for the increasingly popular early Friday night family services that many synagogues sponsor, sometimes as often as once a month. Also watch for community Friday night dinners in the synagogue, which can be good opportunities for Shabbat celebration in a new and different way.

Havurot Shabbat Dinners

Many havurot (small friendship groups containing up to ten families) report great success in alternating Shabbat dinners in different members' homes. This can be extremely important in communities where extended families are the exception rather than the rule. It is also a great idea for singles, single-parent families, and empty-nesters to get together for Shabbat dinner celebrations.

These Shabbat activities can be chosen by the family as a group, or each person can take the responsibility for planning the Shabbat activity for one week. Establish a pattern of these types of family experiences on Shabbat, and your search for "quality time" with your family will be over.

A Shabbat Bible Search and Discussion

Here is an idea to get your Shabbat Seder study sessions going. Just look up the biblical verses listed for each activity, read aloud, and then do the activity for family fun and learning.

Create-a-Song-a-Thon

Psalm 96:1—"Sing unto the Lord a song."

One person chooses a topic, e.g. "love." Members of the family sing as many songs as possible with the word "love" in it. Create teams for added fun.

Create-a-Costume

Genesis 37:3—Jacob gives Joseph a coat.

Choose clothes and accessories from your closets. Dress up like famous biblical characters or animals, and do impromptu skits.

Create-an-Exercise

Genesis 1:26—Body Awareness.

Warm up your family with some fun exercise. Gather together and do some simple running in place, jumping jacks, or other exercises. End with some tumbling activities and good old-fashioned wrestling.

Create-a-Crazy-Poem

Genesis 1:2—"Unformed and void."

Nonsense is the rule. One person creates an original poem, reciting only one line. The next person creates the next line, setting the rhyming pattern. Each person adds a line.

Shabbat Discussion Topics

Here are a few suggestions of Shabbat themes to explore with your family.

1. Shabbat is compared to a bride and a queen. What images do you see in your mind when you hear these comparisons?
2. Discuss the significance of the Fourth Commandment: "Remember the Shabbat and keep it holy." Include a discussion of your favorite Shabbat rituals that serve to make the Shabbat special.
3. The Torah tells us that God completed the work of creation in six days, and on the seventh day God rested. Discuss your workday schedules and how the Shabbat day of rest becomes a re-creation of God's renewal and refreshment.
4. "More than Israel has kept the Shabbat, the Shabbat has kept Israel." Discuss this famous quotation from Ahad Ha-Am and how it relates to your family and Jewish communal life today.

A Famous Shabbat Story

The Roman emperor Hadrian asked Rabbi Joshua ben Ḥananyah, "Why does the Shabbat meal smell so good?" Rabbi Joshua replied, "We have a certain seasoning and its name is the Shabbat, which we put into our food to produce a wonderful aroma." Hadrian immediately requested some of the spice. Rabbi Joshua said to him, "Whoever keeps the Shabbat finds how the spice works for him or her, but whoever does not keep the Shabbat finds that the spice does no good" (Talmud *Shabbat* 119a).

Shabbat Customs around the World

Shabbat is celebrated by Jews all over the world. Even though Jews from different countries celebrate the holiday in unique ways, the fact that Shabbat is observed simultaneously by so many is a thread connecting Jews everywhere.

Did you know that the Falashas, the black Jews from Ethiopia, celebrate every seventh Shabbat in a special way? On the eve of this Shabbat, the Falashas gather in their synagogue to pray, and they stop only for the meal. Then they continue to pray and sing throughout the night and the following day.

Did you know that Sephardi Jews have several interesting Shabbat customs that differ from the Ashkenazi practices? For example:

- Among the Jews of Syria, the husband is responsible for doing all the shopping for Shabbat and for setting up the candlesticks for his wife to light. Many of their families still use oil and wick lights for Shabbat candle-lighting. And many use twelve small *ḥallah* rolls for *Hamotzi*, symbolic of the twelve showbreads once used in the Temple.
- In the Moroccan Jewish community, if a new fruit appears in the marketplace during the week, it is purchased for eating on Shabbat, at which time the *Sheheḥeyanu* prayer is recited. There used to be a very interesting custom of having a pre-Shabbat snack of cake and radishes, which they called *"Bo'i Kallah,"* "Welcome, Queen (Shabbat)." They found that this little social occasion before Shabbat calmed the emotions

of family members and relieved the pressures everyone felt in rushing to complete Shabbat preparations.

- The Jews of Spain bless their children after the Kiddush and then kiss the hand of their parents or grandparents. After the traditional Hebrew blessing, it is customary for the parents to add an additional personal blessing for each child being blessed. They sing *Zemirot* in their language—Ladino—a mixture of Hebrew and Spanish, and in Hebrew, sometimes using both languages in the same song!

- The Spanish and Portuguese Jews who live in Holland do not sing *Shalom Aleikhem* or recite *Eishet Hayil* because these prayers are Kabbalistic in origin—a trend they generally do not follow.

- Many Sephardim recite the entire *Shir Hashirim* (Song of Songs) just before Shabbat begins.

- Most Sephardim recite a version of *Birkat Hamazon* that is different in several ways from the Ashkenazi version. For example, the *Zimmun*, the invitation to bless, begins *Nevarekh she'akhalnu mishelo*, "Let us bless (our God) of whose food we have eaten." The response is *Barukh she'akhalnu mishelo uevetuvo hagadol hayinu*, "Blessed is (our God) of whose bounty we have eaten and through whose great goodness we live!'

Recipes

"Chicken Again?"

Have you ever heard this complaint on Friday night? We spoke to several families who told us that the ubiquitous chicken dinner is still very much a tradition in many homes. Here are three chicken recipes from different cultures that could spice up your Shabbat menu.

Chinese Chicken Delight

You'll need:

    10 tbsp. safflower oil
    5 lb. chicken parts
    cornstarch
    6 tbsp. soy sauce
    1 can water chestnuts, sliced
    ½ lb. bean sprouts
    ½ lb. mushrooms, sliced
    4 large onions, diced
    2 cups pineapple, diced
    2 tsp. brown sugar
    slivered almonds for garnish

Here's how:

Place 5 tablespoons oil in a large frying pan, and heat. Dust chicken with cornstarch. Place chicken in pan, and cook, covered, until half done. Add soy sauce and cook until tender. Remove and set aside. Add 5 remaining tablespoons of oil, water chestnuts, bean sprouts, mushrooms, diced onion, and pineapple, and stir-fry for 5 to 6 minutes. Add brown sugar, and return chicken to the pot until heated through. Serve with cooked brown rice sprinkled with slivered almonds. Serves 8.

Chicken Marengo à la France

You'll need:

    1 chicken, cut into eight pieces
    oil for frying
    ¼ tsp. light salt
    ¼ tsp. pepper
    12 small white pearl onions
    12-18 medium-size mushrooms
    2 cloves garlic, crushed
    1 small can whole tomatoes
    1½ cups chicken stock
    ½ cup white kosher wine

Here's how:

In a frying pan, brown chicken in small amount of oil. Add seasonings, onions, mushrooms, garlic, and tomatoes. Cover the pan, and place in oven at 350 degrees F. for 1½ hours. While cooking, add 1 cup chicken stock and baste occasionally. When tender, remove to a hot platter. Add ½ cup stock and ½ cup white wine to sauce in pan. Cook over high flame until thickened. Pour sauce over chicken, and serve. Serves 4.

Arroz Con Pollo from Spain

You'll need:
    3–4 lb. chicken parts
    ½ cup olive oil
    ¾ cup diced onion
    ¾ tsp. salt
    2 cloves garlic, crushed
    1 bay leaf
    1 cup uncooked rice
    1 cup chopped green pepper
    ½ cup chopped red pepper
    ½ cup sliced green olives

Here's how:

In a large frying pan, brown chicken in oil. When evenly browned, remove chicken. Cook onions. Replace chicken; add seasonings, tomatoes, and rice. Cook gently over low heat until rice is fluffy (approximately one hour). Stir once after half an hour of cooking time has elapsed. Serve on a warm platter garnished with green and red peppers and olives.

Suzan Weingarten's Cholent Recipe

You'll need:

    1 box Telma onion soup mix

    1–1½ lbs. stew beef

    1 flanken (ask the butcher—they are Jewish short ribs)

    ½ cup each of:

        lentils

        pink beans

        baby lima beans

        small white beans

        pearl barley

    1 whole onion

    2 large carrots, peeled and cut in halves

    3 small potatoes, peeled and cut in quarters

    ½ tsp. sugar

    1 tsp. paprika

    2 bay leaves

    ½ cup ketchup

    salt and pepper to taste

Here's how:

Rinse all beans in colander. Place in Crock Pot or slow cooker, along with the barley. Add all other ingredients. Cover with boiling water, approximately 4 to 5 cups. Turn pot on high for half an hour, then set on low until served the following day. Serves 6 to 8.

Yael Neinstein's Lukshen Kugel

You'll need:
      16 oz. fine noodles
      4 eggs
      1 cup sugar
      3 apples, peeled and diced
      ½ cup raisins
      3 tbsp. oil
      slivered almonds
      cinnamon and sugar to taste

Here's how:
Cook noodles until tender, and drain. Mix all other ingredients well, and pour into a large, greased, glass baking dish. Sprinkle the top with a mixture of cinnamon and sugar and sliced almonds. Bake in a 325-degree F. oven until browned. When cool, cut into squares and reheat for a few minutes.

Susan Rappaport's Never-Fail (So Far!) _Hallah_ Recipe

You'll need:
      ½ cup oil
      4 tsp. salt
      ¾ cup sugar
      1 cup boiling water
      ½ cup cold water
      2 packages dry yeast
      ⅓ cup warm (bath temperature) water—about 110 degrees F.
      3 large or extra-large eggs, plus one more egg for the top
      7–8 cups flour, unbleached, bleached, or "Better for Bread"
      Sesame seeds, poppy seeds, or raisins (optional)

Here's how:

1. Pour the oil, salt, and sugar into a large mixing bowl.
2. Add 1 cup boiling water, and stir.
3. Add ½ cup cold water and stir.
4. Dissolve the two packages dry yeast in ⅓ cup warm water by sprinkling the yeast into the water and mixing until mixture is cloudy and yeast is dissolved. It is okay if some of the yeast clumps.
5. Beat the three eggs with a fork and add to the oil and water mixture. Stir.
6. Add the dissolved yeast, and stir.
7. Add seven cups flour. Either stir after each cup, or add all at once and stir well.
8. If the batter looks very wet and sticky, add another ¼ to ½ cup of flour.
9. Turn dough out on a lightly floured board, table, or pastry cloth. Now is the time to "take *ḥallah*" (see below).
10. Fill bowl up to the top with hot water, and let it sit to make it easier to clean.
11. Knead the dough for ten minutes.
12. Pour water out of bowl. Rinse and dry completely. Using a paper towel, spread oil over entire inside surface of the bowl.
13. Put dough into the bowl, and turn it a few times so that the surface of the dough is lightly oiled.
14. Put a pan of water in the bottom of your oven, and heat the oven for one minute. Any temperature will do. Turn oven off.
15. Cover the bowl with slightly damp dish towel, and put in the oven. Let sit for an hour to an hour and a half until doubled in bulk. If the dough is poked with a finger, the indentation should remain.
16. Punch the dough down with your fist.
17. Turn the dough out on a floured surface, and knead gently for about one minute. If desired, you can knead in raisins.
18. Decide how many *ḥallot* you wish to make, and multiply that number by three to determine into how many pieces you will cut the dough. This recipe will make one huge *ḥallah* or two very big ones or four large or six medium or eight small.
19. Cut the dough into the number of pieces you will need. A poultry scissors makes cutting the dough very easy.

20. Knead each piece with a little flour for a few seconds until no longer sticky.
21. Let the pieces sit and rest while you grease two cookie sheets with a light layer of oil, vegetable shortening, or a spray such as Pam.
22. Roll three pieces of dough, one at a time, between the palms of your hands until the strands are equal in length and about one inch thick. Their length will depend upon the size ḥallah you are making.
23. Braid the strands, pinch the ends together, and tuck ends under. Put ḥallah on greased cookie sheet.
24. Repeat with remaining pieces of dough. Divide ḥallot between the two cookie sheets.
25. Cover ḥallot with dish towels, and let stand at room temperature for 45 minutes.
26. Preheat oven to 375 degrees F.
27. Beat remaining egg, and brush it on top of ḥallot.
28. Sprinkle tops with poppy or sesame seeds if desired.
29. Bake loaves 30–45 minutes, depending on size, or until tops are light brown.
30. Note: extra loaves may be stored in the freezer in plastic bags after they have cooled. To serve, remove them from freezer about three hours before needed. Heat in a paper bag with a few drops of water.

ENJOY!

On "taking" ḥallah: In the days of the Temple, a portion of one's dough was taken and given to the priests. Since the destruction of the Temple, those who bake ḥallah fulfill this mitzvah by separating a small piece of dough before baking and burning it in the oven. The blessing to be recited before this ritual action is

Barukh attah Adonai, Eloheinu melekh ha'olam, asher kidshanu bemitzvotav vetzivanu lehafrish ḥallah.

Praised are You, Adonai, our God, Ruler of the universe; who has made us holy through the commandments and commanded us to separate ḥallah.

Shabbat Hiddur Mitzvah *Crafts*

Before Shabbat, gather your family to make these clever crafts for the embellishment of your Shabbat table.

A Shabbat Queen Bottle Stopper

You'll need:
> wine bottle cork
> white fabric strips
> Ping-Pong ball
> felt pens
> glue
> scissors
> a ring

Here's how:
> Place the wine cork in the bottle to mark off where to end the design. Remove the cork and wrap it with white fabric cut to size. Glue Ping-Pong ball to the top of the cork. Drape it with more white fabric. Glue the ring on top of the draped fabric. Draw a face onto the Ping-Pong ball with markers. Let dry.

A Batik Shabbat Tablecloth or *Hallah* Cover

You'll need:
> fabric
> wax
> charcoal
> dye
> iron
> newspaper

Here's how:

Paint Shabbat and holiday symbols on fabric with warm melted wax. (Hint: draw your simple designs in charcoal first; when dry, tie-dye in a bucket. Follow directions for dyeing on the commercially available dye packets.) Let fabric dry, and iron it, covering cloth with newspaper for wax absorption.

AFTERWORD

Mazal tov—"Good luck"—is a familiar Jewish expression, used to congratulate someone on a significant occasion. Yet, I want to extend a somewhat more appropriate salutation to the reader of this text: *Yasher Ko'aḥ!* It means "may you be strengthened": strengthened to continue the work you have begun, strengthened to continue to make Shabbat an important part of your life and the life of your family, strengthened to continue to learn and enact the art of Jewish living.

As you do, please share with me your experiences in creating Shabbat. Your feedback will be invaluable to our research and teaching efforts. I am interested in reports on all aspects of your attempt to learn about and establish a Shabbat Seder in your home—the successes and the failures, the rewards and the challenges. We are especially interested in creative ideas for Shabbat celebration that we may share with others.

Send your comments to

Dr. Ron Wolfson
University of Judaism
15600 Mulholland Drive
Los Angeles, CA 90077

Thanks, and *Shabbat Shalom!*

APPENDIX: COMPLETE TEXT OF *BIRKAT HAMAZON* FOR SHABBAT

Shir haMa'alot
Beshuv Adonai et shivat Tzion
hayinu keholmim.
Az yimalei sehok pinu
ulshoneinu rinah.
Az yomru vagoyim:
"Higdil Adonai la'asot im eileh."
Higdil Adonai la'asot imanu
hayinu semeihim.
Shavuah Adonai et sheviteinu
ka'afikim baNegev.
Hazor'im bedim'ah
berinah yiktzoru;
Halokh yeleikh uvakhoh
nosei meshekh hazara—
bo yavo verinah,
nosei alumotav.

A song of ascents:
When Adonai restores the fortunes of Zion,
we will be as in a dream.
Then our mouths will be filled with laughter
and our tongues (filled with) songs of joy.
Then they will say among the nations:
"Adonai did great things for them."
Adonai will do great things for us;
we will be happy.
The Lord will restore our fortune
like streams in the Negev.
Those who sow in tears,
with songs they shall reap;
One who walks along and weeps,
carrying a sack of seeds—
that one will come back with song,
carrying sheaves.

Leader:

Haveirai nevarekh.

My friends, let us praise.

Everyone:

Yehi shem Adonai mevorakh
mei'attah ve'ad olam.

May Adonai's name be praised from
now and until forever.

שִׁיר הַמַּעֲלוֹת

בְּשׁוּב יְיָ אֶת־שִׁיבַת צִיּוֹן

הָיִינוּ כְּחֹלְמִים:

אָז יִמָּלֵא שְׂחוֹק פִּינוּ

וּלְשׁוֹנֵנוּ רִנָּה

אָז יֹאמְרוּ בַגּוֹיִם

הִגְדִּיל יְיָ לַעֲשׂוֹת עִם־אֵלֶּה:

הִגְדִּיל יְיָ לַעֲשׂוֹת עִמָּנוּ

הָיִינוּ שְׂמֵחִים:

שׁוּבָה יְיָ אֶת־שְׁבִיתֵנוּ

כַּאֲפִיקִים בַּנֶּגֶב:

הַזֹּרְעִים בְּדִמְעָה

בְּרִנָּה יִקְצֹרוּ:

הָלוֹךְ יֵלֵךְ וּבָכֹה

נֹשֵׂא מֶשֶׁךְ־הַזָּרַע

בֹּא־יָבוֹא בְרִנָּה

נֹשֵׂא אֲלֻמֹּתָיו:

חֲבֵרַי נְבָרֵךְ

יְהִי שֵׁם יְיָ מְבֹרָךְ

מֵעַתָּה וְעַד עוֹלָם.

Leader:

Yehi shem Adonai mevorakh	May Adonai's name be praised
mei'attah ve'ad olam.	from now and until forever.
Birshut ḥavei	With the consent of my friends,
nevarekh (Eloheinu)	let us praise (our God) the One
she'akhalnu mishelo.	of whose food we have eaten.

Everyone:

Barukh (Eloheinu)	Praised is (our God) the One
she'akhalnu mishelo	of whose (food) we have eaten,
uvtuvo ḥayinu.	and by whose goodness we live.

Leader:

Barukh (Eloheinu)	Praised is (our God) the One
she'akhalnu mishelo	of whose (food) we have eaten,
uvtuvo ḥayinu.	and by whose goodness we live.

Everyone:

Barukh hu uvarukh shemo.	Praised be God and praised be God's name.

Barukh attah Adonai	Praised are You, Adonai,
Eloheinu melekh ha'olam	Our God, Ruler of the universe,
hazan et ha'olam	who feeds the world,
kulo betuvo	all of it with goodness,
behen beḥesed uvraḥamim.	with graciousness, with love, and with compassion.
Hu notein leḥem lekhol basar	God provides food to every creature
ki le'olam ḥasdo.	because Divine love (endures) forever.
Uvtuvo hagadol	And through God's great goodness
tamid lo ḥasar lanu	we have never lacked,
ve'al yeḥsar lanu mazon le'olam va'ed	and will never lack food
ba'avur shemo hagadol	for the sake of God's great name.
Ki hu El zan umfarnes lakol	Because God who feeds provides for all,
umeitiv lakol	and does good for all,

יְהִי שֵׁם יְיָ מְבֹרָךְ

מֵעַתָּה וְעַד עוֹלָם.

בִּרְשׁוּת חֲבֵרַי

נְבָרֵךְ (אֱלֹהֵינוּ)

שֶׁאָכַלְנוּ מִשֶּׁלּוֹ.

בָּרוּךְ (אֱלֹהֵינוּ)

שֶׁאָכַלְנוּ מִשֶּׁלּוֹ

וּבְטוּבוֹ חָיִינוּ.

בָּרוּךְ (אֱלֹהֵינוּ)

שֶׁאָכַלְנוּ מִשֶּׁלּוֹ

וּבְטוּבוֹ חָיִינוּ.

בָּרוּךְ הוּא וּבָרוּךְ שְׁמוֹ:

בָּרוּךְ אַתָּה יְיָ

אֱלֹהֵינוּ מֶלֶךְ הָעוֹלָם

הַזָּן אֶת הָעוֹלָם

כֻּלּוֹ בְּטוּבוֹ

בְּחֵן בְּחֶסֶד וּבְרַחֲמִים

הוּא נוֹתֵן לֶחֶם לְכָל־בָּשָׂר

כִּי לְעוֹלָם חַסְדּוֹ

וּבְטוּבוֹ הַגָּדוֹל

תָּמִיד לֹא חָסַר לָנוּ

וְאַל יֶחְסַר לָנוּ מָזוֹן לְעוֹלָם וָעֶד

בַּעֲבוּר שְׁמוֹ הַגָּדוֹל

כִּי הוּא אֵל זָן וּמְפַרְנֵס לַכֹּל

וּמֵטִיב לַכֹּל

umeikhin mazon lekhol beriyotav	and prepares food for all creatures
asher bara.	which God created.
Barukh attah Adonai	Praised are You, Adonai,
Hazan et hakol.	the Provider of food for all.
Nodeh lekha, Adonai, Eloheinu,	We thank you, Adonai, Our God,
al shehinhalta la'avoteinu:	for Your inheritance to our ancestors:
eretz hemdah, tovah, urhavah,	a land—desirable, good, and spacious,
ve'al shehotzeitanu,	and for liberating us,
Adonai, Eloheinu,	Adonai, Our God,
me'eretz Mitzrayim,	from the land of Egypt
ufditanu mibeit avadim.	and for redeeming us from slavery
Ve'al britkha	And for Your Covenant
shehatamta bivsareinu,	which You sealed in our flesh,
ve'al toratkha shelimadtanu,	and for Your Torah that You taught us,
ve'al hukekha shehoda'tanu,	and for Your laws that You made known to us,
ve'al hayim, hen vahesed	and for life, which You so graciously
shehonantanu,	granted to us,
ve'al akhilat mazon	and for the food that we have eaten
she'attah zan	with which You nourish us
umfarnes otanu tamid—	and provide for us always—
b'khol yom uvkhol eit	every day and every season,
uvkhol sha'ah.	and every hour.

וּמֵכִין מָזוֹן לְכֹל בְּרִיּוֹתָיו
אֲשֶׁר בָּרָא.

בָּרוּךְ אַתָּה יְיָ
הַזָּן אֶת הַכֹּל:

נוֹדֶה לְךָ יְיָ אֱלֹהֵינוּ
עַל שֶׁהִנְחַלְתָּ לַאֲבוֹתֵינוּ
אֶרֶץ חֶמְדָּה טוֹבָה וּרְחָבָה
וְעַל שֶׁהוֹצֵאתָנוּ
יְיָ אֱלֹהֵינוּ
מֵאֶרֶץ מִצְרַיִם
וּפְדִיתָנוּ מִבֵּית עֲבָדִים
וְעַל בְּרִיתְךָ
שֶׁחָתַמְתָּ בִּבְשָׂרֵנוּ
וְעַל תּוֹרָתְךָ שֶׁלִּמַּדְתָּנוּ
וְעַל חֻקֶּיךָ שֶׁהוֹדַעְתָּנוּ
וְעַל חַיִּים חֵן וָחֶסֶד
שֶׁחוֹנַנְתָּנוּ
וְעַל אֲכִילַת מָזוֹן
שָׁאַתָּה זָן
וּמְפַרְנֵס אוֹתָנוּ תָּמִיד
בְּכָל־יוֹם וּבְכָל־עֵת
וּבְכָל־שָׁעָה:

On Hanukkah add:

(We thank You also)

Al hanisim ve'al hapurkan,	for the wonders and for the deliverance,
ve'al hagevurot ve'al hatshu'ot,	and for the victory and for the liberation,
ve'al hamilhamot	and for the battles
she'asita la'avoteinu	that you fought for our ancestors
bayamim hahem, bazeman hazeh.	In those days, at this season.

Bimei Matityahu,	In the days of Mattathias,
ben Yohanan kohen gadol,	son of Yohanan the High Priest
Hashmona'i uvanav,	and his sons, the Hasmoneans,
keshe'amdah malkhut yavan harsha'ah,	the cruel Hellenist kingdom rose up
al amkha Yisra'el,	against Your people Israel
lehashkiham toratekha	to make them forget Your Torah
uleha'aviram mehukei retzonekha.	and to turn them away from the statutes of Your will.
Ve'attah, berahamekha harabim,	And You, in Your abundant mercy,
amadta lahem be'et tzaratam.	stood by them in their time of sorrow.
Ravta et rivam,	You defended their cause,
danta et dinam,	You judged their grievances,
nakamta et nikmatam.	You avenged them.
Masarta giborim beyad halashim;	You delivered the mighty into the hands of the weak;
verabim beyad me'atim,	the many into the hands of the few,
utmei'im beyad tehorim,	the impure into the hands of the pure,
ursha'im beyad tzadikim,	the wicked into the hands of the righteous,
vezedim beyad oskei toratekha.	and the tyrants into the hands of the devoted students of Your Torah.

Ulkha asita	And You made Yourself
shem gadol vekadosh be'olamekha.	a great and holy name in Your world.
Ul'amkha Yisra'el	And for Your people Israel
asita teshuah gedolah	You performed a great deliverance
ufurkan kehayom hazeh.	and redemption to this very day.
Ve'ahar ken ba'u vanekha	Afterwards, Your children entered

עַל הַנִּסִּים וְעַל הַפֻּרְקָן

וְעַל הַגְּבוּרוֹת וְעַל הַתְּשׁוּעוֹת

וְעַל הַמִּלְחָמוֹת

שֶׁעָשִׂיתָ לַאֲבוֹתֵינוּ

בַּיָּמִים הָהֵם בַּזְּמַן הַזֶּה.

בִּימֵי מַתִּתְיָהוּ

בֶּן יוֹחָנָן כֹּהֵן גָּדוֹל

חַשְׁמוֹנַאי וּבָנָיו

כְּשֶׁעָמְדָה מַלְכוּת יָוָן הָרְשָׁעָה

עַל עַמְּךָ יִשְׂרָאֵל

לְהַשְׁכִּיחָם תּוֹרָתֶךָ

וּלְהַעֲבִירָם מֵחֻקֵּי רְצוֹנֶךָ.

וְאַתָּה בְּרַחֲמֶיךָ הָרַבִּים

עָמַדְתָּ לָהֶם בְּעֵת צָרָתָם

רַבְתָּ אֶת רִיבָם

דַּנְתָּ אֶת דִּינָם

נָקַמְתָּ אֶת נִקְמָתָם

מָסַרְתָּ גִּבּוֹרִים בְּיַד חַלָּשִׁים

וְרַבִּים בְּיַד מְעַטִּים

וּטְמֵאִים בְּיַד טְהוֹרִים

וּרְשָׁעִים בְּיַד צַדִּיקִים

וְזֵדִים בְּיַד עוֹסְקֵי תוֹרָתֶךָ

וּלְךָ עָשִׂיתָ

שֵׁם גָּדוֹל וְקָדוֹשׁ בְּעוֹלָמֶךָ

וּלְעַמְּךָ יִשְׂרָאֵל

עָשִׂיתָ תְּשׁוּעָה גְדוֹלָה

וּפֻרְקָן כְּהַיּוֹם הַזֶּה

וְאַחַר כֵּן בָּאוּ בָנֶיךָ

lidvir beitekha,	the Holy of Holies of Your Temple,
ufinu et heikhalekha,	cleared Your Temple,
vetiharu et mikdashekha,	cleansed Your sanctuary,
vehidliku nerot behatzrot kodshekha,	and kindled lights in Your holy courtyards,
vekav'u shemonat yemei Hanukkah eilu	and instituted these eight days of Hanukkah
lehodot ulhalel leshimkha hagadol.	to thank and praise Your great name.

Ve'al hakol,	And for all this,
Adonai, Eloheinu,	Adonai, Our God,
anahnu modim lakh	we thank You
umvarkhim otakh.	and we praise You.
Yitbarakh shimkha	May Your name be praised
befi khol hai tamid le'olam va'ed.	by the mouths of all living things forever.

Kakatuv:	As it is written:
"ve'akhalta	"And (when) you have eaten
vesavata	and are satisfied
uverakhta et Adonai, Elohekha,	(and) you shall praise Adonai, your God,
al ha'aretz hatovah asher natan lakh."	for the good land that God gave to you."
Barukh attah Adonai	Praised are You, Adonai,
al ha'aretz ve'al hamazon.	for the land and for the sustenance.

Rahem, Adonai, Eloheinu,	Show compassion, Adonai, Our God,
al Yisra'el amekha,	on Israel Your people,
ve'al Yerushalayim, irekha,	and on Jerusalem, Your city,
ve'al Tzion, mishkan kevodekha,	and on Zion, the home of your glory,
ve'al malkhut beit David meshihekha,	and on the kingdom of the House of David Your anointed,
ve'al habayit hagadol vehakadosh	and on the great and holy Temple
shenikra shimkha alav.	which is called by Your name.
Eloheinu, Avinu, re'einu, zuneinu,	Our God, Our Parent, tend us, nourish us,

לִדְבִיר בֵּיתֶךָ

וּפִנּוּ אֶת הֵיכָלֶךָ

וְטִהֲרוּ אֶת מִקְדָּשֶׁךָ

וְהִדְלִיקוּ נֵרוֹת בְּחַצְרוֹת קָדְשֶׁךָ

וְקָבְעוּ שְׁמוֹנַת יְמֵי חֲנֻכָּה אֵלּוּ

לְהוֹדוֹת וּלְהַלֵּל לְשִׁמְךָ הַגָּדוֹל.

וְעַל הַכֹּל

יְיָ אֱלֹהֵינוּ

אֲנַחְנוּ מוֹדִים לָךְ

וּמְבָרְכִים אוֹתָךְ

יִתְבָּרַךְ שִׁמְךָ

בְּפִי כָּל חַי תָּמִיד   לְעוֹלָם וָעֶד.

כַּכָּתוּב:

וְאָכַלְתָּ

וְשָׂבָעְתָּ

וּבֵרַכְתָּ אֶת יְיָ אֱלֹהֶיךָ

עַל הָאָרֶץ הַטֹּבָה אֲשֶׁר נָתַן לָךְ:

בָּרוּךְ אַתָּה יְיָ

עַל הָאָרֶץ וְעַל הַמָּזוֹן:

רַחֶם נָא יְיָ אֱלֹהֵינוּ

עַל יִשְׂרָאֵל עַמֶּךָ

וְעַל יְרוּשָׁלַיִם עִירֶךָ

וְעַל צִיּוֹן מִשְׁכַּן כְּבוֹדֶךָ

וְעַל מַלְכוּת בֵּית דָּוִד מְשִׁיחֶךָ

וְעַל הַבַּיִת הַגָּדוֹל וְהַקָּדוֹשׁ

שֶׁנִּקְרָא שִׁמְךָ עָלָיו.

אֱלֹהֵינוּ אָבִינוּ רְעֵנוּ זוּנֵנוּ

parneseinu, vekhalkeleinu, veharviheinu,	maintain us, sustain us, relieve us,
veharvah lanu, Adonai, Eloheinu,	and grant us relief, Adonai, Our God,
meheirah mikol tzaroteinu.	speedily from all our troubles.
Vena al tatzrikheinu,	And may we never be in need,
Adonai, Eloheinu,	Adonai, Our God,
lo lidei matnat basar vadam,	of the gifts of flesh and blood,
velo lidei halva'atam,	nor of their loans,
ki im leyadkha hamlei'ah,	but only of Your helping hand,
hapetuhah, hakedoshah, veharhavah,	which is open, holy, and generous,
shelo nevosh	so that we may not be shamed
velo nikalem	or humiliated
le'olam va'ed.	ever.
Retzei vehahalitzeinu,	May it please You to strengthen us,
Adonai, Eloheinu,	Adonai, Our God,
bemitzvotekha,	with Your commandments,
uvmitzvat yom hashvi'i—	and with the commandment of the seventh day,
Hashabbat hagadol, vehakadosh hazeh.	this great holy Shabbat.
Ki yom zeh gadol	For this day is great
vekadosh hu lefanekha	and holy before You
lishbot bo velanu'ah bo,	to cease work on it and to rest on it,
be'ahavah, kemitzvat retzonekha.	with love, according to Your will.
Uvirtzonkha haniah lanu,	And by Your will grant us rest,
Adonai, Eloheinu,	Adonai, Our God,
shelo tehei tzarah, veyagon, va'anahah	that there be no trouble, or sorrow, or sighing
beyom menuhateinu.	on the day of our rest.
Vehar'einu, Adonai, Eloheinu,	Show us, Adonai, Our God,
benehamat Tzion, irekha,	the consolation of Zion, Your city,
uvevinyan Yerushalayim, ir kodshekha,	and rebuild Jerusalem, Your holy city,
ki attah hu ba'al hayeshu'ot	for You are the Master of deliverance
uva'al hanehamot.	and the Master of consolation.

פַּרְנְסֵנוּ וְכַלְכְּלֵנוּ וְהַרְוִיחֵנוּ
וְהַרְוַח לָנוּ יְיָ אֱלֹהֵינוּ
מְהֵרָה מִכָּל צָרוֹתֵינוּ
וְנָא אַל תַּצְרִיכֵנוּ
יְיָ אֱלֹהֵינוּ
לֹא לִידֵי מַתְּנַת בָּשָׂר וָדָם
וְלֹא לִידֵי הַלְוָאָתָם
כִּי אִם לְיָדְךָ הַמְּלֵאָה
הַפְּתוּחָה הַקְּדוֹשָׁה וְהָרְחָבָה
שֶׁלֹּא נֵבוֹשׁ
וְלֹא נִכָּלֵם
לְעוֹלָם וָעֶד:

רְצֵה וְהַחֲלִיצֵנוּ
יְיָ אֱלֹהֵינוּ
בְּמִצְוֹתֶיךָ
וּבְמִצְוַת יוֹם הַשְּׁבִיעִי
הַשַּׁבָּת הַגָּדוֹל וְהַקָּדוֹשׁ הַזֶּה.
כִּי יוֹם זֶה גָּדוֹל
וְקָדוֹשׁ הוּא לְפָנֶיךָ
לִשְׁבָּת־בּוֹ וְלָנוּחַ בּוֹ
בְּאַהֲבָה כְּמִצְוַת רְצוֹנֶךָ
וּבִרְצוֹנְךָ הָנִיחַ לָנוּ
יְיָ אֱלֹהֵינוּ
שֶׁלֹּא תְהֵא צָרָה וְיָגוֹן וַאֲנָחָה
בְּיוֹם מְנוּחָתֵנוּ
וְהַרְאֵנוּ יְיָ אֱלֹהֵינוּ
בְּנֶחָמַת צִיּוֹן עִירֶךָ
וּבְבִנְיַן יְרוּשָׁלַיִם עִיר קָדְשֶׁךָ
כִּי אַתָּה הוּא בַּעַל הַיְשׁוּעוֹת
וּבַעַל הַנֶּחָמוֹת:

On Rosh Hodesh (the New Moon)
and festivals add:

Eloheinu veilohei avoteinu,	Our God and God of our ancestors,
ya'aleh veyavo,	may there ascend, come,
veyagi'a veyera'eh,	reach, and appear,
veyeratzeh veyishama,	be accepted and heard,
veyipaked veyizakher:	counted and recalled,
zikhroneinu ufikdoneinu	our remembrance and our reckoning:
vezikhron avoteinu,	the remembrance of our ancestors,
vezikhron mashiah ben David avdekha,	the remembrance of the Messiah, the seed of David, Your servant,
vezikhron Yerushalayim, ir kodshekha,	the remembrance of Jerusalem, Your holy city,
vezikhron kol amkha beit Yisra'el lefanekha;	the remembrance of all Your people, the House of Israel, before you;
lifleitah letovah,	for deliverance and for good,
lehen, ulhesed, ulrahamim,	for favor, kindness, and mercy;
lehayim ulshalom,	for life and for peace;
beyom	on this day of the:
(on Rosh Hodesh) rosh hahodesh hazeh.	New Moon
(on Pesah) hag hamatzot hazeh	Feast of Unleavened Bread
(on Shavuot) hag hashavu'ot hazeh.	Feast of Weeks
(on Rosh Hashanah) hazikaron hazeh.	New Year
(on Sukkot) hag hasukkot hazeh.	Feast of Tabernacles
(on Shemini Atzeret and Simhat Torah) hashemini hag ha'atzeret hazeh.	Eighth Day Feast
Zokhrenu, Adonai, Eloheinu,	Remember us, Adonai, Our God,
bo letovah;	on this day for well-being;
ufokdeinu vo livrakha,	be mindful of us for blessing,
vehoshi'einu vo lehayim.	and save us for life.
Uvidvar yeshu'ah verahamim,	With a promise of salvation and mercy,
hus vehonenu,	spare us and favor us,

אֱלֹהֵינוּ וֵאלֹהֵי אֲבוֹתֵינוּ

יַעֲלֶה וְיָבֹא

וְיַגִּיעַ וְיֵרָאֶה

וְיֵרָצֶה וְיִשָּׁמַע

וְיִפָּקֵד וְיִזָּכֵר

זִכְרוֹנֵנוּ וּפִקְדוֹנֵנוּ

וְזִכְרוֹן אֲבוֹתֵינוּ

וְזִכְרוֹן מָשִׁיחַ בֶּן דָּוִד עַבְדֶּךָ

וְזִכְרוֹן יְרוּשָׁלַיִם עִיר קָדְשֶׁךָ

וְזִכְרוֹן כָּל־עַמְּךָ בֵּית יִשְׂרָאֵל לְפָנֶיךָ

לִפְלֵיטָה לְטוֹבָה

לְחֵן וּלְחֶסֶד וּלְרַחֲמִים

לְחַיִּים וּלְשָׁלוֹם

בְּיוֹם

רֹאשׁ הַחֹדֶשׁ הַזֶּה

חַג הַמַּצּוֹת הַזֶּה

חַג הַשָּׁבֻעוֹת הַזֶּה

הַזִּכָּרוֹן הַזֶּה

חַג הַסֻּכּוֹת הַזֶּה

הַשְּׁמִינִי חַג הָעֲצֶרֶת הַזֶּה

זָכְרֵנוּ יְיָ אֱלֹהֵינוּ

בּוֹ לְטוֹבָה

וּפָקְדֵנוּ בוֹ לִבְרָכָה

וְהוֹשִׁיעֵנוּ בוֹ לְחַיִּים

וּבִדְבַר יְשׁוּעָה וְרַחֲמִים חוּס וְחָנֵּנוּ

verahem aleinu vehoshi'einu,	have mercy on us and save us,
ki elekha eineinu	for our eyes look to You
ki El melekh hanun verahum attah.	because You, O God, are a gracious and merciful Ruler.

Uvnei Yerushalayim,	Rebuild Jerusalem,
ir hakodesh,	the holy city,
bimherah veyameinu.	soon in our days.
Barukh attah, Adonai,	Praised are You, Adonai,
boneh verahamav Yerushalayim,	who in compassion rebuilds Jerusalem:
Amen.	Amen.

Barukh attah, Adonai,	Praised are You, Adonai,
Eloheinu, melekh ha'olam,	Our God, Ruler of the universe,
ha'El, avinu, malkeinu,	God, Our Parent, Our Ruler,
adireinu, bor'einu,	Our Mighty One, Our Creator,
go'aleinu, yotzreinu,	Our Redeemer, Our Maker,
kedosheinu, kedosh Ya'akov,	Our Holy One, Holy One of Jacob,
ro'einu ro'ei Yisra'el,	our Shepherd, Shepherd of Israel,
hamelekh hatov vehametiv lakol.	the good Ruler who does good for all.
Shebekhol yom vayom	Every single day
hu hetiv,	God has been good,
hu metiv	God is good,
hu yeitiv lanu.	God will be good to us.
Hu gemalanu,	God bestowed upon us,
hu gomleinu,	God bestows upon us,
hu yigmeleinu la'ad	God will bestow upon us forever
lehen, lehesed, ulrahamim,	grace and kindness and compassion
ul'revah hatzalah,	and relief and rescue,
vehatzlahah, berakhah,	success, blessing,
vishu'ah, nehamah, parnasah,	deliverance, consolation, prosperity,

268

וְרַחֵם עָלֵינוּ וְהוֹשִׁיעֵנוּ

כִּי אֵלֶיךָ עֵינֵינוּ

כִּי אֵל מֶלֶךְ חַנּוּן וְרַחוּם אָתָּה:

וּבְנֵה יְרוּשָׁלַיִם

עִיר הַקֹּדֶשׁ

בִּמְהֵרָה בְיָמֵינוּ.

בָּרוּךְ אַתָּה יְיָ

בּוֹנֵה בְרַחֲמָיו יְרוּשָׁלָיִם.

אָמֵן:

בָּרוּךְ אַתָּה יְיָ

אֱלֹהֵינוּ מֶלֶךְ הָעוֹלָם,

הָאֵל אָבִינוּ מַלְכֵּנוּ

אַדִּירֵנוּ בּוֹרְאֵנוּ

גּוֹאֲלֵנוּ יוֹצְרֵנוּ

קְדוֹשֵׁנוּ קְדוֹשׁ יַעֲקֹב

רוֹעֵנוּ רוֹעֵה יִשְׂרָאֵל.

הַמֶּלֶךְ הַטּוֹב וְהַמֵּטִיב לַכֹּל

שֶׁבְּכָל־יוֹם וָיוֹם

הוּא הֵטִיב

הוּא מֵטִיב

הוּא יֵיטִיב לָנוּ.

הוּא גְמָלָנוּ

הוּא גוֹמְלֵנוּ

הוּא יִגְמְלֵנוּ לָעַד

לְחֵן לְחֶסֶד וּלְרַחֲמִים

וּלְרֶוַח הַצָּלָה

וְהַצְלָחָה בְּרָכָה

וִישׁוּעָה נֶחָמָה פַּרְנָסָה

vekhalkalah,
verahamim, vehayim, veshalom,
vekhol tov;
umikol tuv
le'olam al yehasreinu.

sustenance,
mercy, life, peace,
and everything good;
and of everything good
may God never deprive us.

Harahaman, hu yimlokh aleinu
le'olam va'ed.

May the Merciful One reign over us
forever.

Harahaman, hu yitbarakh
bashamayim uva'aretz.

May the Merciful One be praised
in heaven and on earth.

Harahaman, hu yishtabah
ledor dorim,
veyitpa'ar banu la'ad
ulnetzah netzahim,
veyit'hadar banu la'ad
ul'olmei olamim.

May the Merciful One be praised
in every generation
be glorified through us forever
and through all eternity,
and be exalted through us
for time everlasting.

Harahaman
hu yefarneseinu
bekhavod.

May the Merciful One
allow us to earn our livelihood
with honor.

Harahaman, hu yishbor uleinu,
me'al tzavareinu,
v'hu yolikheinu kom'miyut le'artzeinu.

May the Merciful One break the yoke (of foreign rule)
from off our necks,
and lead us in dignity to our land.

Harahaman, hu yishlah lanu
berakhah merubah babayit hazeh
ve'al shulhan zeh she'akhalnu alav.

May the Merciful One send us
abundant blessing to this home
and to this table at which we have eaten.

וְכַלְכָּלָה
וְרַחֲמִים וְחַיִּים וְשָׁלוֹם
וְכָל־טוֹב
וּמִכָּל־טוּב
לְעוֹלָם אַל יְחַסְּרֵנוּ:

הָרַחֲמָן, הוּא יִמְלוֹךְ עָלֵינוּ
לְעוֹלָם וָעֶד.

הָרַחֲמָן, הוּא יִתְבָּרַךְ
בַּשָּׁמַיִם וּבָאָרֶץ.

הָרַחֲמָן, הוּא יִשְׁתַּבַּח
לְדוֹר דּוֹרִים.
וְיִתְפָּאַר בָּנוּ לָעַד
וּלְנֵצַח נְצָחִים
וְיִתְהַדַּר בָּנוּ לָעַד
וּלְעוֹלְמֵי עוֹלָמִים.

הָרַחֲמָן
הוּא יְפַרְנְסֵנוּ
בְּכָבוֹד.

הָרַחֲמָן הוּא יִשְׁבּוֹר עֻלֵּנוּ
מֵעַל צַוָּארֵנוּ
וְהוּא יוֹלִיכֵנוּ קוֹמְמִיּוּת לְאַרְצֵנוּ.

הָרַחֲמָן הוּא יִשְׁלַח לָנוּ
בְּרָכָה מְרֻבָּה בַּבַּיִת הַזֶּה
וְעַל שֻׁלְחָן זֶה שֶׁאָכַלְנוּ עָלָיו.

Haraḥaman, hu yishlaḥ lanu	May the Merciful One send us
et Eliyahu Hanavi, zakhur latov,	Elijah the Prophet, whose good deeds we
	remember,
yevaser lanu besorot tovot,	may he bring us good tidings,
yeshu'ot veneḥamot.	deliverance, and comfort.
Haraḥaman, hu yevarekh	May the Merciful One bless
et eretz megureinu	this land in which we dwell
veyagen aleha.	and protect it.
Haraḥaman, hu yevarekh	May the Merciful One bless
et medinat Yisra'el,	the State of Israel,
reishit tzemiḥat ge'ulateinu.	the beginning of the flowering of our redemption.
Haraḥaman, hu yevarekh	May the Merciful One bless
et aḥeinu benei Yisra'el,	(those among) our people, the children of Israel,
hanetunim betzarah	who are in trouble,
veyotzi'em me'afela le'orah.	and bring them out of darkness into light.

Blessings for those at the table.
When the leader is the father and
there are no guests, begin:

Haraḥaman, hu yevarekh	May the Merciful One bless
oti, ve'et ishti, ve'et zari (you may add	me, my wife, and my children,
the Hebrew names of your children),	
ve'et kol asher li...	and all that is mine....

When at the table of parents, begin:

Haraḥaman, hu yevarekh	May the Merciful One bless
et avi, mori,	my father, my teacher,
ba'al habayit hazeh,	the host of this home;

הָרַחֲמָן הוּא יִשְׁלַח לָנוּ
אֶת אֵלִיָּהוּ הַנָּבִיא זָכוּר לַטּוֹב

וִיבַשֶּׂר לָנוּ בְּשׂוֹרוֹת טוֹבוֹת
יְשׁוּעוֹת וְנֶחָמוֹת.

הָרַחֲמָן הוּא יְבָרֵךְ
אֶת־אֶרֶץ מְגוּרֵנוּ
וְיָגֵן עָלֶיהָ.

הָרַחֲמָן הוּא יְבָרֵךְ
אֶת־מְדִינַת יִשְׂרָאֵל
רֵאשִׁית צְמִיחַת גְּאֻלָּתֵנוּ.

הָרַחֲמָן הוּא יְבָרֵךְ
אֶת־אַחֵינוּ בְּנֵי יִשְׂרָאֵל
הַנְּתוּנִים בְּצָרָה
וְיוֹצִיאֵם מֵאֲפֵלָה לְאוֹרָה.

הָרַחֲמָן הוּא יְבָרֵךְ אוֹתִי
וְאֶת אִשְׁתִּי וְאֶת זַרְעִי

וְאֶת־כָּל אֲשֶׁר לִי.

הָרַחֲמָן הוּא יְבָרֵךְ
אֶת־אָבִי מוֹרִי
בַּעַל הַבַּיִת הַזֶּה

ve'et imi, morati,	my mother, my teacher,
ba'alat habayit hazeh,	the hostess of this home;
otam, ve'et beitam, ve'et zar'am,	them, their household, their children
ve'et kol asher lahem...	and everything that is theirs....

**When you are the leader at
another's table, begin:**

Harahaman, hu yevarekh	May the Merciful One bless
et ba'al habayit hazeh	the host of this home,
oto, ve'et ishto ba'alat habayit hazeh	him, his wife, the hostess of this home;
otam ve'et beitam ve'et zar'am	them, their household, their children,
ve'et kol asher lahem	and everything that is theirs...

**When there are guests at the table,
add either the Hebrew names of all
present or this all-inclusive statement:**

ve'et kol hamesubin kan	and all who are seated here.

In all cases, continue:

otanu, ve'et kol asher lanu,	Ours and all that is ours,
kemo shenitbarkhu avoteinu	just as our ancestors were blessed,
Avraham, Yitzhak, veYa'akov—	Abraham, Isaac, and Jacob—
"bakol," "mikol," "kol"	"in all things," "from everything," "with everything,"
ken yevarekh otanu, kulanu yahad	so God may bless us, all of us together
bivrakha shlemah,	with complete blessing,
venomar: Amen.	and let us say: Amen.

Bamarom yelamdu	From on high may there be invoked
aleihem ve'aleinu	upon them and upon us
zekhut shetehei lemishmeret shalom;	the merit to insure peace;
Venisa verakhah me'et Adonai,	Then we shall receive blessing from Adonai

וְאֶת־אִמִּי מוֹרָתִי
בַּעֲלַת הַבַּיִת הַזֶּה,
אוֹתָם וְאֶת־בֵּיתָם וְאֶת־זַרְעָם
וְאֶת כָּל אֲשֶׁר לָהֶם.

הָרַחֲמָן הוּא יְבָרֵךְ
אֶת־בַּעַל הַבַּיִת הַזֶּה,
אוֹתוֹ וְאֶת אִשְׁתּוֹ בַּעֲלַת הַבַּיִת הַזֶּה
אוֹתָם וְאֶת־בֵּיתָם וְאֶת־זַרְעָם
וְאֶת־כָּל־אֲשֶׁר לָהֶם.

אֶת־כָּל־הַמְסֻבִּין כָּאן

אוֹתָנוּ וְאֶת כָּל אֲשֶׁר לָנוּ
כְּמוֹ שֶׁנִּתְבָּרְכוּ אֲבוֹתֵינוּ
אַבְרָהָם יִצְחָק וְיַעֲקֹב:
בַּכֹּל, מִכֹּל, כֹּל.
כֵּן יְבָרֵךְ אוֹתָנוּ כֻּלָּנוּ יַחַד.
בִּבְרָכָה שְׁלֵמָה
וְנֹאמַר אָמֵן:

בַּמָּרוֹם יְלַמְּדוּ
עֲלֵיהֶם וְעָלֵינוּ זְכוּת
שֶׁתְּהֵא לְמִשְׁמֶרֶת שָׁלוֹם
וְנִשָּׂא בְרָכָה מֵאֵת יְיָ

utzedakah me'Elohei yish'einu.   and we shall receive justice from the God of our deliverance.

Ve'nimtza ḥen ve'sekhel tov be'einei Elohim ve'adam. And may we find favor and good understanding in the eyes of God and people.

Haraḥaman, hu yanḥileinu yom shekulo Shabbat, umnuḥa leḥayei ha'olamim. May the Merciful One give us as an inheritance a day that is completely Shabbat and rest in life everlasting.

On Rosh Hodesh add:

Haraḥaman, hu y'ḥadesh aleinu et haḥodesh hazeh letovah velivrakhah. May the Merciful One renew for us this month for good and for blessing.

On festivals add:

Haraḥaman, hu yanḥileinu yom shekulo tov. May the Merciful One give us for an inheritance a day that is completely good.

On Rosh Hashanah add:

Haraḥaman, hu yeḥadesh aleinu et hashanah hazot letovah velivrakhah. May the Merciful One renew for us this year for good and for blessing.

On Sukkot add:

Haraḥaman, hu yakim lanu et sukkat David hanofelet. May the Merciful one restore for us the fallen sukkah of David.

Add at all times:

Haraḥaman, hu yezakeinu limot hamashiaḥ ulḥayei ha'olam haba. May the Merciful One make us worthy of the Messianic Age and the life of the world to come.

וּצְדָקָה מֵאֱלֹהֵי יִשְׁעֵנוּ

וְנִמְצָא חֵן וְשֵׂכֶל טוֹב
בְּעֵינֵי אֱלֹהִים וְאָדָם:
הָרַחֲמָן הוּא יַנְחִילֵנוּ
יוֹם שֶׁכֻּלוֹ שַׁבָּת
וּמְנוּחָה לְחַיֵּי הָעוֹלָמִים.

הָרַחֲמָן הוּא יְחַדֵּשׁ עָלֵינוּ
אֶת־הַחֹדֶשׁ הַזֶּה
לְטוֹבָה וְלִבְרָכָה.

הָרַחֲמָן הוּא יַנְחִילֵנוּ
יוֹם שֶׁכֻּלוֹ טוֹב.

הָרַחֲמָן הוּא יְחַדֵּשׁ עָלֵינוּ
אֶת הַשָּׁנָה הַזֹּאת
לְטוֹבָה וְלִבְרָכָה.

הָרַחֲמָן הוּא יָקִים לָנוּ
אֶת סֻכַּת דָּוִד הַנּוֹפֶלֶת.

הָרַחֲמָן הוּא יְזַכֵּנוּ
לִימוֹת הַמָּשִׁיחַ
וּלְחַיֵּי הָעוֹלָם הַבָּא.

Migdol yeshu'ot malko,	God is a tower of deliverance to the king,
ve'oseh hesed limshiho—	and shows kindness to the anointed One—
leDavid ulzaro ad olam.	to David and his descendants forever.
Oseh shalom bimromav,	God who makes peace in the heavens,
hu ya'aseh shalom	make peace
aleinu, ve'al kol Yisra'el,	for us and for all Israel,
ve'imru: Amen.	and let us say: Amen.
Yeru et Adonai, kedoshav,	Revere Adonai, you (God's) holy ones,
ki ein mahsor lirei'av.	for those who revere God know no want.
Kefirim rashu vera'eivu,	Even young lions may feel want and hunger,
vedorshei Adonai	but those who seek Adonai
lo yahseru khol tov.	shall not be deprived of any good thing.
Hodu l'Adonai ki tov,	Give thanks to Adonai, for God is good,
ki le'olam hasdo.	for God's mercy endures forever.
Potei'ah et yadekha,	You open Your hand,
umasbi'a lekhol hai ratzon.	and satisfy the needs of every living being.
Barukh hagever asher yivtah b'Adonai,	Blessed are those who trust in Adonai,
vehayah Adonai mivtaho.	whose trust is in Adonai.
"Na'ar hayiti gam zakanti,	"I have been young and now I am old,
velo ra'iti tzadik ne'ezav,	Yet I have not seen the righteous forsaken,
vezaro mevakesh lahem."	nor their children begging for bread."
Adonai oz le'amo yiten,	Adonai will give strength to God's people,
Adonai yevarekh et amo vashalom.	Adonai will bless God's people with peace.

מִגְדּוֹל יְשׁוּעוֹת מַלְכּוֹ

וְעֹשֶׂה חֶסֶד לִמְשִׁיחוֹ

לְדָוִד וּלְזַרְעוֹ עַד עוֹלָם:

עֹשֶׂה שָׁלוֹם בִּמְרוֹמָיו

הוּא יַעֲשֶׂה שָׁלוֹם

עָלֵינוּ וְעַל כָּל יִשְׂרָאֵל

וְאִמְרוּ אָמֵן:

יְראוּ אֶת יְיָ קְדֹשָׁיו

כִּי אֵין מַחְסוֹר לִירֵאָיו:

כְּפִירִים רָשׁוּ וְרָעֵבוּ

וְדוֹרְשֵׁי יְיָ

לֹא יַחְסְרוּ כָל טוֹב:

הוֹדוּ לַיְיָ כִּי טוֹב

כִּי לְעוֹלָם חַסְדּוֹ:

פּוֹתֵחַ אֶת יָדֶךָ

וּמַשְׂבִּיעַ לְכָל חַי רָצוֹן:

בָּרוּךְ הַגֶּבֶר אֲשֶׁר יִבְטַח בַּיְיָ

וְהָיָה יְיָ מִבְטַחוֹ:

נַעַר הָיִיתִי גַּם זָקַנְתִּי

וְלֹא רָאִיתִי צַדִּיק נֶעֱזָב

וְזַרְעוֹ מְבַקֶּשׁ לָחֶם:

יְיָ עֹז לְעַמּוֹ יִתֵּן

יְיָ יְבָרֵךְ אֶת עַמּוֹ בַשָּׁלוֹם:

SELECTED BIBLIOGRAPHY OF SHABBAT RESOURCES

The following books and materials contain information and resources for enriching your understanding and observance of the Shabbat Seder.

For Background Reading

Cardin, Nina Beth. *The Tapestry of Jewish Time: A Spiritual Guide to Holidays and Life-Cycle Events.* Springfield, N.J.: Behrman House, 2000.

Friedland, Ronnie, and Edmund Case, eds. *The Guide to Jewish Interfaith Family Life: An InterfaithFamily.com Handbook.* Woodstock, Vt.: Jewish Lights Publishing, 2000.

Garfinkel, Stephen. *Slow Down and Live: A Guide to Shabbat Observance and Enjoyment.* New York: United Synagogue of Conservative Judaism, Department of Youth Activities.

Green, Arthur. *These Are the Words: A Vocabulary of Jewish Spiritual Life.* Woodstock, Vt.: Jewish Lights Publishing, 2000.

Heschel, Abraham Joshua. *The Sabbath.* New York: Farrar, Straus & Giroux, 1975.

Hoffman, Lawrence A., ed. *My People's Prayer Book—Traditional Prayers, Modern Commentaries, Vol. 7: Introduction to Friday Night Shabbat Service.* Woodstock, Vt.: Jewish Lights Publishing, est. pub. 2003.

———. *The Way Into Jewish Prayer.* Woodstock, Vt.: Jewish Lights Publishing, 2000.

Kula, Irwin, and Vanessa L. Ochs, eds. *The Book of Jewish Sacred Practices: CLAL's Guide to Everyday and Holiday Rituals and Blessings.* Woodstock, Vt.: Jewish Lights Publishing, 2000.

Matlins, Stuart M., ed. *The Jewish Lights Spirituality Handbook: A Guide to Understanding, Exploring, and Living a Spiritual Life.* Woodstock, Vt.: Jewish Lights Publishing, 2000.

Sonsino, Rifat. *Six Jewish Spiritual Paths: A Rationalist Looks at Spirituality*. Woodstock, Vt.: Jewish Lights Publishing, 2000.

Strassfeld, Michael; Richard Siegel; and Sharon Strassfeld; eds. *The First Jewish Catalog*. Philadelphia, Pa.: Jewish Publication Society, 1989.

For Family Reading and Doing

Abrams, Judith Z. *Shabbat—A Family Service*. Rockville, Md.: Kar-Ben Copies, 1992.

Artson, Bradley Shavit. *It's a Mitzvah!: Step-By-Step to Jewish Living*. Springfield, N.J.: Behrman House, 1995.

Dardashti, Danielle, and Roni Sarig. *The Jewish Family Fun Book: Holiday Projects, Home Activities, and Travel Ideas with Jewish Themes*. Woodstock, Vt.: Jewish Lights Publishing, 2002.

Elkins, Dov Peretz. *A Shabbat Reader—Universe of Cosmic Joy*. New York: Union of American Hebrew Congregations, 1999.

Greenberg, Irving. *The Jewish Way: Living the Holidays*. New York: Touchstone Books, 1993.

Kahn, Katherine Janus. *Shabbat Fun for Little Hands*. Rockville, Md.: Kar-Ben Copies, 1994.

Perelson, Ruth. *An Invitation to Shabbat*. New York: Union of American Hebrew Congregations, 1997.

Children's Literature

Fishman, Cathy Goldberg. *On Shabbat*. New York: Atheneum, 2001.

Jaffe, Nina. *Tales for the Seventh Day: A Collection of Sabbath Stories*. New York: Scholastic Trade, 2000.

Jules, Jacqueline. *Once Upon A Shabbos*. Rockville, Md.: Kar-Ben Copies, 1998.

Kobre, Faige. *A Sense of Shabbat*. Los Angeles: Torah Aura Productions, 1999.

Kress, Camille. *Tot Shabbat*. New York: Union of American Hebrew Congregations, 1997.

Kripke, Dorothy. *Let's Talk about the Sabbath*. Los Angeles: Alef Design Group, 1999.

Musleah, Rahel, and Michael Klayman. *Sharing Blessings: Children's Stories for Exploring the Spirit of the Jewish Holidays*. Woodstock, Vt.: Jewish Lights Publishing, 1997.

Mykoff, Moshe. *7th Heaven: Celebrating Shabbat with Rebbe Nachman of Breslov*. Woodstock, Vt.: Jewish Lights Publishing, 2003.

Nerlove, Miriam. *Shabbat*. Morton Grove, Ill.: Albert Whitman, 2000.

Rouss, Sylvia A. *Sammy Spider's First Shabbat*. Rockville, Md.: Kar-Ben Copies, 1998.

Schwartz, Amy. *Mrs. Moskowitz and the Sabbath Candlesticks*. Philadelphia, Pa.: Jewish Publication Society, 1991.

Schwartz, Howard, and Barbara Rush. *The Sabbath Lion: A Jewish Folktale from Algeria*. New York: HarperTrophy, 1996.

Simpson, Lesley. *The Shabbat Box*. Rockville, Md.: Kar-Ben Copies, 2001.

Swartz, Daniel J. *Bim and Bom—A Shabbat Tale*. Rockville, Md.: Kar-Ben Copies, 1996.

Topek, Susan Remick. *Shalom, Shabbat: A Book For Havdalah*. Rockville, Md.: Kar-Ben Copies, 1998.

Weilerstein, Sadie Rose. *The Best of K'tonton*. Philadelphia, Pa.: The Jewish Publication Society of America, 1988.

Wickler, Madeline. *Let's Celebrate Shabbat*. Rockville, Md.: Kar-Ben Copies, 1999.

Zerwin, Raymond E., and Audrey Friedman Marcus. *Shabbat Can Be*. New York: Union of American Hebrew Congregations, 1998.

Jewish Calendars

Kar-Ben Copies. Lerner Publishing Group, 1251 Washington Avenue North, Minneapolis, MN 55401. 1-800-4-KARBEN. www.kar-ben.com.

United Synagogue of Conservative Judaism. 155 Fifth Avenue, New York, NY 10010-6802. (212)533-7800. www.uscj.org.

Local Jewish bookstores, synagogues, and mortuaries.

Recipe Books

Brown, Michael. *The Jewish Gardening Cookbook: Growing Plants and Cooking for Holidays and Festivals.* Woodstock, Vt.: Jewish Lights Publishing, 1998.

Cohen, Jayne. *The Gefilte Variations: 200 Inspired Re-Creations of Classics from The Jewish Kitchen, with Menus, Stories and Traditions for the Holidays and Year-Round.* New York: Scribner, 2000.

Friedland, Susan R. *Shabbat Shalom: Recipes and Menus for the Sabbath.* Boston: Little, Brown, 1999.

Song Books

The Book of Songs and Blessings. New York: United Jewish Appeal, 1982.

Pasternak, Velvel. *Shabbat Melodies.* Owings Mills, Md.: Tara Publications, 1978.

Bible Study

Goldstein, Elyse. *ReVisions: Seeing Torah through a Feminist Lens.* Woodstock, Vt.: Jewish Lights Publishing, 2001.

Goldstein, Elyse, ed. *The Women's Torah Commentary: New Insights from Women Rabbis on the 54 Weekly Torah Portions.* Woodstock, Vt.: Jewish Lights Publishing, 2000.

Grishaver, Joel Lurie et al. *Being Torah: A First Book of Torah Texts.* Los Angeles: Torah Aura Productions, 1986.

Lieber, David L., ed. *Etz Hayim: Torah and Commentary.* Philadelphia: the Rabbinical Assembly/the United Synagogue for Conservative Judaism, produced by Jewish Publication Society, 2001.

ABOUT THE FEDERATION OF JEWISH MEN'S CLUBS

The Federation of Jewish Men's Clubs is the male volunteer arm of Conservative/Masorti Judaism.

Designed to "involve Jewish men in Jewish life," the FJMC has been enriching the quality of Jewish life since 1929. Most recent efforts have resulted in *The Ties That Bind,* a dynamic film teaching the mitvah of tefillin and its programmatic component; The World Wide Wrap; and the Hearing Men's Voices Initiative, which consists of a series of books devoted to men's issues. *Building the Faith: A Book of Inclusion for Dual Faith Families,* one of our most recent and far-reaching publications, was released in the fall of 2001.

For a complete list of our publications, films, and services visit our webpage at www.fjmc.org.

ABOUT THE UNIVERSITY OF JUDASIM

The University of Judaism in Los Angeles is a fully accredited institution of higher Jewish learning that includes a four year undergraduate College of Arts and Sciences, the Ziegler School of Rabbinic Studies, graduate professional schools in Jewish education and business administration, an extensive Department of Continuing Education, as well as a variety of cultural arts programs and academic think tanks. The Whizin Center for the Jewish Future hosts the Whizin Institute for Jewish Family Life, a leading resource for Jewish family education, and Synagogue 2000, a transdenominational institute for the synagogue of the 21st century.

Notes

Notes

Notes

Notes

Notes

About JEWISH LIGHTS Publishing

People of all faiths and backgrounds yearn for books that attract, engage, educate, and spiritually inspire.

Our principal goal is to stimulate thought and help all people learn about who the Jewish People are, where they come from, and what the future can be made to hold. While people of our diverse Jewish heritage are the primary audience, our books speak to people in the Christian world as well and will broaden their understanding of Judaism and the roots of their own faith.

We bring to you authors who are at the forefront of spiritual thought and experience. While each has something different to say, they all say it in a voice that you can hear.

Our books are designed to welcome you and then to engage, stimulate, and inspire. We judge our success not only by whether or not our books are beautiful and commercially successful, but by whether or not they make a difference in your life.

We at Jewish Lights take great care to produce beautiful books that present meaningful spiritual content in a form that reflects the art of making high quality books. Therefore, we want to acknowledge those who contributed to the production of this book.

Stuart M. Matlins, Publisher

PRODUCTION
Tim Holtz, Martha McKinney & Bridgett Taylor

EDITORIAL
Amanda Dupuis, Polly Short Mahoney,
Lauren Seidman & Emily Wichland

COVER DESIGN
Bridgett Taylor

TYPESETTING
Peter Bertolami, Brookfield, Connecticut

JACKET / TEXT PRINTING & BINDING
Transcontinental Printing, Peterborough, Ontario

Spirituality

The Dance of the Dolphin
Finding Prayer, Perspective and Meaning in the Stories of Our Lives
by *Karyn D. Kedar*

Helps you decode the three "languages" we all must learn—prayer, perspective, meaning—to weave the seemingly ordinary and extraordinary together.
6 x 9, 176 pp, HC, ISBN 1-58023-154-3 **$19.95**

Does the Soul Survive?
A Jewish Journey to Belief in Afterlife, Past Lives & Living with Purpose
by *Rabbi Elie Kaplan Spitz*; Foreword by *Brian L. Weiss, M.D.*

Spitz relates his own experiences and those shared with him by people he has worked with as a rabbi, and shows us that belief in afterlife and past lives, so often approached with reluctance, is in fact true to Jewish tradition.
6 x 9, 288 pp, Quality PB, ISBN 1-58023-165-9 **$16.95**; HC, ISBN 1-58023-094-6 **$21.95**

The Gift of Kabbalah
Discovering the Secrets of Heaven, Renewing Your Life on Earth
by *Tamar Frankiel, Ph.D.*

Makes accessible the mysteries of Kabbalah. Traces Kabbalah's evolution in Judaism and shows us its most important gift: a way of revealing the connection between our "everyday" life and the spiritual oneness of the universe. 6 x 9, 256 pp, HC, ISBN 1-58023-108-X **$21.95**

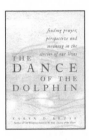 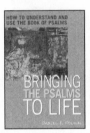   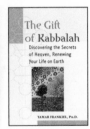

God Whispers: *Stories of the Soul, Lessons of the Heart*
by Karyn D. Kedar 6 x 9, 176 pp, Quality PB, ISBN 1-58023-088-1 **$15.95**

Bringing the Psalms to Life: *How to Understand and Use the Book of Psalms*
by Rabbi Daniel F. Polish
6 x 9, 208 pp, Quality PB, ISBN 1-58023-157-8 **$16.95**; HC, ISBN 1-58023-077-6 **$21.95**

The Empty Chair: *Finding Hope and Joy—*
Timeless Wisdom from a Hasidic Master, Rebbe Nachman of Breslov AWARD WINNER!
4 x 6, 128 pp, Deluxe PB, 2-color text, ISBN 1-879045-67-2 **$9.95**

The Gentle Weapon: *Prayers for Everyday and Not-So-Everyday Moments*
Adapted from the Wisdom of Rebbe Nachman of Breslov
4 x 6, 144 pp, Deluxe PB, 2-color text, ISBN 1-58023-022-9 **$9.95**

Or phone, fax, mail or e-mail to: **JEWISH LIGHTS** Publishing
Sunset Farm Offices, Route 4 • P.O. Box 237 • Woodstock, Vermont 05091
Tel: (802) 457-4000 • Fax: (802) 457-4004 • www.jewishlights.com
Credit card orders: **(800) 962-4544** (8:30AM–5:30PM ET Monday–Friday)
Generous discounts on quantity orders. SATISFACTION GUARANTEED. Prices subject to change.

Spirituality/Jewish Meditation

Aleph-Bet Yoga
Embodying the Hebrew Letters for Physical and Spiritual Well-Being
by *Steven A. Rapp*; Foreword by *Tamar Frankiel & Judy Greenfeld*; Preface by *Hart Lazer*

Blends aspects of hatha yoga and the shapes of the Hebrew letters. Connects yoga practice with Jewish spiritual life. Easy-to-follow instructions, b/w photos.

7 x 10, 128 pp, Quality PB, b/w photos, ISBN 1-58023-162-4 **$16.95**

The Rituals & Practices of a Jewish Life
A Handbook for Personal Spiritual Renewal
by *Rabbi Kerry M. Olitzky* and *Rabbi Daniel Judson*; Foreword by *Vanessa L. Ochs*; Illustrated by *Joel Moskowitz*

This easy-to-use handbook explains the why, what, and how of ten specific areas of Jewish ritual and practice: morning and evening blessings, covering the head, blessings throughout the day, daily prayer, tefillin, tallit and *tallit katan*, Torah study, kashrut, *mikvah*, and entering Shabbat.

6 x 9, 272 pp, Quality PB, Illus., ISBN 1-58023-169-1 **$18.95**

  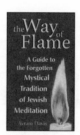  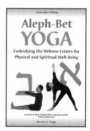

Discovering Jewish Meditation: *Instruction & Guidance for Learning an Ancient Spiritual Practice* by Nan Fink Gefen 6 x 9, 208 pp, Quality PB, ISBN 1-58023-067-9 **$16.95**

The Handbook of Jewish Meditation Practices: *A Guide for Enriching the Sabbath and Other Days of Your Life* by Rabbi David A. Cooper
6 x 9, 208 pp, Quality PB, ISBN 1-58023-102-0 **$16.95**

Meditation from the Heart of Judaism: *Today's Teachers Share Their Practices, Techniques, and Faith* Ed. by Avram Davis 6 x 9, 256 pp, Quality PB, ISBN 1-58023-049-0 **$16.95**

The Way of Flame: *A Guide to the Forgotten Mystical Tradition of Jewish Meditation* by Avram Davis 4½ x 8, 176 pp, Quality PB, ISBN 1-58023-060-1 **$15.95**

Minding the Temple of the Soul: *Balancing Body, Mind, and Spirit through Traditional Jewish Prayer, Movement, and Meditation* by Tamar Frankiel and Judy Greenfeld
7 x 10, 184 pp, Quality PB, Illus., ISBN 1-879045-64-8 **$16.95**

Entering the Temple of Dreams: *Jewish Prayers, Movements, and Meditations for the End of the Day* by Tamar Frankiel and Judy Greenfeld
7 x 10, 192 pp, Illus., Quality PB, ISBN 1-58023-079-2 **$16.95**

Spirituality

My People's Prayer Book: *Traditional Prayers, Modern Commentaries*
Ed. by *Dr. Lawrence A. Hoffman*

Provides a diverse and exciting commentary to the traditional liturgy, helping modern men and women find new wisdom in Jewish prayer, and bring liturgy into their lives. Each book includes Hebrew text, modern translation, and commentaries *from all perspectives* of the Jewish world.

Vol. 1—*The Sh'ma and Its Blessings*, 7 x 10, 168 pp, HC, ISBN 1-879045-79-6 **$23.95**
Vol. 2—*The Amidah*, 7 x 10, 240 pp, HC, ISBN 1-879045-80-X **$23.95**
Vol. 3—*P'sukei D'zimrah* (Morning Psalms), 7 x 10, 240 pp, HC, ISBN 1-879045-81-8 **$24.95**
Vol. 4—*Seder K'riat Hatorah* (The Torah Service), 7 x 10, 264 pp, HC, ISBN 1-879045-82-6 **$23.95**
Vol. 5—*Birkhot Hashachar* (Morning Blessings), 7 x 10, 240 pp, HC, ISBN 1-879045-83-4 **$24.95**
Vol. 6—*Tachanun and Concluding Prayers*, 7 x 10, 240 pp, HC, ISBN 1-879045-84-2 **$24.95**

 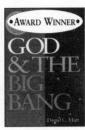   

Six Jewish Spiritual Paths: *A Rationalist Looks at Spirituality*
by Rabbi Rifat Sonsino
6 x 9, 208 pp, Quality PB, ISBN 1-58023-167-5 **$16.95**; HC, ISBN 1-58023-095-4 **$21.95**

Becoming a Congregation of Learners
Learning as a Key to Revitalizing Congregational Life by Isa Aron, Ph.D.;
Foreword by Rabbi Lawrence A. Hoffman, Co-Developer, Synagogue 2000
6 x 9, 304 pp, Quality PB, ISBN 1-58023-089-X **$19.95**

Self, Struggle & Change
Family Conflict Stories in Genesis and Their Healing Insights for Our Lives
by Dr. Norman J. Cohen 6 x 9, 224 pp, Quality PB, ISBN 1-879045-66-4 **$16.95**

Voices from Genesis: *Guiding Us through the Stages of Life*
by Dr. Norman J. Cohen 6 x 9, 192 pp, Quality PB, ISBN 1-58023-118-7 **$16.95**

Ancient Secrets: *Using the Stories of the Bible to Improve Our Everyday Lives*
by Rabbi Levi Meier, Ph.D. 5½ x 8½, 288 pp, Quality PB, ISBN 1-58023-064-4 **$16.95**

The Business Bible: *10 New Commandments for Bringing Spirituality &*
Ethical Values into the Workplace
by Rabbi Wayne Dosick 5½ x 8½, 208 pp, Quality PB, ISBN 1-58023-101-2 **$14.95**

Being God's Partner: *How to Find the Hidden Link Between Spirituality and Your Work*
by Rabbi Jeffrey K. Salkin; Intro. by Norman Lear AWARD WINNER!
6 x 9, 192 pp, Quality PB, ISBN 1-879045-65-6 **$16.95**; HC, ISBN 1-879045-37-0 **$19.95**

God & the Big Bang
Discovering Harmony Between Science & Spirituality AWARD WINNER!
by Daniel C. Matt 6 x 9, 224 pp, Quality PB, ISBN 1-879045-89-3 **$16.95**

Soul Judaism: *Dancing with God into a New Era*
by Rabbi Wayne Dosick 5½ x 8½, 304 pp, Quality PB, ISBN 1-58023-053-9 **$16.95**

Finding Joy: *A Practical Spiritual Guide to Happiness* AWARD WINNER!
by Rabbi Dannel I. Schwartz with Mark Hass
6 x 9, 192 pp, Quality PB, ISBN 1-58023-009-1 **$14.95**; HC, ISBN 1-879045-53-2 **$19.95**

Healing/Wellness/Recovery

Jewish Paths toward Healing and Wholeness
A Personal Guide to Dealing with Suffering
by *Rabbi Kerry M. Olitzky*; Foreword by *Debbie Friedman*

Why me? Why do we suffer? How can we heal? Grounded in personal experience with illness and Jewish spiritual traditions, this book provides healing rituals, psalms and prayers that help readers initiate a dialogue with God, to guide them along the complicated path of healing and wholeness. 6 x 9, 192 pp, Quality PB, ISBN 1-58023-068-7 **$15.95**

Healing of Soul, Healing of Body
Spiritual Leaders Unfold the Strength & Solace in Psalms
Ed. by *Rabbi Simkha Y. Weintraub, CSW*, for The National Center for Jewish Healing

For those who are facing illness and those who care for them. Inspiring commentaries on ten psalms for healing by eminent spiritual leaders reflecting all Jewish movements make the power of the psalms accessible to all.
6 x 9, 128 pp, Quality PB, Illus., 2-color text, ISBN 1-879045-31-1 **$14.95**

Jewish Pastoral Care
A Practical Handbook from Traditional and Contemporary Sources
Ed. by *Rabbi Dayle A. Friedman*

Gives today's Jewish pastoral counselors practical guidelines based in the Jewish tradition.
6 x 9, 464 pp, HC, ISBN 1-58023-078-4 **$35.00**

Twelve Jewish Steps to Recovery: *A Personal Guide to Turning from Alcoholism & Other Addictions—Drugs, Food, Gambling, Sex . . .* by Rabbi Kerry M. Olitzky & Stuart A. Copans, M.D. Preface by Abraham J. Twerski, M.D.; "Getting Help" by JACS Foundation 6 x 9, 144 pp, Quality PB, ISBN 1-879045-09-5 **$14.95**

One Hundred Blessings Every Day: *Daily Twelve Step Recovery Affirmations, Exercises for Personal Growth & Renewal Reflecting Seasons of the Jewish Year* by Rabbi Kerry M. Olitzky 4½ x 6½, 432 pp, Quality PB, ISBN 1-879045-30-3 **$14.95**

Recovery from Codependence: *A Jewish Twelve Steps Guide to Healing Your Soul* by Rabbi Kerry M. Olitzky 6 x 9, 160 pp, Quality PB, ISBN 1-879045-32-X **$13.95**

Renewed Each Day: *Daily Twelve Step Recovery Meditations Based on the Bible* by Rabbi Kerry M. Olitzky & Aaron Z. *Vol. I: Genesis & Exodus*; *Vol. II: Leviticus, Numbers and Deuteronomy*
Vol. I: 6 x 9, 224 pp, Quality PB, ISBN 1-879045-12-5 **$14.95**
Vol. II: 6 x 9, 280 pp, Quality PB, ISBN 1-879045-13-3 **$14.95**

Spirituality—The Kushner Series
Books by Lawrence Kushner

The Way Into Jewish Mystical Tradition
Explains the principles of Jewish mystical thinking, their religious and spiritual significance, and how they relate to our lives. A book that allows us to experience and understand the Jewish mystical approach to our place in the world.
6 x 9, 224 pp, HC, ISBN 1-58023-029-6 **$21.95**

Jewish Spirituality: *A Brief Introduction for Christians*
Addresses Christian's questions, revealing the essence of Judaism in a way that people whose own tradition traces its roots to Judaism can understand and appreciate.
5½ x 8½, 112 pp, Quality PB, ISBN 1-58023-150-0 **$12.95**

Eyes Remade for Wonder: *The Way of Jewish Mysticism and Sacred Living*
A Lawrence Kushner Reader Intro. by *Thomas Moore*

Whether you are new to Kushner or a devoted fan, you'll find inspiration here. With samplings from each of Kushner's works, and a generous amount of new material, this book is to be read and reread, each time discovering deeper layers of meaning in our lives.
6 x 9, 240 pp, Quality PB, ISBN 1-58023-042-3 **$18.95**; HC, ISBN 1-58023-014-8 **$23.95**

   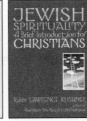 

Invisible Lines of Connection: *Sacred Stories of the Ordinary* AWARD WINNER!
5½ x 8½, 160 pp, Quality PB, ISBN 1-879045-98-2 **$15.95**

Honey from the Rock: *An Introduction to Jewish Mysticism* SPECIAL ANNIVERSARY EDITION
6 x 9, 176 pp, Quality PB, ISBN 1-58023-073-3 **$15.95**

The Book of Letters: *A Mystical Hebrew Alphabet* AWARD WINNER!
Popular HC Edition, 6 x 9, 80 pp, 2-color text, ISBN 1-879045-00-1 **$24.95**; *Deluxe Gift Edition,* 9 x 12, 80 pp, HC, 4-color text, ornamentation, slipcase, ISBN 1-879045-01-X **$79.95**; *Collector's Limited Edition,* 9 x 12, 80 pp, HC, gold-embossed pages, hand-assembled slipcase. With silkscreened print. Limited to 500 signed and numbered copies, ISBN 1-879045-04-4 **$349.00**

The Book of Words: *Talking Spiritual Life, Living Spiritual Talk* AWARD WINNER!
6 x 9, 160 pp, Quality PB, 2-color text, ISBN 1-58023-020-2 **$16.95**; HC, ISBN 1-879045-35-4 **$21.95**

God Was in This Place & I, i Did Not Know: *Finding Self, Spirituality and Ultimate Meaning*
6 x 9, 192 pp, Quality PB, ISBN 1-879045-33-8 **$16.95**

The River of Light: *Jewish Mystical Awareness* SPECIAL ANNIVERSARY EDITION
6 x 9, 192 pp, Quality PB, ISBN 1-58023-096-2 **$16.95**

Because Nothing Looks Like God
by Lawrence and Karen Kushner; Full-color illus. by Dawn W. Majewski
11 x 8½, 32 pp, HC, Full-color illus., ISBN 1-58023-092-X **$16.95** For ages 4 & up

Life Cycle/Grief/Divorce

Divorce Is a Mitzvah: *A Practical Guide to Finding Wholeness and Holiness When Your Marriage Dies*
by *Rabbi Perry Netter;*
Afterword—"Afterwards: New Jewish Divorce Rituals"—by *Rabbi Laura Geller*

What does Judaism tell you about divorce? This first-of-its-kind handbook provides practical wisdom from biblical and rabbinic teachings and modern psychological research, as well as information and strength from a Jewish perspective for those experiencing the challenging life-transition of divorce. 6 x 9, 224 pp, Quality PB, ISBN 1-58023-172-1 **$16.95**

Against the Dying of the Light
A Parent's Story of Love, Loss and Hope
by *Leonard Fein*

The sudden death of a child. A personal tragedy beyond description. Rage and despair deeper than sorrow. What can come from it? Raw wisdom and defiant hope. In this unusual exploration of heartbreak and healing, Fein chronicles the sudden death of his 30-year-old daughter and reveals what the progression of grief can teach each one of us.
5½ x 8½, 176 pp, HC, ISBN 1-58023-110-1 **$19.95**

Mourning & Mitzvah, 2nd Ed.: *A Guided Journal for Walking the Mourner's Path through Grief to Healing* with *Over 60 Guided Exercises*
by *Anne Brener, L.C.S.W.*

For those who mourn a death, for those who would help them, for those who face a loss of any kind, Brener teaches us the power and strength available to us in the fully experienced mourning process. Revised and expanded. 7½ x 9, 304 pp, Quality PB, ISBN 1-58023-113-6 **$19.95**

Grief in Our Seasons: *A Mourner's Kaddish Companion*
by *Rabbi Kerry M. Olitzky*

A wise and inspiring selection of sacred Jewish writings and a simple, powerful ancient ritual for mourners to read each day, to help hold the memory of their loved ones in their hearts. Offers a comforting, step-by-step daily link to saying Kaddish.
4½ x 6½, 448 pp, Quality PB, ISBN 1-879045-55-9 **$15.95**

Tears of Sorrow, Seeds of Hope
A Jewish Spiritual Companion for Infertility and Pregnancy Loss
by Rabbi Nina Beth Cardin   6 x 9, 192 pp, HC, ISBN 1-58023-017-2 **$19.95**

A Time to Mourn, A Time to Comfort
A Guide to Jewish Bereavement and Comfort
by Dr. Ron Wolfson   7 x 9, 336 pp, Quality PB, ISBN 1-879045-96-6 **$18.95**

When a Grandparent Dies
A Kid's Own Remembering Workbook for Dealing with Shiva and the Year Beyond
by Nechama Liss-Levinson, Ph.D.
8 x 10, 48 pp, HC, Illus., 2-color text, ISBN 1-879045-44-3 **$15.95**   **For ages 7–13**

Theology/Philosophy

Love and Terror in the God Encounter
The Theological Legacy of Rabbi Joseph B. Soloveitchik
by *Dr. David Hartman*

Renowned scholar David Hartman explores the sometimes surprising intersection of Soloveitchik's rootedness in halakhic tradition with his genuine responsiveness to modern Western theology. An engaging look at one of the most important Jewish thinkers of the twentieth century.
6 x 9, 240 pp, HC, ISBN 1-58023-112-8 **$25.00**

These Are the Words: *A Vocabulary of Jewish Spiritual Life*
by *Arthur Green*

What are the most essential ideas, concepts and terms that an educated person needs to know about Judaism? From *Adonai* (My Lord) to *zekhut* (merit), this enlightening and entertaining journey through Judaism teaches us the 149 core Hebrew words that constitute the basic vocabulary of Jewish spiritual life. 6 x 9, 304 pp, Quality PB, ISBN 1-58023-107-1 **$18.95**

Broken Tablets: *Restoring the Ten Commandments and Ourselves*
Ed. by *Rabbi Rachel S. Mikva*; Intro. by *Rabbi Lawrence Kushner* AWARD WINNER!

Twelve outstanding spiritual leaders each share profound and personal thoughts about these biblical commands and why they have such a special hold on us.
6 x 9, 192 pp, Quality PB, ISBN 1-58023-158-6 **$16.95**; HC, ISBN 1-58023-066-0 **$21.95**

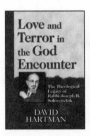   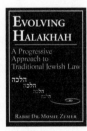 

A Heart of Many Rooms: *Celebrating the Many Voices within Judaism* AWARD WINNER!
by Dr. David Hartman 6 x 9, 352 pp, Quality PB, ISBN 1-58023-156-X **$19.95**; HC, ISBN 1-58023-048-2 **$24.95**

A Living Covenant: *The Innovative Spirit in Traditional Judaism* AWARD WINNER!
by Dr. David Hartman 6 x 9, 368 pp, Quality PB, ISBN 1-58023-011-3 **$18.95**

Evolving Halakhah: *A Progressive Approach to Traditional Jewish Law*
by Rabbi Dr. Moshe Zemer 6 x 9, 480 pp, HC, ISBN 1-58023-002-4 **$40.00**

The Death of Death: *Resurrection and Immortality in Jewish Thought* AWARD WINNER!
by Dr. Neil Gillman 6 x 9, 336 pp, Quality PB, ISBN 1-58023-081-4 **$18.95**

The Last Trial: *On the Legends and Lore of the Command to Abraham to Offer Isaac as a Sacrifice* by Shalom Spiegel 6 x 9, 208 pp, Quality PB, ISBN 1-879045-29-X **$17.95**

Tormented Master: *The Life and Spiritual Quest of Rabbi Nahman of Bratslav*
by Dr. Arthur Green 6 x 9, 416 pp, Quality PB, ISBN 1-879045-11-7 **$18.95**

The Earth Is the Lord's: *The Inner World of the Jew in Eastern Europe*
by Abraham Joshua Heschel 5½ x 8, 128 pp, Quality PB, ISBN 1-879045-42-7 **$14.95**

A Passion for Truth: *Despair and Hope in Hasidism* by Abraham Joshua Heschel
5½ x 8, 352 pp, Quality PB, ISBN 1-879045-41-9 **$18.95**

Your Word Is Fire: *The Hasidic Masters on Contemplative Prayer* Ed. by Dr. Arthur Green and Dr. Barry W. Holtz 6 x 9, 160 pp, Quality PB, ISBN 1-879045-25-7 **$15.95**

Children's Spirituality

Cain & Abel   AWARD WINNER!
Finding the Fruits of Peace
by *Sandy Eisenberg Sasso*
Full-color illus. by *Joani Keller Rothenberg*

For ages 5 & up

A sensitive recasting of the ancient tale shows we have the power to deal with anger in positive ways. Provides questions for kids and adults to explore together. "Editor's Choice"—American Library Association's *Booklist*

9 x 12, 32 pp, HC, Full-color illus., ISBN 1-58023-123-3 **$16.95**

For Heaven's Sake   AWARD WINNER!
For ages 4 & up

by *Sandy Eisenberg Sasso*; Full-color illus. by *Kathryn Kunz Finney*
Everyone talked about heaven, but no one would say what heaven was or how to find it. So Isaiah decides to find out. 9 x 12, 32 pp, HC, Full-color illus., ISBN 1-58023-054-7 **$16.95**

God Said Amen   AWARD WINNER!
For ages 4 & up

by *Sandy Eisenberg Sasso*; Full-color illus. by *Avi Katz*
Inspiring tale of two kingdoms: one overflowing with water but without oil to light its lamps; the other blessed with oil but no water to grow its gardens. The kingdoms' rulers ask God for help but are too stubborn to ask each other. Shows that we need only reach out to each other to find God's answer to our prayers. 9 x 12, 32 pp, HC, Full-color illus., ISBN 1-58023-080-6 **$16.95**

God in Between   AWARD WINNER!
For ages 4 & up

by *Sandy Eisenberg Sasso*; Full-color illus. by *Sally Sweetland*
If you wanted to find God, where would you look? This magical, mythical tale teaches that God can be found where we are: within all of us and the relationships between us.
9 x 12, 32 pp, HC, Full-color illus., ISBN 1-879045-86-9 **$16.95**

Noah's Wife: *The Story of Naamah*
For ages 4 & up

by *Sandy Eisenberg Sasso*; Full-color illus. by *Bethanne Andersen* AWARD WINNER!
Opens religious imaginations to new ideas about the story of the Flood. When God tells Noah to bring the animals onto the ark, God also calls on Naamah, Noah's wife, to save each plant on Earth. 9 x 12, 32 pp, HC, Full-color illus., ISBN 1-58023-134-9 **$16.95**

But God Remembered   AWARD WINNER!
Stories of Women from Creation to the Promised Land
For ages 8 & up

by *Sandy Eisenberg Sasso*; Full-color illus. by *Bethanne Andersen*
Vibrantly brings to life four stories of courageous and strong women from ancient tradition; all teach important values through their actions and faith.
9 x 12, 32 pp, HC, Full-color illus., ISBN 1-879045-43-5 **$16.95**

Children's Spirituality

In Our Image
God's First Creatures   AWARD WINNER!
by *Nancy Sohn Swartz*
Full-color illus. by *Melanie Hall*

For ages 4 & up

A playful new twist on the Creation story—from the perspective of the animals. Celebrates the interconnectedness of nature and the harmony of all living things. "The vibrantly colored illustrations nearly leap off the page in this delightful interpretation." —*School Library Journal*
9 x 12, 32 pp, HC, Full-color illus., ISBN 1-879045-99-0 **$16.95**

 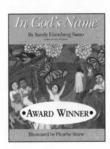 

God's Paintbrush   AWARD WINNER!
by *Sandy Eisenberg Sasso*; Full-color illus. by *Annette Compton*

For ages 4 & up

Invites children of all faiths and backgrounds to encounter God openly in their own lives. Wonderfully interactive; provides questions adult and child can explore together at the end of each episode. 11 x 8½, 32 pp, HC, Full-color illus., ISBN 1-879045-22-2 **$16.95**

*Also available: A Teacher's Guide: **A Guide for Jewish & Christian Educators and Parents***
8½ x 11, 32 pp, PB, ISBN 1-879045-57-5 **$8.95**

God's Paintbrush Celebration Kit 9½ x 12, HC, Includes 5 sessions/40 full-color Activity Sheets and Teacher Folder with complete instructions, ISBN 1-58023-050-4 **$21.95**

In God's Name   AWARD WINNER!
by *Sandy Eisenberg Sasso*; Full-color illus. by *Phoebe Stone*

For ages 4 & up

Like an ancient myth in its poetic text and vibrant illustrations, this award-winning modern fable about the search for God's name celebrates the diversity and, at the same time, the unity of all people. 9 x 12, 32 pp, HC, Full-color illus., ISBN 1-879045-26-5 **$16.95**

What Is God's Name? (A Board Book)
An abridged board book version of award-winning *In God's Name.*
5 x 5, 24 pp, Board, Full-color illus., ISBN 1-893361-10-1 **$7.95** A SKYLIGHT PATHS Book

For ages 0–4

The 11th Commandment: *Wisdom from Our Children*
by *The Children of America*   AWARD WINNER!

For all ages

"If there were an Eleventh Commandment, what would it be?" Children of many religious denominations across America answer this question—in their own drawings and words. "A rare book of spiritual celebration for all people, of all ages, for all time."—*Bookviews*
8 x 10, 48 pp, HC, Full-color illus., ISBN 1-879045-46-X **$16.95**

Children's Spirituality

Because Nothing Looks Like God
by *Lawrence and Karen Kushner*
Full-color illus. by *Dawn W. Majewski*

For ages 4 & up

MULTICULTURAL, NONDENOMINATIONAL, NONSECTARIAN

What is God like? The first collaborative work by husband-and-wife team Lawrence and Karen Kushner introduces children to the possibilities of spiritual life. Real-life examples of happiness and sadness—from goodnight stories, to the hope and fear felt the first time at bat, to the closing moments of life—invite us to explore, together with our children, the questions we all have about God, no matter what our age.

11 x 8½, 32 pp, HC, Full-color illus., ISBN 1-58023-092-X **$16.95**

Also available: **Teacher's Guide,** 8½ x 11, 22 pp, PB, ISBN 1-58023-140-3 **$6.95** For ages 5–8

Where Is God?
What Does God Look Like?
How Does God Make Things Happen? (Board Books)

For ages 0–4

by *Lawrence and Karen Kushner;* Full-color illus. by *Dawn W. Majewski*

Gently invites children to become aware of God's presence all around them. Three board books abridged from *Because Nothing Looks Like God* by Lawrence and Karen Kushner.
Each 5 x 5, 24 pp, Board, Full-color illus. **$7.95** SKYLIGHT PATHS Books

Sharing Blessings
Children's Stories for Exploring the Spirit of the Jewish Holidays

For ages 6 & up

by *Rahel Musleah* and *Rabbi Michael Klayman;* Full-color illus.

What is the spiritual message of each of the Jewish holidays? How do we teach it to our children? Through stories about one family's life, *Sharing Blessings* explores ways to get into the *spirit* of thirteen different holidays.
8½ x 11, 64 pp, HC, Full-color illus., ISBN 1-879045-71-0 **$18.95**

The Book of Miracles   AWARD WINNER!
A Young Person's Guide to Jewish Spiritual Awareness
by *Lawrence Kushner*

For ages 9 & up

Introduces kids to a way of everyday spiritual thinking to last a lifetime. Kushner, whose award-winning books have brought spirituality to life for countless adults, now shows young people how to use Judaism as a foundation on which to build their lives.
6 x 9, 96 pp, HC, 2-color illus., ISBN 1-879045-78-8 **$16.95**

Women's Spirituality

The Women's Torah Commentary: *New Insights from Women Rabbis on the 54 Weekly Torah Portions* Ed. by *Rabbi Elyse Goldstein*

For the first time, women rabbis provide a commentary on the entire Five Books of Moses. More than twenty-five years after the first woman was ordained a rabbi in America, these inspiring teachers bring their rich perspectives to bear on the biblical text. In a week-by-week format; a perfect gift for others, or for yourself. 6 x 9, 496 pp, HC, ISBN 1-58023-076-8 **$34.95**

Moonbeams: *A Hadassah Rosh Hodesh Guide*

Ed. by *Carol Diament, Ph.D.*

This hands-on "idea book" focuses on *Rosh Hodesh*, the festival of the new moon, as a source of spiritual growth for Jewish women. A complete sourcebook that will initiate or rejuvenate women's study groups, it is also perfect for women preparing for *bat mitzvah*, or for anyone interested in learning more about *Rosh Hodesh* observance and what it has to offer. 8½ x 11, 240 pp, Quality PB, ISBN 1-58023-099-7 **$20.00**

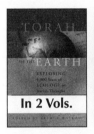    

Lifecycles In Two Volumes **AWARD WINNERS!**
V. 1: *Jewish Women on Life Passages & Personal Milestones*
Ed. and with Intros. by Rabbi Debra Orenstein
V. 2: *Jewish Women on Biblical Themes in Contemporary Life*
Ed. and with Intros. by Rabbi Debra Orenstein and Rabbi Jane Rachel Litman
V. 1: 6 x 9, 480 pp, Quality PB, ISBN 1-58023-018-0 **$19.95**
V. 2: 6 x 9, 464 pp, Quality PB, ISBN 1-58023-019-9 **$19.95**

ReVisions: *Seeing Torah through a Feminist Lens* AWARD WINNER!
by Rabbi Elyse Goldstein 5½ x 8½, 224 pp, Quality PB, ISBN 1-58023-117-9 **$16.95**;
208 pp, HC, ISBN 1-58023-047-4 **$19.95**

The Year Mom Got Religion: *One Woman's Midlife Journey into Judaism*
by Lee Meyerhoff Hendler 6 x 9, 208 pp, Quality PB, ISBN 1-58023-070-9 **$15.95**

Ecology

Torah of the Earth: *Exploring 4,000 Years of Ecology in Jewish Thought*
In 2 Volumes Ed. by *Rabbi Arthur Waskow*

An invaluable key to understanding the intersection of ecology and Judaism. Leading scholars provide a guided tour of Jewish ecological thought.
Vol. 1: *Biblical Israel & Rabbinic Judaism*, 6 x 9, 272 pp, Quality PB, ISBN 1-58023-086-5 **$19.95**
Vol. 2: *Zionism & Eco-Judaism*, 6 x 9, 336 pp, Quality PB, ISBN 1-58023-087-3 **$19.95**

Ecology & the Jewish Spirit: *Where Nature & the Sacred Meet* Ed. and with Intros.
by Ellen Bernstein 6 x 9, 288 pp, Quality PB, ISBN 1-58023-082-2 **$16.95**

The Jewish Gardening Cookbook: *Growing Plants & Cooking for Holidays & Festivals*
by Michael Brown 6 x 9, 224 pp, Illus., Quality PB, ISBN 1-58023-116-0 **$16.95**;
HC, ISBN 1-58023-004-0 **$21.95**

Spirituality & More

The Jewish Lights Spirituality Handbook
A Guide to Understanding, Exploring & Living a Spiritual Life
Ed. by *Stuart M. Matlins, Editor in Chief, Jewish Lights Publishing*

Rich, creative material from over fifty spiritual leaders on every aspect of Jewish spirituality today: prayer, meditation, mysticism, study, rituals, special days, the everyday, and more.
6 x 9, 456 pp, Quality PB, ISBN 1-58023-093-8 **$18.95**; HC, ISBN 1-58023-100-4 **$24.95**

The Story of the Jews: *A 4,000-Year Adventure—A Graphic History Book*
Written and illustrated by *Stan Mack*

Through witty cartoons and accurate narrative, illustrates the major characters and events that have shaped the Jewish people and culture. For all ages.
6 x 9, 304 pp, Quality PB, Illus., ISBN 1-58023-155-1 **$16.95**

The Jewish Prophet: *Visionary Words from Moses and Miriam to Henrietta Szold and A. J. Heschel*
by *Rabbi Dr. Michael J. Shire*

This beautifully illustrated collection of Jewish prophecy features the lives and teachings of thirty men and women, from biblical times to modern day. Provides an inspiring and informative description of the role each played in their own time, and an explanation of why we should know about them in our time. Illustrated with illuminations from medieval Hebrew manuscripts.
6½ x 8½, 128 pp, HC, 123 full-color illus., ISBN 1-58023-168-3 **$25.00**

 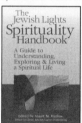   

The Enneagram and Kabbalah: *Reading Your Soul*
by Rabbi Howard A. Addison 6 x 9, 176 pp, Quality PB, ISBN 1-58023-001-6 **$15.95**

Cast in God's Image: *Discover Your Personality Type Using the Enneagram and Kabbalah*
by Rabbi Howard A. Addison 7 x 9, 176 pp, Quality PB, ISBN 1-58023-124-1 **$16.95**

Mystery Midrash: *An Anthology of Jewish Mystery & Detective Fiction* AWARD WINNER!
Ed. by Lawrence W. Raphael 6 x 9, 304 pp, Quality PB, ISBN 1-58023-055-5 **$16.95**

Criminal Kabbalah: *An Intriguing Anthology of Jewish Mystery & Detective Fiction*
Ed. by Lawrence W. Raphael; Foreword by Laurie R. King
6 x 9, 256 pp, Quality PB, ISBN 1-58023-109-8 **$16.95**

Sacred Intentions: *Daily Inspiration to Strengthen the Spirit, Based on Jewish Wisdom*
by Rabbi Kerry M. Olitzky & Rabbi Lori Forman
4½ x 6½, 448 pp, Quality PB, ISBN 1-58023-061-X **$15.95**

Restful Reflections: *Nighttime Inspiration to Calm the Soul, Based on Jewish Wisdom*
by Rabbi Kerry M. Olitzky & Rabbi Lori Forman
4½ x 6½, 448 pp, Quality PB, ISBN 1-58023-091-1 **$15.95**

Embracing the Covenant: *Converts to Judaism Talk About Why & How* Ed. by Rabbi
Allan Berkowitz & Patti Moskovitz 6 x 9, 192 pp, Quality PB, ISBN 1-879045-50-8 **$16.95**

Wandering Stars: *An Anthology of Jewish Fantasy & Science Fiction* Ed. by Jack Dann;
Intro. by Isaac Asimov 6 x 9, 272 pp, Quality PB, ISBN 1-58023-005-9 **$16.95**

Israel—A Spiritual Travel Guide: *A Companion for the Modern Jewish Pilgrim* AWARD WINNER!
by Rabbi Lawrence A. Hoffman 4¾ x 10, 256 pp, Quality PB, ISBN 1-879045-56-7 **$18.95**

Life Cycle & Holidays

The Jewish Family Fun Book: *Holiday Projects, Everyday Activities, and Travel Ideas with Jewish Themes*

by *Danielle Dardashti* & *Roni Sarig;* Illustrated by *Avi Katz*

With almost 100 easy-to-do activities to re-invigorate age-old Jewish customs and make them fun for the whole family, this complete sourcebook details activities for fun at home and away from home, including meaningful everyday and holiday crafts, recipes, travel guides, enriching entertainment and much, much more. Illustrated.
6 x 9, 288 pp, Quality PB, Illus., ISBN 1-58023-171-3 **$18.95**

The Book of Jewish Sacred Practices
CLAL's Guide to Everyday & Holiday Rituals & Blessings

Ed. by *Rabbi Irwin Kula* & *Vanessa L. Ochs, Ph.D.*

A meditation, blessing, profound Jewish teaching, and ritual for more than one hundred everyday events and holidays. 6 x 9, 368 pp, Quality PB, ISBN 1-58023-152-7 **$18.95**

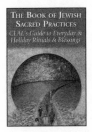    

Celebrating Your New Jewish Daughter: *Creating Jewish Ways to Welcome Baby Girls into the Covenant—New and Traditional Ceremonies*
by Debra Nussbaum Cohen; Foreword by Rabbi Sandy Eisenberg Sasso
6 x 9, 272 pp, Quality PB, ISBN 1-58023-090-3 **$18.95**

The New Jewish Baby Book AWARD WINNER!
Names, Ceremonies & Customs—A Guide for Today's Families
by Anita Diamant 6 x 9, 336 pp, Quality PB, ISBN 1-879045-28-1 **$18.95**

Parenting As a Spiritual Journey
Deepening Ordinary & Extraordinary Events into Sacred Occasions
by Rabbi Nancy Fuchs-Kreimer 6 x 9, 224 pp, Quality PB, ISBN 1-58023-016-4 **$16.95**

Putting God on the Guest List, 2nd Ed. AWARD WINNER!
How to Reclaim the Spiritual Meaning of Your Child's Bar or Bat Mitzvah
by Rabbi Jeffrey K. Salkin 6 x 9, 224 pp, Quality PB, ISBN 1-879045-59-1 **$16.95**

The Bar/Bat Mitzvah Memory Book: *An Album for Treasuring the Spiritual Celebration* by Rabbi Jeffrey K. Salkin and Nina Salkin
8 x 10, 48 pp, Deluxe HC, 2-color text, ribbon marker, ISBN 1-58023-111-X **$19.95**

For Kids—Putting God on Your Guest List
How to Claim the Spiritual Meaning of Your Bar or Bat Mitzvah
by Rabbi Jeffrey K. Salkin 6 x 9, 144 pp, Quality PB, ISBN 1-58023-015-6 **$14.95**

Bar/Bat Mitzvah Basics, 2nd Ed.: *A Practical Family Guide to Coming of Age Together*
Ed. by Cantor Helen Leneman 6 x 9, 240 pp, Quality PB, ISBN 1-58023-151-9 **$18.95**

Hanukkah, 2nd Ed.: *The Family Guide to Spiritual Celebration*—The Art of Jewish Living
by Dr. Ron Wolfson 7 x 9, 240 pp, Quality PB, Illus., ISBN 1-58023-122-5 **$18.95**

Shabbat, 2nd Ed.: *Preparing for and Celebrating the Sabbath*—The Art of Jewish Living
by Dr. Ron Wolfson 7 x 9, 320 pp, Quality PB, Illus., ISBN 1-58023-164-0 **$19.95**

Passover, 2nd Ed.: *The Family Guide to Spiritual Celebration*—The Art of Jewish Living
by Dr. Ron Wolfson 7 x 9, 352 pp, Quality PB, ISBN 1-58023-174-8 **$19.95**

  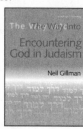